The Fate of the Jews of Rzeszów 1939-1944: Chronicle of those days

English translation by Gabrielle Eisen

Written by **Franciszek Kotula**

First published in Polish in 1999 from a journal hand-written during World War II.
Original edit by **Wanda Tarnawska.**

This edition translated into English by **Gabrielle Eisen.**
Edited by **Peter Levy,** who has tried to maintain the integrity of the original text, regardless of the correctness of the grammar.
Acknowledgments from Gabrielle Eisen
I would like to thank:
My husband **Hans Eisen,** without whose input and support this project could not have reached fruition.
Peter Levy, ever helpful and available to discuss the many issues of putting this work together.
Anna Blay who recommended Peter Levy as editor and publisher.
Krystyna Kynst who edited a part of the book.
Krystyna Duszniak who helped me to find **Mrs. Wanda Tarnawska**, the editor in Poland of the first edition of the original Franciszek Kotula manuscript, which he compiled from his hand-written notes in 1947. Her advice is also very appreciated.
Sharon Hurst for the layout.
Alex Nutman (a.e.nutman@gmail.com) for preparing the files for upload.
Mish Eisen for her technical support in text and photos.

Photos/artwork from **The Regional Museum of Rzeszow, Lukas and Boguslaw Kotula, Janusz Witowicz** and **Alexander Hadala.**
Cover-Monument to the victims of the Holocaust founded by Rzeszow survivors in the place of mass graves in Czekaj cemetery
Back- Monument on the site of mass killings in Bor near Glogow dedicated in June 1995
ISBN 978-0-578-75822-0

Published 2020 by IngramSpark US

TABLE OF CONTENTS

FROM THE ORIGINAL PUBLISHER

The fate of the Jews of Rzeszów 1939-1944. Chronicle of those days is the second book prepared by the Social Issues Committee of the Works of Franciszek Kotula from his rich legacy.

This is no ordinary book. Franciszek Kotula had an extraordinary passion for documenting important events he witnessed in his community. From the earliest days of German occupation in Rzeszów, with full awareness of the serious consequences, he noted in real time, everything he regarded as significant. Before long he observed the markedly different character of the Germans' attitude towards the Jewish community, thus from the cards of his 'Diary of Occupation' he selected the notes which concerned Jews and kept them separately. To the administrative work at the City Museum and Archives, directed by Kotula, were assigned some Jews often known to him before the war. Some were even his friends. Therefore it is their reports, supplemented by the author's own observations that contributed to this chronicle. Its value is mainly due to the fact that it was conducted 'in real time,' thus documenting the state of information and social atmosphere of those days, without the distance and subsequent comments, typical of diaries written 'post factum.' The account of Kotula is a living work, whose mood, details, atmosphere and language, even the best historian is not able to capture years later, relying only on documents.

Reading his Chronicle one gets the impression that particularly in Rzeszów, the Germans were somehow rushing to the 'Final Solution of the Jewish question.' Today we know that Endlosung plans were prepared beforehand and the Rzeszów Kreishauptmann Ehaus was probably more zealous and wanted to show off *(it was said that he was the brother in law of Himmler.)* Killing defenseless Jews was in this situation the easiest matter. As early as March 1941, a special supplement in the 'Krakauer Zeitung,' published on the occasion of the conference for the Divisions of Economic Councils of the General Government, was devoted in its entirety, to the 'model' of the Rzeszów solutions - the first city of GG, which completely 'cleared the economy from the Jewish element.' This, however, was not enough for Ehaus. He therefore 'immortalized' his achievements on a copper plate that he placed on the wing of the German eagle, which crowned the castle tower from the year 1942. The inscription proclaimed: 'This eagle, the German symbol of ascendancy and victory, was placed here in connection with the liberation of Rzeszów of all Jews in July 1942. The installation of it occurred under the head councillor and commander of the County Rzeszów District NSDAP, SS-Sturmbannfuhrer Dr. Heinz Ehaus.' It was, however, on reading the evidence, a premature propaganda of success.

Franciszek Kotula's book, prepared for the first time for print in 1947, went through general enough various vicissitudes. For political reasons it was always blocked at the last minute. In the eighties, the author sent the manuscript to the National Publishing Agency, but there he could not obtain permission to publish, despite the substantial alteration of text and numerous reviews. Only in 1990, an independent "SAN Weekly" published extensive excerpts from the manuscript.

This current version is the closest to the original. It has been prepared on the basis of the manuscript and the typescript of 1947 - which includes a preface by the author. The round parentheses appearing in the text apply F. Kotula. The square brackets contain explanations from the current publisher.

The book is richly illustrated with original photographs from the period of the war, many of which were not known to the author, because they were only recently discovered. Not all have been thoroughly researched, but knowing their provenance, we can conclude that they only concern Rzeszów and its closest surroundings. Some of the photographs in this book are contemporary and represent what was left of the Jewish community in Rzeszów: cemeteries, monuments and memorial plaques.

The plan of the Rzeszów ghetto was developed by Januarius Nowak, Mark Zielinski and Zbigniew Grzysia, based on a small map made by Bozena Gąsiorowska under the direction of Franciszek Kotula. Much of the information was obtained from Rzeszów Jews who currently live outside of Poland.

Few Jewish inhabitants of Rzeszów survived, but some still maintain contact with Poland and their native town to this day. They include Klara Maayan, who heads in Israel, Moshe Oster and Zygmunt Gross, who often visit Rzeszów. Their correspondence, reports, opinions and comments gave rise to a supplement to the journal of Kotula. The Social Issues Committee of Works of Franciszek Kotula intends to release it after collecting further opinions concerning this book.

All comments and correspondence should be addressed to:
Social Issues Committee of Works of Franciszek Kotula
(Wanda Tarnawska or Mark Czarnota)
35-016 Rzeszów, ul. Kraszewski.
Rzeszów, January 1999.

FOREWORD

What was the proportion of the Jewish population in Rzeszów in the time preceding the events described in the Chronicle of Franciszek Kotula? I understand that living in the city were 14.5 thousand people of Jewish nationality and that was 35 percent of the general population. Among the 8260 people of working age were:
- workers and hired hands - 2400 people
- employed in wholesale trade - 200 people
- employed in retail trade - 550 people
- employed as craftsmen - 600 people
- employed in industry - 70 people
- professions - 400 people

Of the total of 707 handicraft workshops, 442 were Jewish. Of the 1500 wholesale trade businesses, 1083 were Jewish, including 294 food retail trade establishments of which 227 were Jewish. Jews owned 50-60 percent of the town's real estate.

This structure of ownership and of the professions to some extent reflects the division between 'rich and poor' which later, during the occupation, was to witness the disproportional allocation of unjust favors (redeeming of the rich,) as imposed by the Germans and the Judenrat.

E. Podkowizer-Sandel (the extermination of the Jews in the district of Kraków, the Bulletin of the Jewish Historical Institute, Warsaw, April-June 1959, no. 30) estimates the number of the population as 14,000. In the collective work, Rzeszów Jews, Memorial Book, Tel-Aviv, in 1967, it was rated at 15.2 thousand.

ZK Wojcik (*1935 to 1939 History of Rzeszów, Rzeszów 1994)* writes that in 1939 the Jewish population was about 14 thousand people, certainly not exceeding 15,000.

In the Rzeszów city council of a total of 32 councillors, 12 represented the interests of the Jewish population.

There were many Jewish associations, political, religious, economic, educational, cultural, charitable, and sporting. Political associations had 3320 people, of whom 300 were communists.

Jewish youth attended public schools in the city. There was a coeducational primary school, a coeducational middle school and a middle and a public technical college of the Jewish School Society. There was a Jewish Cultural Centre with a hall for theatre performances and screenings of contemporary films. There was a drama section, 'The Stage,' at the Jewish gymnastic and sports society, Samson. The Jewish Hospital, initially on Copernicus Street, moved to a newly erected building on Leszczynski Street in 1938. It had 30 beds.

When the September 1939 campaign ended with the occupation, many Jews thought that reasonable relations with the Germans would be able to be arranged somehow and that they would manage to survive to the end of the war. The Supreme Commander of the German army, Walter von Brauchitsch, in a speech to the Polish population on September 1, 1939, stated that 'in areas outside the border of the Reich, occupied by German troops ... the armed forces do not see civilians as their enemy. All aspects of international law will be respected.' Moreover in a radio speech on 4 September he assured the Jews that they can be confident of their situation. These were assurances without any guarantees. Even before the beginning of the war with Poland, a plan was developed in general terms for 'the final solution of the Jewish question'- Endlosung der Judenfrage, whose ultimate goal was to be the biological destruction of the Jewish population. So there would be no doubt, the regulation by Wachter, the head of the district of Kraków dated 18 November 1939, referred to the signage of Jews in the district of Kraków [it concerned the wearing of armbands with the Star of David - JP.] It stated that a Jew is one who is or was of Mosaic religion.

In a particular manner, contrary to the above assurances instituted by Brauchitsch, work for Jews was controlled by the regulation of the Governor General, 12 December 1939: 'All Jewish residents in the General Government who are older than 14 and to the completion of their 60th year are generally subject to forced labor. The duration of compulsory labor is in principle two years; the prolonging of it will occur **'if the educational purpose of the forced labor has not been attained in that time.'** [My emphasis - it allowed optional assessment of the work - JP.] As to what could be the consequences of failure to comply with this coercion, the call of 24 January 1940 left no doubt: 'The Jewish Religious Council in Rzeszów is calling all Jewish men between the ages of 16-60, to appear every morning at 6:30 at the council premises Rynek 21 to carry out work on snow removal. In view of severe consequences, unconditional obedience is called for.'

In his Chronicle, Kotula showed how constantly throughout the occupation, the practical implementation of the educational purpose of forced labor of the Jews enabled treatment that was not responsible before any law: beating, shooting, lack of nutrition, the lack of any precautions relating to safety and health to the rapid destruction of the body. The motive driving the subjects was fear of beating and being killed and the delusive hope of survival through various documents confirming the right to work - thus to life.

To what work?

The statement of Hans Frank 22 January 1941: 'As long as there are Jews they have to work, obviously not in the way they did before. Yet there are still remnants of humanitarian dreamers and those who, because of the German emotionality, tend to sift the history of the world. You cannot demand from us that we still have any consideration for the Jews, from us who stand in this struggle together with the Führer for twenty years. When the Jews in the world today are asking for sympathy we are not moved.'

Kotula showed in his Chronicle how without any formal procedures, without even a semblance of law, from the beginning of the occupation to the Endlosung, continual demands in cash and in kind, contributions, requisitions were demanded of the Jewish population to be carried out immediately or in the shortest possible time until the move to the ghetto limited the freedom of living in the town and the possibility of employment. Participation in cultural and social organizations was also forbidden.

Such treatment of the Jews was far from the assurances of Brauchitsch of September 1939.

Hans Frank declared on 23rd April 1940, honestly, but not clearly at that time, 'Jews do not interest me at all.' However on 19th April 1941 he announced: 'The Führer has promised me that the General Government will be the first area liberated from the Jews.' And on 16 December of that year: 'I will say openly gentlemen that we have to finish with the Jews one way or another.' From these alleged statements of Frank, the order warning against 'sentimentality' is evident though not directly spoken. Therefore the behavior of the Rzeszów authorities did not differ from the 'norm' and were not due to special local favor.

Until a program that provided for the 'end of the Jews' appeared, ghettos created in designated cities were to serve the purpose. They were officially called Jewish residential districts - Jüdische Wohnbezirk.

Also designated by the Germans in place of the previous Jewish Communes was the Jewish Council - the Judenrat, also known as Council of Elders - Altesten Rate, which were often unofficially called kahals.

Of what truth about ghettos did the Nazi propaganda want to convince the population?

Dr. du Prel, author of 'Handbook for the General Government' wrote inter alia that the Jews were left a kind of government in the General Government, and that the Council elders were entitled to act as official representatives of the Jewish part of the population to the German authorities.

Yet, on 21st September 1939 the Security Police chief, Heydrich, stated that the ghetto is to be a means to the ultimate goal, namely the liquidation of the Jewish population by moral, mental and physical destruction. In a telephonogram to commanders of operating groups of the Security Police he commanded: 'In every Jewish community a Jewish Council of Elders is to be installed who should be charged with full responsibility in the whole sense of the word to the accurate and timely performance of any issued commands.' The appointment of boards was designed to prepare for the total extermination of the Jewish population. A subsidiary body of the council was the Jewish Order Service or police (Ordnungsdienst,) both often regarded by the people trapped in the ghettos as worse than the Gestapo.

This opinion is also repeated several times in Kotula's original Chronicle, p.11

The Rzeszów ghetto was closed on the night of 20th to 21st December 1941. Kotula reported the herding of Jews from other territories to the Rzeszów ghetto. This was in accordance with the previously quoted Heydrich's order of 21st September 1939: '.. we should seek to ensure that [the Jews] should be concentrated in a small number of cities. Few points of concentration should be created, thus facilitating the subsequent steps.' The police and the Gestapo had the right without warning to shoot anyone leaving the ghetto. Through the words of the Chronicle, hunger weaves continuously and shows with great clarity that starvation was part of the planned policy of the occupation once the Jews were locked in the ghetto with a minimal possibility of escaping from it.

Hans Frank said on the 23rd April 1940: 'Whether [the Jews] have something to eat or not, does not concern me in the least.' And at the meeting of the General Government on the 16th December 1941: 'Jews are in our opinion harmful gluttons.'

There is a lack of data for Rzeszów, but the average daily provisions for Warsaw in the years of occupation are shown in the following table.

Description	Grams			Calories
	Protein	Fats	Carbohydrates	
Before the war Polish worker with average earnings	61,4	45,4	472,5	2602,0
Physiological norm	70,0	50,0	400,0	2400,0
Unemployed in 1932.	48,0	33,0	384,0	2087,0
The allocation for the Polish population year: 1940	12,1	1,1	163,0	740,0
1941	12,9	3,3	142,0	669,0
1942	11,1	1,6	125,0	576,0
1943	7,0	0,9	93,0	414,9
The allocation for the German population in 1941	82,4	95,6	338,0	2613,0
The allocation for the Jewish population in 1941	3,2	0,2	41,0	184,0

The situation was tragic for the inhabitants of the ghetto in terms of fuel for heating. Allocations were not supplied and winters were severe. In December 1941 they had to turn over all their fur products including the smallest scraps. With the organism extremely weakened by famine and the working conditions, illness and mortality increased sharply.

Kotula noted: 'the fate of Jews confined in the ghetto in the winter of 1941/42 was tragic. Heavy frosts, a complete lack of fuel, and hunger ... They burned everything that could be burned, rafters, floors, ceilings, unnecessary doors and windows - the district was in fact a ruin.'

Many Jews, unable to endure such conditions committed suicide by ingesting poison, as is mentioned in the Chronicle ... But such a death was then a luxury. In the Lwów ghetto at the turn of 1942/43 up to three thousand złoty was paid for one portion of cyanide at black market price of one dollar equal to 53 złoty.'

On 20th January 1942, at a conference in the nearby village of Wannsee, the decision for Endlosung was taken: 'The Final Solution of the Jewish question.' There, the Secretary of State, Buhler, said that 'the General Government would be happy if the solution to this problem was started from there. ... Jews must be removed from the territory of General Government as quickly as possible, because it is here that the Jew is a big danger as an epidemic carrier, besides he constantly induces disturbances in the economic structure of the country due to constantly practicing illicit trade dealings. Moreover of the approximately 2.5 million Jews concerned, the majority is unfit for work.'

'Solving the problem' in the form of pogroms and mass deportations to extermination sites began - as amply shown in the Chronicle ... in July 1942. The Rzeszów district was the first district of Kraków, whose Jewish population was annihilated. Of 14.5 thousand of Jews, residents of Rzeszów (not counting those transported from nearby areas,) only two hundred people survived.

Julius PETRUS

FROM THE AUTHOR

It may seem strange to many a reader that a Pole undertook to describe the fate of Jews during the German occupation and who after all did not have anything to do directly with the ghetto. It may be even stranger that he allows himself some generalizations, and even an evaluation of these and other events or phenomena. Because the Jews reserved this right essentially only for themselves. Therefore from the author of the following work some clarification is required so that he will not be misunderstood.

I first encountered Jews as a schoolboy in the public school and later as an adult and a teacher with students and their parents. I paid less attention to the latter. I was particularly interested in the youth which I considered as a thumbnail of the Jewish community, its true reflection. Here I want to point out that my observations were primarily at the school, not the religious, political or social sphere.

As a teacher I tried as well as I could to introduce and maintain a friendly atmosphere in the classroom. So I could not help noticing that in the classroom, Jews, who sometimes formed a third of the total number of students, were a closed group, and besides study they lived a separate life. Although from time to time it happened that a friendship was formed between the Polish and Jewish boys, it was generally rare. And it was a peculiar friendship. It happened only at school, and mostly broke off outside it. Friendship which existed outside the school was not a common occurrence but it happened sometimes.

Looking beyond young people at Jewish society, I could not understand how such a social group who had lived hundreds of years next to the numerically larger communities was so able to isolate itself. It happened that a Jewish boy coming to school did not know and did not understand the Polish language. Even among educated

Jews it was rare to speak without a specific accent but otherwise quite correctly.

On the other hand one cannot exclude influences that mutual nationalities living side by side for centuries exert on one another. Therefore, while observing my Jewish students, I tried to extract those features that could be the result of the influence of the Polish environment. And when I found them, it was much more common in girls than in boys, because girls were less isolated than young Jews. They had a lot of coquetry and femininity. Young girls often mixed with Polish boys who gladly flirted with Jewish girls, and sometimes they married them. I also had friendships among Jewish girls.

Until one day when I met Jews who for generations were raised not in the city but in rural areas. Meeting and getting to know these people was quite a revelation to me. Those rural Jews were very different from those in urban areas. I would not say that they had more Polish features or less. They were Jews, but very different from the city ones! When I shared with them my observations, they explained to me that the land and life among the fields 'forms' a man differently than the town. Then I came to the conclusion (though not only I but so have others, and often confirmed by Jews themselves,) that certain characteristics unpleasant, negative and repulsive are not necessarily exclusively Jewish, that one meets quite often in others, and were the result of the abnormal conditions in which that nation has lived for centuries. Consequently in cities and towns, in the alleys among stalls in the narrow streets of the ghetto developed a unique human type to whom even rural Jews could not relate. There were frequent and intense quarrels between them.

It was an indisputable fact that only a few Jews wanted to understand and be understood. Generally the majority did not recognize that they were a foreign body in the Polish organism. And it is a natural biological tendency of every living organism to get rid of a foreign body even with a feverish reaction and in such a way arose anti-Semitism. And its sources were not religious or ethnic reasons, of course not in the concept of later nationalism. Actually Jewish organizations, already of a very nationalistic character, saw the source of anti-Semitism on an ethnic basis.

To the sources of anti-Semitism also quite incorrectly was joined another aspect concerning Jews, namely the economic. The fact is that the Polish proletariat, which numbered a great percentage of the Polish people, looked adversely at a Jew if he was a wealthy man, often very rich having the best of everything. But they looked the same way at a wealthy Pole. This thesis is supported by the fact of cooperation of Poles and Jews, especially in the proletariat, namely the Polish Socialist Party with the Bund, and later in the activity of the Polish Communist Party.

War broke out, and soon the occupation of Poland by a nation whose leaders put forward the war on Judaism as one of the main banners of its National Socialist party program. This slogan was carried out with German thoroughness. Therefore Polish Jews expected something similar on Polish territory. And when the Germans began at once the biological destruction of the Polish nation, in this respect the Jews encountered a pleasant surprise. The economic blows they received in the beginning were very distressing for those displaced from other territories and resettled in Rzeszów.

For the local people it was often like the bite of a fly.

As a teacher who worked many years in a Rzeszów school known for its large number of Jews, and having many friends among them, I could observe closely the

German-Jewish relations in the first two years of the war. These observations were a revelation for me. To be certain, I always checked them with the opinion of many Jews. My observations were generally accurate.

In the winter of 1940 to 1941, when the Germans were preparing for war with Russia and arranged the setting up of military hospitals, the collection of the Rzeszów Museum located in one of the schools designated for a hospital, was thrown out and placed in a dilapidated old house in the Square (then No. 8, now 6.)

Restoration of the collection began and continued until the spring of 1944. Jews were assigned for non-professional work. And because there were orders at the same time to organize the Municipal Archive which the Germans initially intended to burn, it happened that in the Museum worked daily dozens of Jews, men and women, common people and intellectuals, merchants and proletarians, often my good friends and former students. There were also others deported from West Poland as well as from Germany itself who could not speak Polish at all.

Polish language during the occupation, was 'enriched' with new terms and expressions. And so the place of work to which Jews were assigned was called a posting. The Museum was one of these 'postings' and I was the 'boss.'

What sort of boss is not my business to judge myself. I will only point out that for getting this work in July 1942, after the terrible murders at that time, the distributors of work in the ghetto were paid big bribes. Still later, the specially favored, or more precisely, family members of the Judenrat, were assigned to me.

I was 'director of the institution' for a number of years. In addition of the possibility to observe the behavior of Jews in special circumstances, I received the latest news from them directly from the source. Every morning before work, 'hot off the press,' they told me everything (they preferred to talk rather than work) with details of whatever happened in the ghetto, about the conditions, about people, their behavior in those living conditions, and so on. I listened carefully to these reports, and noted them down immediately, I tried to be as objective as possible, a truthful chronicle. And so from these cards will speak people who have now been shadows for a long time.

War is a veritable mine of insights for psychologists. What strange forces emerge from the deep layers of the human soul! And so, many observers have noted that people who fell into the trap, and were able to assume that they were in a hopeless situation, became suddenly sincere, even disclosing the most sensitive secrets. It was as if they were under an irresistible compulsion. This strange inner compulsion concealed from people the realization that someone can specifically be lurking for their confession. In particular this symptom could be observed in the prison cells, and not only among simple people. It was used by the Gestapo who inserted their own informers who cleverly drew out the suspects' confessions. Then came the confrontation and the man was 'ready.'

For untold years a legend was created around Jews and the fantastic virtue of their discretion; that to tell something to a Jew is to throw a stone into the sea. But the period of occupation and the ghetto completely dispelled this myth. As if suddenly, even the most powerful brakes had been destroyed. Regarding themselves, they were simply naively honest. About others, it was sometimes even in the nature of denunciation, although this was not intended at all. They hid nothing, they declared everything. Apparently the burden that oppressed them was so heavy that they had to unburden themselves of their troubles and discard out of themselves all that was no longer necessary.

In the ghetto very disgraceful events occurred. Those Jews who did not pass through this hell readily condemn those people and do not have words of justification or forgiveness for them. I would not say that they are unjustly righteous. They do not know, did not experience that in a very difficult circumstances a man becomes a wolf toward fellow man. It is a fact as old as the mountains. It was therefore in the ghetto that the other legend, the proverbial Jewish solidarity also burst like a soap bubble. I do not claim to know why in the ghetto so many people became wolves. Therefore against this general background emerged certain individuals who resisted numerous pressures and did not succumb to this illness. I also came in contact with these individuals, the brightest of them were: Simon Landesman, the farmer from Kraczkowa, a Jewish peasant of fervent faith, almost a prophet, devotedly loving of his only daughter; Miriam Henz, a young girl who graduated in 1939, passionately loving her people and having a great heart; Sabina Reissowa, embroiderer, proletarian, quiet, obliging, humble; Dr. Levi Speiser, a lawyer, and this 'other' Jew, wise, noble, and a great soul. I pay tribute to their shadows.

The reports that I was receiving, my own observations and reflections, tormented and worried me.

Are they accurate, correct, and fair?

I compared them with those of both Polish and Jewish intelligentsia. These judgements and hypotheses set forth below are not just mine, but also of my many interlocutors. Here I owe a lot to the intellectual, Dr. Levi Speiser, my friend who was a Polish officer mobilized in 1939 and who successfully survived the September campaign. He escaped from German captivity somewhere in the vicinity of the city of Lwów. He spoke Ukrainian, and between the years 1939-1941 was a school teacher in eastern Ukraine.

Thanks to the fact that at the home of his sister in law in Rzeszów lived the Orstkommandant (governor of the city, more about him below) he received permission to return to Rzeszów. When the ghetto was not yet closed and the Poles were allowed to enter it, I used to visit him. I talked a lot with him, exchanging ideas and opinions. At the time of the closing of the ghetto 'he stood up' to the Germans who shot him.

Reports obtained only from Jews, which to some extent could have been one sided, would not be sufficient to produce a complete picture.

Thanks to my many acquaintances in the area, as well as several 'dark blue' police officers who remained to the end, most faithful Poles and brave men, I learned many kinds of details.

My notes were taken directly, honestly and objectively under the influence of the interest awakened. While still at school in my work as a teacher I produced the material for this book which does not claim to be the decisive answer to certain problems. First of all it is a chronicle. I tried to avoid any side influences and I hope I have succeeded.

Whoever survived the German occupation would realize what the consequences would be for the one taking such notes if found by the Germans. Thus they passed many channels, changed hiding places, discretion covered them, and also damp soil. Maybe it is not a miracle, but in any case it is a happy coincidence, that they survived at all. They owe much to my father, Walentyn, and brother, Stefan, who had them in their care.

F.K.

Rzeszów, 1947

ILLUSIONS OF THE YEAR 1939

In the spring of 1939, the political sky of Europe darkened forever. The black and threatening clouds billowing over Germany were moving towards Poland. In this situation almost all Poles became political meteorologists.

Much of the public sincerely prayed that the threat of war would be dispelled and that peace would return. Many preserved our specific Polish optimism that somehow all will be resolved. There were also those who wanted the war as the only solution to the German problem. From these conflicting desires were born different moods, and these again had a surprising influence on human behavior.

It is known that a large part of the Polish population were Jews. On the whole they did not believe in war. This view was held by the older generation who knew Germany, but of former times. They simply could not imagine that the sensible German nation could be carried away by war against almost the whole of Europe. This belief was so strong that buyers greedily profited from the boom year and took easy credit to fill storehouses and shops with all manner of goods. Later it became evident that certain stores worth millions arose.

When in August, mobilization was announced in Poland, Jews became really worried. It was apparent in the fact that traders were willing to give goods on credit; they persuaded buyers without even asking for money. And today it is difficult to say whether it was only a traders' argument, when they said: 'Take it Sir. There may be a war. Later you will settle it in cents, bearing in mind the situation after the First World War.'

They convinced some who took huge quantities of goods, often not paying a penny for it, because there was no one there any more to receive the money.

On the first of September the predictions came true:

war broke out. Jews became very anxious, and many were seized by a real panic when after just a few days of the war, at first a handful, but soon multitudes of Poles appeared fleeing from the Germans. They sowed unbelievable fear. Among those fleeing were many Jews.

Up to 8th September about five thousand Jews left Rzeszów. It was mainly the wealthy who fled, having their own cars or being able to afford to buy or hire horses.

Many young people were leaving, especially those with left-wing views, as well as those courageous and more enterprising. The refugees took with them mainly gold, jewelry, U.S. dollars and cash.

On the roads leading east were often seen wagons completely covered in black, with destitute figures, who, while hiding from air raids in fields and woods or seeking accommodation for the night, were childishly helpless. Especially Jews from the larger cities whose only habitat was the street, the square, the shop, or the pavement. They stayed, waiting in terror for what would happen. Many were prepared for the worst. These pessimistic assumptions were based on news from Germany. 'Let it be God's will!' They replied with that specific note of Jewish fatalism to the warnings of Poles who asked why they did not go east.

The Germans entered Rzeszów on dawn of the 9th September. The very next day the leading units of the Wehrmacht pasted on the walls of the city, and in every little town and village, a proclamation by the Commander of the German Army, von Brauchitsch, in which everyone could read that all international law would be respected. This notice allowed a more optimistic outlook of the situation, especially as in the early days there was not a single murder of Jews. Hope entered their hearts. Lowered heads were raised.

But already, the next day, another regulation was posted

relating exclusively to Jews. It was issued by the Chief of Civil Administration in the areas occupied by German troops, and his principal and first paragraph read:

'The storage, sale, or gifting of every kind of movable asset or immovable property being in whole or in part owned by Jews is prohibited.'

Simultaneously with the posting of the proclamation of the Commander, soldiers- maybe even the same ones-began the barbaric demolition of Rzeszów synagogues and minor houses of prayer held by various religious fraternities. Valuable old furnishings were destroyed, benches were burned, and precious liturgical items were stolen, huge candelabras smashed, while horses and soldiers were led into the synagogues. The Germans encouraged the lowest rabble of the street composed of delinquent elements to complete the destruction. After several days the interiors of synagogues and prayer houses were in complete ruins.

Targeted anti-Jewish action was commenced for the time being in the least painful manner because it was financial.

11th September. The military commander of the city, Captain Lorenz, arrived in Rzeszów. On the same day he issued a 16-point announcement whose precise content ordered the immediate opening of shops, selling of goods in small quantities and only for cash or redeemable receipts. Again this concerned mainly Jews in whose hands was found a large percentage of stores and warehouses.

13th September. The Head of Civil Administration issued a decree that all Jewish businesses or those financed by Jews should be immediately marked by the sign of the 'Star of David.' Disobedience would be punished.

On the same day, the commander of the city issued a notice which ordered that each store must have a sign with the words 'Aryan shop.' Finally, 'all Jewish shops will have Aryan administrators appointed by the Municipal

Board, and paid by non-Aryan owners. Shops of non-Aryan owners who left the city will be handed over to the administrator, who would deposit the money into the treasury of the City Council for the goods sold to an account of the shop owners.

The regulation on Jewish property from the date of 6th September and actually posted on 10th September was repeated on 22nd September with an additional final remark that it applied retrospectively from 1st September 1939.

September 25th. The first regulation signed by the Landrat (Starosta) Eisenlohr, appeared which indicated the beginning of civil operations. In the city itself the Polish council still officiated.

In the city centre were two large Jewish cemeteries and a third small one near the old synagogue. In the largest and oldest one, between Sobieski, Żeromski and Copernicus streets, were graves from the sixteenth century. The second, slightly smaller, was at the corner of Żeromski and Sobieski streets. Both were surrounded by walls and were thickly overgrown with bushes and trees. Naturally, once they had been outside the city, but over time found themselves within its precinct. They fulfilled the role of lungs for the city if not a park. At the same time they cancelled any planning regulations in the area, for as it is known, the Mosaic religion forbids the digging up of cemeteries.

Somewhere in the middle of October, the news spread quickly through the city that the walls of the Jewish cemeteries were being torn down. In fact the German authorities ordered Jews to destroy the walls. Long stretches of walls were pulled down and once on the ground were broken up into bricks. Within a few days all trees and shrubs were cut down, and in place of dense shrubbery arose a wide open space bristling only with thousands of grave stones. It was later ordered to dig them up and place them in stacks. The damaged ones were used to repair roads, and thicker ones were laid in some streets as foundations under the pavement.

At the same time the extension to the old synagogue was demolished because it blocked the passage from Żeromski to Mickiewicz streets. A small square in front of the synagogue on Mickiewicz Street was also eliminated.

After the announcement of 13th September (repeated on the 22nd) no public regulation against the Jews appeared for some time. The proclamations had slight impact because they applied only in the material sense. Every Jewish shop indeed acquired an 'Aryan manager,' a local Pole, usually well known to the owner, who hung around the shop, served customers, assisted in opening and closing the store, took minor payment most often in the form of goods, while the owner of the shop collected the money and quietly took it home.

It must be said that in September and October at the time of the great movement of troops there was no looting of shops. Regulations concerning only the Jews were placed with the Kahal, the administration of the Jewish community. Due to the reopening of stores from mid-September, over several weeks from dawn, crowds of people were waiting for their opening especially in front of textile warehouses. They were mainly those from the countryside who waited patiently for hours before going in and buying a few yards of material or other commodity. Memory of the First World War was still alive regarding how difficult it had been to obtain certain goods.

Jews were surprised by the behavior of the Germans. They expected murders, robberies, rapes, and yet nothing like that occurred. Admittedly, it happened very often that groups of German soldiers came into haberdasheries shouting, 'los' [get lost!] scattering stubborn Polish crowds and bought as much they could carry, or spent how much money they had with them. Some paid the required price, while others took what they wanted and left. It convinced people that the order to open the stores was issued so that German soldiers could take benefit from the war.

Jewish owners of the shops acted in various ways. Some sold off goods as soon as possible and bought U.S. dollars or gold, paying incredible prices of more than 200 złoty for one dollar! Others however tried all they could to save the majority of their merchandise and ultimately fared badly.

Already in the second half of September, when the German troops under the August agreement with Russia [the Ribbentrop - Molotov pact,] left eastern Poland, ceding those areas to the Soviet forces, when German troops and Ukrainian nationalists, who probably had an understanding for many years with the Germans, arrived in Rzeszów. Across the demarcation line of the San River they moved stealthily in substantial groups and settled in various cities of the subsequent General Government. Ukrainians, almost without exception, offered the Germans their services.

From the beginning, the Germans did not trust the Poles. Unable to fill all the top positions in the offices and institutions, they gave them to the Ukrainians. In particular, economic, administrative and political positions were only for the Germans.

In Rzeszów, the Ukrainian colony was very large. There were not enough official positions. Polish managers were removed from Jewish stores and replaced by Ukrainians. Materially, it was an unfortunate turn for the Jews because the new managers had no scruples. In the first place they took care of themselves.

Hundreds of these Ukrainian immigrants, often with their families, had to be accommodated somewhere. So the German authorities took the larger Jewish houses and gave them to the Ukrainians.

Of course with furnishings, because naturally no one transported furniture across the border.

In addition to the more or less wealthy retail stores in Rzeszów, there were several warehouses mainly of textiles. These were quickly sealed and announced as German property. There were warehouses worth millions. Huge vehicles pulled up to them and transported mountains of goods to Germany. The tears and pleading of wives and children of the owners were to no avail.

In order that something from this loot was left for the Germans who were sent to Rzeszów as officials or other functionaries, a huge depot with all kinds of goods taken from Jewish stores was installed in a large hall in the Town Hall. The loot was later distributed to Germans, both in Rzeszów and in the surrounding area.

The arrival of Germans was felt much more painfully by Jews in small towns. There the looting of shops was commonplace. What the soldiers could not take away themselves, they 'generously' gave out to the rabble that gathered at such moments.

In addition to the overt acts of plunder and requisitions, there were also hidden ones carried out without warning in true bandit manner, because the Germans, soon after arriving in town, had wide and excellent knowledge about people and property. In the first days of occupation it became clear that German intelligence had been working very well on Polish territory for years. In various institutions, especially in factories, were people who were regarded as the best Poles and activists, however after the Germans entered they immediately revealed themselves as Germans.

For how many years had they acted as informers and spies?

Just a few days after 9th September, a few men in

military or civilian clothing came to wealthy Jews in the night, as well as by day, and forcefully demanded money and jewelry threatening them at gunpoint. Who knows if they were not members of the advance Gestapo, who the very next day after the occupation of Rzeszów arrived and established themselves in a big new hotel near Asnyk Street. How they looted items of high value at that time!

From the first days after the invasion of Rzeszów, the Germans daily demanded from the Kahal a certain number of people for work, to clean barracks, repair roads, street cleaning, etc. At first, only the poor went to work, firstly in their own right, then for the more notable and rich, who paid the substitutes.

By the end of September, shortly after the end of invasion activity, mass transports of a few thousand Jews arrived in Rzeszów from the western half of Poland. Most of them were residents of Lodz and Kalisz, suddenly expelled from their homes and shops in minutes, and at the same time robbed of anything valuable. What were they allowed to take with them? The official 20 złoty and some bedding and clothing. Probably a few managed to hide something or to smuggle it. They came as paupers, whereas at home they had been very wealthy.

They were received coldly and even unwillingly by their Rzeszów co-religionists. But people had to cede a part of their houses to help the newcomers materially.

The fate of the newcomers was from the beginning very sad and at times became simply tragic. They were pushed into forced labor, taken advantage of, and often denied meagre assistance. Therefore, in the square near the Synagogue, they sold off en masse 'as trash' the remnants of their clothing or bedding, sad and resigned, as only Jews can be.

Various German agencies and institutions arrived in Rzeszów at different times. They settled anywhere temporarily. After a while those that were to remain in the city began to look for suitable permanent premises.

The earliest of the authorities that settled was Ortskommandantur (the military area command,) and most likely at the same time, half of the Gestapo also. A little later came the Board of Civil Authority, then the County Council, and finally the Municipal Council. The Orstkommandant officiated for some time in a private apartment at Grundwalska Street, in the home of the merchant Michael Gottman. Later, he took the Council building at 3 May Street where he remained until the end of the war. The Gestapo first installed itself in a new hotel on Asnyk Street, then in the Polish Bank building, and finally took two modern best decorated houses in Rzeszów belonging to the brothers Wang at 17 Jagiellonian Street (they also remained there until the end of the occupation.) In contrast, the Board of Civil Administration took the premises of the Jewish Club at 3 May Street after the first days of arrival, then moved to the County Council building on Kraków Street. But when Dr. Heinz Ehaus took the position of Kreishauptmann (at the beginning of January 1940,) he moved to the Castle, which was the courthouse, where he resided until his escape at the end of July 1944.

Finally, the German city government arrived in Rzeszów and began to officiate on the 19th October. As it later turned out, the entire management of Rzeszów city was delegated from Rathenow, near Berlin. A large group of people arrived, both men and women, most likely those who were prepared to achieve the objectives of 'Drang nach Osten,' and the slogans of the Führer. Indeed, the authorities were not disappointed in them. They were even proud of them.

Soon it became clear that these people came, frankly speaking, to gouge. The first 'sacrificial cows' became the Jews. 'Kulturtragerom' (to look around) only a few days were enough, because among the former minor city officials they usually found one perfectly familiar with the city and the prevailing conditions. As it was generally said, he was an exceptional informant.

By that autumn you could observe how at times a Jew or Jewess went to the county council with smaller or larger packages. This one for Dr. Hahn, this one for David, this for Frisch, Mrs. Tauber or Werk. For others, the 'poor' and the 'needy' brought shoes, dresses, coats ... Germans had high living standards.

If the Germans needed or wanted to know something, they turned directly to the Board of the Jewish Community that was located at 2 Matejko Street. The director designated from the beginning of the occupation was a lawyer, Dr. Kleinmann. Jews for centuries were brought up under specific conditions, anomalous in comparison with other societies, and thus mostly in cities, and were mainly involved in trade. Scattered throughout the country, without larger clusters, they were physically weak. But each man and society sought strength; Jews also. Their strength became primarily money. Thus among the Jews existed the cult of money. With the start of the occupation, Jews quickly realized that the Germans were hungry for material goods, especially money. So at once, they started an offensive known and practiced for centuries, often with masterly skill, that aimed to overcome the opponent, not physically, but by satisfying him, disarming him, weakening his blows even oversaturating him. Jews are great psychologists: they applied excellent, but unfortunately, already outdated tactics. They did not realize that Hitler armed the German psyche not only for the offensive, but with a modern defensive weapon just against this kind of action that was used by Jews.

The Jews fooled themselves that their tactic was

bringing excellent results experiencing, in the beginning, quite benign though finally unpleasant consequences of German behavior. They continued to fight the Germans with the tactic of satisfying them, fulfilling all their whims. They were happy seeing the satisfaction of their clients who were often in wonder at the sight of this or that commodity which in Germany was only a legend. So when, after the first, but not very severe, blows were followed with fairly normal conditions, the Jews grew confident that their very old tactic was the most correct. In any case, they did not consider any others, and did not take any others into account, with the exception of perhaps a few individuals. Thus came the belief at the beginning of the occupation that the devil was not as dreadful as he was portrayed and that the Jews would manage. Anyone who thought otherwise was rather frowned upon.

If not Hitler, then in any case the upper leaders of the Germans, knew the Jewish tactics and the weaknesses of their own people. Therefore great freedom was given to Germans to gratify the old Germanic instinct; robbery and plunder. So the German soldier robbed the Jew, throwing him a few coins for a heap of material. Later, various officials plundered the stock for this or other reason, just single pieces, or very valuable items.

Most cultured Germans had a weakness for fitting out houses. So when various officials ensconced themselves in Rzeszów they began stripping Jewish homes. Under the guise of equipment needed for homes and offices, the best furniture and carpets were taken. In this excelled David, the lame Oberleutnant. Everything was brought to the town hall, piles of high quality carpets (Jews also loved carpets.) And then came the division of spoils and shipping by train to Germany.

At the start of autumn, the installation of the German

casino was undertaken, the 'Deutsches Haus' at the top section of the building KKO - Municipal Savings Bank, which until then had been the municipal Rzeszów casino.

And so that the 'master race' had an appropriate environment, again Jews were fleeced, their club, office equipment and carpets while the most beautiful palm trees were taken from Polish homes.

In October and November, the German authorities 'fur besetzten polnischen Gebiete' [for the occupied Polish territory] were already roughly organized.

Representatives of various authorities arrived and continued to arrive, hence the great demand for accommodation. This department belonged to the Ortskommandantur. Naturally the best rooms in the city centre were taken and in the best furnished homes. And then more and more were needed because during the winter of 1939-1940 in Rzeszów a large military garrison with many officers arrived. Then many of the rooms were also rented with Jews. It soon became clear that a significant proportion of those tenants were not anti-Semitic and in many cases quite the opposite. Jews, with their tactics disarmed a powerful opponent and knowing well the good Germans of old, provided them with comfort, care and cleanliness. In a very short time it was common knowledge that most often both parties were happy with each other. The Jews themselves were saying that German anti-Semitism is just a government program which did not have a mass following.

At that time appeared various small but unpleasant anti-Jewish decrees announced by Kahal in the religious community. For example, Jewish doctors or lawyers were not allowed to have Aryan customers, an Aryan could not be a servant to Jews, etc. But this was not at all dangerous. 'That will not kill you.' said the Jews themselves.

In that unfortunate September, not only thousands of Jews but also thousands of Poles found their way to the East. The latter for somewhat different reasons. The bolder and more resourceful and especially capable of faster decisions came back in September or early October, when the border between the Reich and the Soviet Union was not yet definitively established, and the passage through the San River was not especially difficult. Although the German outposts did not allow the adventurous ones to the other side, they facilitated transit for the escapees from there. However when the German army stood on the line marked out by the politicians when the border was established the bridge on the San River in Przemysl was closed, thousands of people were formally cut off. It took weeks to wait for the reopening of the bridge. Many crossed through the water, but it entailed a sacrifice. The weaker ones if not drowned, caught a deathly cold. Those with cash found risk takers who carried them across. Among those returning were a number of bold Jews who did not believe the rumors about mass murders and pogroms or were driven by concern for their families. They stated that in western Ukraine Jews felt very well. They had equality with all citizens of the USSR. Those with left leaning ideas were especially favored and received outstanding positions and influence, etc.

These reports provoked great excitement. Consequently the more daring people, or perhaps more perceptive of the future, sold whatever possessions they still had for gold or dollars only and with small luggage escaped to the 'other side.' (Russian occupied side)

One feature of the German psyche is a tendency to mysticism. Various 'führers' took advantage of this feature, demanding from their subordinates some or other 'mission.' The same method was used by National Socialism, convincing its followers that the East was the direction of the German mission through Poland, through the vast expanses of Russia, up to the Urals. Thus the grey masses of the Wehrmacht soldiers were saying with conviction, that in place of oppression, poverty and backwardness, Germans were bringing progress, culture, and wealth into those terrains.

As early as the autumn of 1939, the German administration began the 'Europeanization' of Rzeszów. Of course very cheaply, not only without the expense but also with profit for themselves. They ordered the razing of various old hovels in the area of the city, both wooden and brick. This affected mainly Jews, and especially the Jewish poor, who did not want to leave the city centre, and crowded often in the worst conditions precisely in such slums. This resulted in a further concentration of the population in the remaining houses. As a consequence it provoked intensified clashes, misunderstandings and quarrels, which troubled people's lives. The wealthier were as yet not touched by the Kahal and thus their lives were quite bearable. It was only for the poor that life was getting harder.

Autumn rains finally came and the city, with the passing of thousands of cars and frequent marches of armies, was dirty and muddy 'up to the ears.' Now the Board of the Jewish community had to provide work groups to clean the streets. Mainly the refugees from the West were sent to whom the Kahal paid something out of its funds. So every day in the morning through dragged sad, bent columns, armed with shovels or brooms, some under the control of municipal officers, others of the military to work on the premises occupied by the army.

In the columns directed to the army, were many girls and young women. Among them, Jewish women displaced from Germany and especially from Berlin. They did not know the Polish language at all. They saw Poland for the first time in their life. Poland and hence Polish Jewry were completely foreign to them, a foreign culture, because they had grown up in Germany and had already assimilated into the German culture. These Jewish women, usually at the end of the column, were followed by the German soldiers. They held merry conversations with them and flirted without care. The pleasure of the soldiers could be seen because the Jewish women were very pretty and elegant. Certainly in the souls of those ordinary soldiers there would not be found a penny of 'private' anti-Semitism.

The flirting of Jewish girls with German soldiers was not limited only to the occasions while walking to work or during work itself. Often during the day or night you could meet Jewish girls in the happy company of the soldiers and sometimes with officers. The Jewish girls usually knew the German language and when they chose they could be flirtatious and interesting.

One even heard of real attachments and feelings at that time. But man is only human, and a sign is a sign. Some of the local girls and women before the war did not enjoy a good reputation. Ultimately no one was surprised at the German Jewish women, but looking at the behavior of some of the local women was quite surprising.

It was said quietly, but everyone knew, that some bolder Jews were secretly doing business with the Germans, because in this transitional period the opportunities were extraordinary. In these transactions the Jews gained 'slightly' because they towered in shrewdness over the Germans. There was also some dealing in gold and currency.

Actions against the Jews and similarly against the Poles were still casual, random and capricious. You could see that Germans did not yet have definite tactics. They did whatever came into their heads.

In the second half of October, without any apparent

reason the Gestapo arrested one of the few Jewish judges, Dr. Kessler, along with his wife and son, who were already converts. They took them to the San and moved them to the Soviet side. It was said that only the fact that his wife and son were Catholics saved Dr. Kessler from being shot. But it is strange that something like this was used only for one family.

In early November, several Jews were arrested under some pretense, but it was clear to all that in fact for no reason. Immediately after the Jews began the mass arrests of Poles. In Rzeszów they arrested a lot of intelligentsia, priests, wealthy merchants and townspeople. In the surrounding area, priests, teachers and landowners. In total more than a thousand people. The prison was packed. Horror seized everyone, what would happen?

November 7th 1939. The Gestapo imposed on the Jews, strictly only on the Jewish community, an enormous levy for that time of 150 thousand złoty. The Kahal had to resolve how to spread it over the individual members of the community. After the payment of the ransom, many Jews were released from prison. The earlier policy in relation to them seemed suddenly to soften. Nevertheless, the Jews still slipped over to the east. In conjunction with the contributions, an interesting event happened. Among the notes were found 100 German marks. As a fine, an additional 500 złoty was imposed on the Kahal. As if in Poland counterfeit German marks were made! Most probably some German had previously cheated a Jewish merchant.

After 11th November they began to gradually release the Poles, and some of the wealthier, secretly, for a very high ransom. Then it became clear that these mass arrests were just a kind of particular German terror.

Shortly after these arrests the whole Gestapo contingent was transferred from Rzeszów. Naturally, new ones came, headed by the later infamous Captain Mack. It was whispered that those first mass arrests by the Gestapo were their own idea just to get the ransom. There was an inquiry which concluded that numerous abuses had occurred and the zealots were removed. They robbed many Jews on 30th September, and in October they looted houses of those Poles who had gone to the east. In addition, they committed many other crimes and offenses.

Around the middle of November, Jewish shops were completely cleared of goods. If something was left it was that which no one wanted to buy. Mostly, the store shelves were empty. In the open doorway the manager stood idly by, and somewhere in a corner or behind the counter brooded a sad Jew. However, if the owner had reached an agreement with the caretaker, the latter somehow moved a part of the goods to a private apartment and sold them there at higher prices. The caretaker also gained from the deal. In this respect the community had either more or less grievances towards the caretakers.

The Germans, famous above all for their organizational skills, invaded ever more deeply and strongly all walks of life in the occupied Polish territories. Particularly evident was the desire to master the 'Jewish question.' To this end, through the mediation of the Jewish council, in the second half of November they conducted a detailed census of Jews, together with their professions, their exact address and description of the shop or workshop.

The Germans established a legal term with serious consequences for many, namely 'herrenlos,' which in Polish means 'ownerless.' This referred to the abandoned homes, workshops and stores. Herrenlos was, for instance, a Jewish shop in which lived the whole big family of the owner, only he himself was not there. And he was usually on the 'other side.' On 15th October those shops were sealed and the family of the owners had no further access to it. Whoever had sold the goods or had taken them out quietly had won. The hordes lost. The caretakers were reassured that after inventories they would trade again, but that the money from the takings would be deposited in the municipal cash savings, in fact into German pockets. A new way of exploiting the conquered country.

30th November 1939. All owners of shops together with managers were summoned to the magistrate to carry out the establishment of documents relating to the new management of the shops. The head of the office was a Ukrainian. Stores abandoned by the owner were no longer restored to the family but to the Ukrainians who were waiting 'on hand' for the outcome of the control. By mid-December a lot of Jewish shops were in the hands of Ukrainians. Managers lost their jobs. Completely empty shops located somewhere away from centre were assigned to willing Poles.

Jewish shops whose owners could prove their rights, were relocated gradually to the vicinity of New Town (formerly Freedom Square) and to the streets of Galçzowski and Mickiewicz that is outside the centre. Two shops were even allocated one space. Jewish premises although signed with a Star of David were often visited by the Germans.

Prices jumped up two hundred percent. At the same time, every now and then on the walls of the town and shops, were densely posted bills in German and Polish announcing very strict pricing, which naturally applied to urban merchants and local people.

The Germans looked at the prices and paid accordingly. Sometimes however someone was caught overcharging.

Then enormous penalties were imposed. This happened quite often to Jews, therefore they sold mostly to acquaintances.

At the end of November it was announced that from 1st December, all Jews must wear a white armband with a blue Star of David, located on the right shoulder. Any person infringing this decree would suffer the severest punishment. Jews received this order with indignation. Not because they were told to wear their national sign, but because the sign distinguished them from others, and that by that mark they would be treated as people of a lower category.

At the same time in the same decree it was decided that the armbands were to be worn by those who had once belonged to the Jewish community, even converts, and finally those whose father or mother were Jews. This point was aimed at many Poles. It was known that every year a certain number of Jews accepted baptism, which was not only a change of religion, but also of nationality. The Polish community was generally willing to accept these people into its midst. For them, the band was not only an identifying sign, but actually a kind of stigma. In Rzeszów this applied to many people. Some fearing the future departed, others shut themselves in their homes and did not venture into God's world. However, many almost ostentatiously walked the streets without the bands. Friends watched in fear whether someone malicious or servile would denounce the brave rebels. But there were no such incidents.

EHAUS

At the end of December 1939, the current Landrat, Dr. Eisenlohr, left Rzeszów; he did not leave behind him especially bad memories. Even before his departure the news spread that his successor will be the Landrat from Niska, Dr. Heinz Ehaus, a fanatical Nazi and a pervert. Niska sighed with relief after his departure, Rzeszów awaited him with terror, especially Jews, towards whom Ehaus had been ruthless in Niska.

He arrived. The Council building on Kraków Street was not enough for him anymore. He took possession of the castle from where Polish courts had to move at Christmas and during very severe frosts. The first appearance of the new, no longer Landrat, but a Kreishauptmann, (district governor,) because the county of Kolbuszow had become attached to Rzeszów, confirmed previous rumors. One felt that Ehaus, a Major in the SS, would govern hard and ruthlessly.

8th January 1940. The administrator of the city, Hahn, orders a detailed inventory of all Jewish property in Rzeszów either by the owners or by the managers. Whoever does not declare their possessions will be considered a fugitive, and so lose his fortune, and moreover will be punished.

The first appearance of Ehaus took place on 22nd January 1940. An appearance reminiscent of Middle Ages and the pillory.

Heavy snow had fallen which had to be removed from the road the squares and the sidewalks. German police asked the Kahal for three hundred Jews to work. Actually only about a hundred came. No doubt this was reported to Ehaus, because only he could make the following decision. Once again those who did not come in the morning were called up. Again many of the summoned were absent. German police then brought the entire board of the Jewish community to the market. Chairs were called for and the beating began. It began with the members of the Kahal and ended with those who did not obey the order. They were beaten with whips. Each received an average of about thirty strokes.

Despair overcame the Jews, because from that day on the municipality had to provide people to remove snow without a murmur.

Dr. Kleinmann called to work everyone from sixteen to sixty years old. Every morning it seemed whole battalions marched in German order, in threes, grey, crushed, and bent, with the commandant at the head. It made an unusual impression that they walked quietly, which is so contrary to the Jewish temperament.

In a notice of 26th January, the German city government announced a census of the Rzeszów population in association with the planned introduction of ration cards. This census showed the number of Poles and Jews living in the city. It soon became apparent that while the food assigned to Polish people was very meagre, the Jewish quotas were laughable. The 26th January 1940 also saw the release of an announcement signed in Kraków by the Governor-General Frank, which abruptly pushed the Jewish community in the General Government to the dregs of society. At the same time the Poles were recognized as a second category in relation to the Germans, and even the Ukrainians. This was one of those strokes which was aimed not only at the material condition of the Jews but above of all at their self-esteem.

Under unlimited penalties, Jews were prohibited from travel by rail without the written permission by the authorities. The purpose of the regulation was clear and decisive: it had to nail Jews to one place and get them under control. Jewish trade had to stop, because buying and importing goods became impossible, and yet stocks had to come to an end.

The Germans therefore had noticed the beginning of a Jewish movement within the country. Those more perceptive, more suspicious and having material resources, moved to other cities where they were not known and where they did not always present themselves as Jews. Just in case.

One has to state one thing: the Germans feared Jews. Whether it was due to the acting German propaganda or intuition; the fact is that they feared the Jewish dismantling of Nazi propaganda and sabotage in the ethical sphere. For the Jews knew the German language, were far above the average German in acumen, therefore it was better to settle them in one place.

Something must have happened. From mid-February one could not see either groups or single Jews working or going to work.

Nothing was heard about requisitions and revisions. Everyone ascertained a softening in relation to Jews. There were many conjectures. Jews themselves tried to explain this phenomenon, that apparently after the beatings in January the Kahal appealed to the Governor-General and to some American committee. It is possible that it really worked, but who knew? However this period did not last long.

Jews, like no other nation, have a remarkable ability to adapt to new living conditions. This is understandable on the basis of the history of the Jews, who in the course of their existence had to adapt to different environments. They quickly shook off the first wave of depression, and in spite of everything they decided to stay positive. Constrained in many areas and having limited freedom of movement, they still managed. Their Polish acquaintances arranged many affairs for them, sometimes the Ukrainians, even some Germans. When it was impossible to find it with kindness or through acquaintances, they rode on the old "golden ass."

In spite of everything, there were goods in the Jewish shops that managed to survive. They found middlemen, who brought them commodities from Krakow or Warsaw, or even from Lodz.

One must say that at that time trade in currencies and gold was booming. This area was still held in the hands of Jewish merchants. Intermediaries between Rzeszów and Kraków were Poles who at the same time acquired practice in this complex field of trade. Many of them became independent and soon even became competitors. Meanwhile many Jews conducted excellent business, mediating in the purchase of currencies or gold, even by the Germans. It was whispered that even the Gestapo used Jews for trading. Those who had not resisted the temptation and took on this function later fared badly because as embarrassing witnesses they were quietly 'cleaned up.'

The standard of living of the Jews is extremely varied. There are those who are very well off, and next to them terrible poverty, especially among the previously poor, those in clerical jobs and among those displaced from the West. Sometimes indeed, it happens that the rich help the needy, that a charitable activity is organized by the Municipal Board, but the myth of Jewish solidarity is shattered. More humanity, understanding, heart, is found among the younger generation, by those so sneeringly referred to by the old as 'progressives,' but among the older generation there is great selfishness. And especially among the most affluent. The Jewish solidarity is largely shattered, many think only of themselves. Various craftsmen are well off. They have a lot of work and earn well. They triumph over the merchants. They even have many German customers, who often pay with food.

The occupying administrators try to keep the official anti-Semitism burning not only among the Germans but also among the Poles. In April 1940 a scattered mass of leaflets in Polish basically encourages active anti-Semitism, pointing naturally to official channels by the police. This leaflet obviously lies, throwing blame for all misfortunes and shortages on the Jews. The Poles however are immune to it assessing the situation realistically. They realize that the lack of goods and high prices are not the result of Jewish speculation, but obviously the work of the Germans.

In autumn of 1939 came from beyond the San River very valuable and reassuring messages for Jews: that there Jews were given full rights, that they are officials, managers and wield great influence. Thus 'the other side' has grown to the status of the biblical Promised Land.

But in winter over the back roads started to come worse news. Yes, Jews were granted powers, but it ended their trade and speculation, property and wealth. On the 'other side' there are no shops, private trade or private banks. There the dollar and gold have almost no value and the houses are nationalized. Those who do not want to adapt to the socialist system are deported to the east. These messages smuggled by Jews cooled enthusiasm toward the East, and for Jews whose family members were behind the San, they caused anxiety.

In the spring of 1940 the Germans announced that under an agreement with Russia for the exchange of populations, every Jew can go to the USSR as long as he has family there. At the same time Soviet citizenship rights for their wives and children started to arrive. Very few people took the opportunity to take advantage of emigrating. Finally, the Germans did not even let those go. This in turn alarmed those interested in departure, arising in them a fear of German retaliation.

In summer, hope to connect separated families had already become very vague and very remote. Gloom had deepened even more.

Passover arrived, the Jewish Christmas, always solemnly celebrated. One has to admire the Jewish dedication to tradition. Before these first wartime holidays, as at time of peace, many products increased in price. Butter for instance leapt suddenly from eight to thirteen złoty. This indicated that Jews were arranging holidays in the traditional manner.

A month before the holiday, ten thousand dollars arrived officially to Rzeszów from America, but the Germans paid the Kahal only fifty thousand złoty. If Kahal had received the gift in U.S. currency they would probably have about a million złoty. That money was to be used to pay for those called up to work by the Germans, and especially for the very poor, because the Germans paid almost nothing for the work.

Sometime later, from Romania, Hungary, and even from America came a lot of very white matzah, without which the Passover feast would not have had the appropriate character. In addition matzah was also baked from the locally obtained rather dark flour which was later distributed to the poor Jews. The wealthy and influential got white matzah, and also bought the white one from the poor. So something illegal happened to the American money. One of the disadvantaged must have complained to the Gestapo because many Kahal members were arrested. Dr. Kleinmann eluded this, but complained loudly about the matzah.

The Kahal is hated by nearly all the Jews, only the rich and powerful Jews took positions for themselves in it. The Gestapo itself appointed several of them brought in from Germany. Those are simply spoken of as agents of the Gestapo. The Jews themselves say that in the service of the Gestapo are also a few Jews deported from Lodz. The Jewish population directly accuses the Kahal of their cordial relationship with the Germans, by directing them to where there is still something left that is in helping in the looting of fellow coreligionists. The Kahal undertakes to intervene with the authorities on various matters, Jews are banned to handle matters directly.

But for interventions so often without any result one had to pay thousands. A common secret was that Kahal had to share the payment of the fees with the Gestapo.

The conduct of the Germans, or more precisely the Gestapo, is simply treacherous and totally amoral. It has to be the result of deep study based on knowledge of the human psyche.

Psychologists know that power can intoxicate, pervert, and morally disarm a man, especially one who never had power. These people indulge in power, using it like drunken barbarians.

Jews had never had greater power. The Gestapo deliberately gave the Kahal and its Regulatory Authority, numbering in sum over one hundred seventy people, great power, so that between rulers and ruled would arise an abyss and hatred. They achieved this aim. Their coreligionists had to turn directly for justice to their hated worst enemy. History records such incidents.

After various hearings, five members of the Kahal were arrested. Then the Board turned to the Gestapo asking for their release. The Gestapo, glad of the opportunity, demanded twelve thousand ransom per head, together sixty thousand, a huge amount. The Kahal put further pressure on the whole Jewish community to collect it. But the community resisted. It was pleased that the guilty were in jail and being punished. The bolder loudly said that Kahal was worse than the Gestapo, that it was in cahoots with the Germans, that they paid themselves huge salaries. German sowing bore fruit. Jews were angry with one another.

Abnormal conditions of Jewish life during many centuries did their job. If the Jews, having obtained power, are ruthless in regard to their subordinates, they behave like slaves in relation to someone stronger. Attempts at rebirth of the Jewish nation lasted not long enough to change it. What did it matter that some of the youth are rebelling in shame and rage, but they are powerless. The flirting of Jewish women with Germans, especially in small towns where the German public opinion did not exist is simply indecent. Many of them had completely mastered their admirers.

In spite of it all, the fate of Jews in 1940 was still better than the fate of the Poles. The majority of Jews were not yet arrested, not taken away to camps or forced labor, not shot, not killed with cudgels during investigations.

Jewish tactics towards the Germans, dictated by a sense of their own weakness and dependence but directed with amazing cleverness and high intelligence, began to have effect. It was a tactic of moral diversion, a disarming of the influence of propaganda because many Germans in general did not know any Jews whom they were told to hate. In contact with them, polite and giving service, anticipating and fulfilling wishes, the burden of hatred disappeared. Something else was happening.

In Rzeszów there are a lot of Jews, and it seems as if they are becoming more and more numerous. It is just an illusion. It appears so because a lot of Jews now live on the street.

This mass of people who formerly sat in their shops, in counting houses, ran or travelled somewhere on business, are now forced to be idle. They wander aimlessly, drag about on streets, talking and talking, pouring from empty into nothing. At the same time the black battalions of the poor work, or rather pretend to work. This is a parody of work. Nobody actually hurries them, the more so because they know that they are hungry. Peasants passing by shake their heads in pity. Over the work and over those working. This one or other in a way will say, 'You know, it is God's punishment for the fact that they never did any work and did not respect our work.' Everyone knows that no one is interested in these paupers, least of all those who are doing excellent business.

In the first half of May, dated 8th May 1940, appears a regulation, signed by the Kreishauptmann, which further limits freedom for Jews. This regulation prohibits the access of the Jewish population to the Wislok, over the area from the bridge on Lwów Street up to Lisa Mountain, in a suburban park frequented mostly by mothers with children, and only on Sundays and holidays at prescribed times in streets and squares. Ehaus let all know that he is 'watching.'

This announcement however was only a prelude to another issued three months later, exactly 6th August, and signed by Paul, the deputy Kreishauptmann, while Ehaus was ill. This announcement was a turning point in the history of Jews in the GG [General Government.] It is in fact a decree of slavery which actually has tragic consequences for the Jews, not so much for their businesses but for their food supply. This regulation consisted of five paragraphs. The first of these sets a strict curfew for Jews. But the real importance is in the second paragraph which literally reads:

'It is forbidden to all Jews located within the district to leave limits of the city or town, their permanent residence or permanent shelter even for a short time.'

Other paragraphs are less important, they outline permissions, and penalties for transgressions, etc.

According to the census conducted 1st August 1940, whose contents were not disclosed officially, and really closely concealed, out of 32, 352 inhabitants in Rzeszów, the number of Jews was 11, 617.

Jewish entrepreneurship and resourcefulness was definitely checked. Trade with the villages, mainly barter for food, became severely limited. Jews were limited to purchase only what arrived to the city, and the supply was impeded every day. Naturally, food prices rose. Although there still existed for Jews the opportunity to gain a pass, it was always associated with costs, and, even more often with costly bribes. And once again only the rich could profit from the passes and life of the poor was pushed a few degrees lower.

All this resulted in Jews losing their shops. These pass into the hands of either Ukrainians or Poles. This is determined by a committee of Germans or Ukrainians who occasionally come to the Jewish district and examine which shop is to be liquidated. The Poles also lose their premises in the town centre to the Germans or the Volsdeutsche. But a Jewish shop has to be completely renovated inside and out before one received the permit for a business card. Therefore craftsmen, also Jewish ones, now become very busy. Whole streets are shining bright, fresh and colorful, but there are few goods in the shops.

Impoverishment of the Jews is progressing at a rapid pace and includes new social strata. The poorest are already actually starving. By frequent forced labor the Germans deprive Jews of the opportunity to 'organize' something.

The German authorities make efforts to find work specifically for Jews. And because the city was at that time already cleaned 'to a shine,' someone got into their head that it was necessary to make a typical German park of Lisia Mountain. In fact Lisia was a forest, a wild park, and there lay its whole charm. Lines were laid out with string and compass, hundreds of Jews were driven there, and the 'Europeanization' of this enchanting romantic spot began. After the paths had been dug and swept it was sad to look at it all.

Some Jews, philosophically looking at the world, said with a melancholy irony: 'Jews caused a mess wherever they arrived. Now they clean up not only for themselves but for their ancestors.'

In August a large extension to the New Town Synagogue was destroyed. Jews already looked at that with fatalistic resignation.

Until the defeat of France, Jews felt a kind of grudge against Poland, that it let itself be defeated, which exposed them to this misery. The calamity of France caused among them stronger alarm, and their grief moved to the newly defeated.

Already in autumn 1939, Jewish hopes and dreams turned toward Soviet Russia, whose relations with Germany were entirely correct. Despite this, and despite assurances by the German press of a friendship linking the two countries, in general there was a strong belief that it would come to a conflict. This belief was reinforced by people who legally returned from the 'other side' reporting that the Soviets were preparing for war. Therefore, Jews compulsively watched relations between the 'friendly' countries and carefully wrote down the slightest signs of friction. The decrease of intensity of Soviet transports, the withholding of delivery of letters, someone's words were discussed and examined from every possible aspect. How many times they had to accept disappointments, disillusions, miscalculations at that time.

It is a fact that dreams and wishes affect the way you think. Many Jews already understood that only some extraordinary events in the world could reverse their dangerous fate, whose cold winds grew ever stronger. Hence the desire for something violent, a turning point. Undoubtedly, there lay the source of the fantastic rumors that circulated time and again in the city. That Italy surrendered, that Russia would strike Germany at any moment ... The authors of these rumors were mostly Jews themselves. And because in the Polish community was always the belief that Jews knew everything, any rumor passed on by the Jews was immediately sent from mouth to mouth. No one cared that such reports were mainly untrue, because new more sensational and more revealing ones captured people.

In the first half of August a rumor spread that Jews in Kraków were pressured by the German authorities to leave Kraków and move to other cities. If persuasion brought no result, the Germans would apply coercion especially in relation to owners of comfortable apartments.

At about the same time from the official German seals in the territory of GG, the words 'fur die besetzten polnischen Gebiete' ['the General Government for the occupied Polish territories'] were removed, followed by Frank's famous speech printed in the 'Krakauer Zeitung' 17th August 1940. It stated that Poles must say goodbye to their dreams of Poland whose territory was henceforth included 'forever' in the composition of the great Empire. This statement once again provoked great gloom and bad foreboding in Jews.

A great relief was spread by confirmed rumors that the German air offensive against England had collapsed. 'The black market' which was still ruled by Jews, reacted in the rise of the dollar from thirty to fifty złoty and even more.

Buying of the old Polish złotys also started. But after a few days, returned reality and self-control. The dollar fell to forty złoty. As usual in such situations, some gained, and some lost.

In spring Ehaus became ill and left for treatment somewhere. After a while a rumor spread that he had died. Even the Germans spoke about it. Suddenly, on 24th August he reappeared. He showed up here and there to deny the rumors by his presence. Apparently he was mad with rage when an official informed him that the Poles and the Jews rejoiced at the news of his death. Immediately, his anger landed on the Jews by issuing orders that from 1st September, Jews had to leave Jagiellonian Street, the most modern street of Rzeszów with comfortable apartments.

Between some Jewish families and their German tenants prevail comfortable relations. A Jewish woman advised her tenant about this order. He was a captain, Ortskommandant of the Rzeszów garrison, a university professor in civilian life, a physics scholar who had long been at loggerheads with Ehaus. After this message, the Ortskommandant summoned Ehaus and informed him that he forbade the abandonment of apartments and shifting families with which officers were quartered, and he would not look for new ones. Ehaus had to back down, and the hatred between them intensified.

At the end of August, after a rumor spread around Rzeszów that Jews would not be allowed to live in the city but somewhere out of town where a ghetto would be created, most probably at Budy where barracks would be built. Under these conditions most would die of hunger and disease, and after the war the rest would be transported somewhere. Where to was not known.

There is no ghetto yet, but there is terrible hunger among the Jews, especially among the poor. It is pitiful to look at these unfortunate people. And they themselves say that the hearts of the rich are getting harder.

Apart from all this, on 1st September 1940, there appeared an official announcement signed by the Office of the Jewish Community Education in Rzeszów. It stated that at the instruction of the governor, general compulsory education would be applied, that enrolments would take place in a school building on 10 Bóźnicza St. Of course it applied only to primary school. But it caused a big surprise and some hope.

Teaching began and was held in Polish. Halpern, a teacher of Judaism in a Polish public school, became head of the school. But teaching in the Polish language did not last long. Orders came that teaching will be in the Yiddish dialect or in Hebrew. Of course, few people knew that language, so learning took place in dialect without any textbooks.

In the first half of September, the economic dictator of Rzeszów and the Rzeszów district, 'the demented,' and chimeric Dr. Troschke arrived. Taking authority over the Jewish shops and premises he surrounds himself with an entire staff of Ukrainians, doing what they advise him. He runs around town with them causing panic and confusion everywhere. It is said that his 'staff officers' profit well from the trading and management of premises with remaining goods.

EXPECTATION

9ᵗʰ September 1940. In the evening, Jews half insane with despair, spread the terrible news through the city that the Germans had landed in England, that the royal family had left the country... One could not talk at all with these people.

10ᵗʰ September 1940. In the morning a number of voices have confirmed yesterday's news. Depression such as had not been seen until now. The most excitable people ran to Joselewicz Street, to where the 'stock exchange' had moved, to learn how 'stood' the dollar, and to confirm or deny these rumors. At the 'stock exchange,' Jews instead of talking about dollars, stood motionless with eyes riveted to the 'Krakauer Zeitung.'

'What is the matter?' I ask one friend.

'Now!' He hisses through his teeth and with his palm he makes a characteristic gesture, which means without words: dead!

'You see, only English and German, it is already over, the problem is over!'

'You don't say? But here it is clearly written that the weaker activity of aviation was due to bad weather.' I observed.

'Why, yes!' he exclaimed. 'If it does not work out they say that it was bad weather.' He was still yelling, suddenly elated. 'I am telling you all will be well!' He was happy like a child.

Yesterday's rumors were in fundamental conflict with today's official communication. Therefore, while black pessimism reigned yesterday, today for a change was a crazy joy. At the same time to the factory of the former Polish Aviation Plant, now Flugmotorenwerke, all night drove a number of anti-aircraft guns, and to Jaslo whole columns of cars.

It is already an open secret that the palace in the old city and the court in Jasionka was occupied by the quartermasters of the air force. Around Rzeszów airmen are stretching cables. On the roofs of PZL were installed anti-aircraft machine guns.

11ᵗʰ September 1940. Great movement of cars full of soldiers in airforce uniforms. To the east drove cars with the military and civilians. In the countryside lists of quarters for troops are being drawn up.

Since several days, in broad daylight, singly or a few at a time, a few mysterious planes appear circling so high that their distinguishing marks cannot be identified. Everyone however said they were Soviet.

Traffic fully resembled that of September 1939. That one made one sad, but this one brings joy. The community feels happier, heads are raised. All behave as if they were witnessing the coming of crucial days.

There is widespread belief that the Germans got it in the neck, and war with the Soviets can explode at any moment. Letters from Russia come so ruined that at times they are illegible. All pray for a German-Soviet war as soon as possible.

In mid-September, the political atmosphere suddenly changed. The Germans did not write explicitly that the attack on Britain had failed, but the official German announcements about the bombing of Germany and Berlin indirectly state that England won the air war, and now itself had launched an attack on Germany. If inhabitants of the GG understood this, the Germans themselves certainly understood it.

The 'kindness and thoughtfulness' of the Germans, which was observed after the victory over France, vanished. The mask fell and showed the true face of Germany. Jews who had contact with the Gestapo and who for money, of course, undertook some intervention to get a more lenient sentence for someone or even a parole, distance themselves vehemently from this, nor even want to be advised of some action.

People are full of bad premonitions. At the same time hopes and prayers for the war with Russia look as if beginning to be fulfilled. In Rzeszów, as elsewhere, there is construction of whole housing complexes. It is said for the troops who are yet to arrive. Jews are happy as if they had acquired wings.

The night of 11th to 12th September. Many Jews are dragged from their homes and driven to the station. Terrified, they do not know where they are going: to die? For transport?

At the station they did not wait long. Soon a train full of Germans from the Reich arrived, mostly families of officials living in Rzeszów and refugees from the bombing. Jews had to carry their suitcases and bales to their houses. They heard how these refugees were cursing.

The attitude of the Germans towards Jews is deteriorating by the hour. Masses of hungry and barefoot people are driven to work.

13th September 1940. More than three hundred young men were taken to Zakopane to the quarries. It is said more and more loudly that Jews would be expelled from entire sections of the city and their apartments will be occupied by the refugees from Germany. It weighs heavily on the Jewish spirit.

Whole transports of the army are driving to the East..

A few weeks ago it was announced that anyone who wanted to go to Russia in connection with the exchange of population between Russia and Germany, was to report to the administration. Many Jews applied, especially those who had husbands, brothers, sisters on the other side.

Suddenly the whole action was stopped and it was simply announced that there would be no departures.

The applicants became afraid. It was suspected that the Germans deliberately wanted to make a record of Russian sympathizers to keep an eye on them.

The growing hatred towards the Jews manifests itself more frequently. Once, quite by chance, at a Jewish house in Lwów Street, the Germans found a military can of gasoline, which someone had left at night for himself. The Germans wanted to extract the identity of the owner of the can, but the old Jew was stubborn. He was beaten to death.

The second half of September. The thoughts of the Jews turn from West to East. Faith in Russia is growing every day. More and more troops are going in the direction of Przemysl. Jews look upon them as you look at those sentenced to death. Jews are certain that when the Soviet power will move, the force and momentum of its own weight will crush the Germans to powder. And they know that war is certain, from the Jewish workers who had fled from digging trenches on the San River and had gone to the Soviet side. They were immediately expelled from there and on leaving, they were told: "Do not come to us, but we will come to you!"

A certain group of Jews however have become troubled. News coming from over the San disturb the wealthy.

A large number of soldiers have arrived in Rzeszów. The soldiers quickly learned that village women bring food to the city to sell. So they go beyond the barrier and take everything by force. It affects the Jews for whom that food was mainly intended.

Taking advantage of the heavy circulation, some Jews have ignored the prohibition of walking in the streets. As they became annoyingly visible on September 22nd, a roundup of them was organized. For each one caught, a one thousand złoty penalty was imposed. It was a painful awakening.

A severe prohibition against selling food in free trade was announced. Every morning a mass of police appear who catch people carrying food and take them to the castle. There, after the confiscation of goods, heavy fines are imposed on them. In contrast, it is permitted to sell food to the cooperative from where it goes straight to the Germans. This repression is felt first of all by Jews.

The official anti-Semitic attitude of the Germans is increasing. It is said openly that after the war not a single Jew will remain here. Germans have made a profitable enterprise out of catching Jews. This afternoon, 25th September, once again a raid took place on the 'promenaders.' For a Jew it is hard to sit still. Those caught are sent to the county offices where a penalty 28 złoty is imposed on them. A net profit.

In the first half of October the war temperature rose again. More mysterious aeroplanes are flying and more frequently. The question perturbs people: Soviet or English? In this atmosphere there are even arguments about this. Particularly intriguing people were single planes which drag behind them a long trail of white smoke. Nothing like this has been seen until now. Toward the east there is a constant flow of military transports and all types of weapons.

Near Strzyżow, in the high Żarnowska Mountain, a mysterious construction has begun. A special railway siding has been built. On the summit they are digging a tunnel or perhaps an underground factory. No Poles have access. Everywhere masses of guards.

In the woods behind Głogów, great barracks and something like sheds are being built. It is said that it will be a depot for ammunition. But they are getting ready for war, because the road to Sokolow is being built at lightning speed.

In the area of Debica and Mielec, entire villages are being evacuated and large tracts of woodland are cut down. For what purpose? Apparently for the construction of an airport. From time to time, cars gather hundreds of young Jews take them out in that direction.

There is talk of blackout of windows.

Finally came the news that the Germans have occupied the Romanian oil fields. Will Russia tolerate this?

Jews lift their heads. Faded eyes look knowingly. And suddenly a joke about this, proof that they are once again full of hope:

'Sir, do you know when the Germans will lose the war?'

'I don't know.'

'So, I will tell you: on the eve of the biggest Jewish holiday.'

'Really? Well, that is exactly in a year, in October next year, because today we have the Day of Atonement, the most important Jewish holiday.'

'No! That was in the past, but it will not be the biggest Jewish holiday. The biggest Jewish festival will be when the Jews will celebrate the defeat of Germany. And the defeat will come on the eve of that holiday. Right?'

14ᵗʰ October 1940. On the hot Jewish heads, Ehaus suddenly poured a bucket of ice water. He decreed that Jews in whose homes are officers' quarters have to leave everything and move out by November 1ˢᵗ. The empty apartments will be occupied by Reichs or Volksdeutsche.

Jews raised an unbelievable of lament. But is that surprising? Where were they to move?

And so there was a reaction which Ehaus probably least expected. Phone calls to the Orstkommandant did not stop ringing because the officers strongly and vehemently protested against the change of their hosts to whom they had gotten used and with whom they were very comfortable. Incidentally the Ortskommandant also lived with a Jewish family and his housekeeper was also affected by this regulation.

Given large number of protests, the Ortskommandant went to Ehaus, presented the situation to him and explained that such agitation among the officers is very undesirable.

Ehaus, with great irony, expressed his regret and showed him the order from the governor about which he was powerless and he could not do otherwise. But the commander did not give up. He approached the general, the commander of the division of Rzeszów. The result was that a committee, composed of an officer and an official from the Kreishauptmannschaft, went to the quarters concerned and asked the affected officers whether they were satisfied, checking at the same time the cleanliness of the dwellings, etc. Everywhere they received positive responses and expressions of satisfaction.

In fact this regulation is not the ordinary persecution towards the Jews; probably higher command ordered the governor to give such a regulation. It seems that he knows the situation, knows that the contact between the officers and the Jews, who are after all intellectually superior to the German, can have adverse consequences, that the Jews may have a 'demoralizing effect' on the officer corps, and therefore this state of affairs has to be changed immediately.

Did the governor expect such a reaction? What conclusion will he reach from this? What impact can this have on further proceedings against the Jews?

Fundamentally, the Jewish action of 'moral disarmament' of the Germans, as far as this could be called, also worked in favor of the Poles. Still many Poles explicitly condemn this attitude of the Jews toward the Germans. They believe that such subservience toward those who so maltreat and harass them shows a lack of honor, is simply something shameful. They even say that giving the Germans quarters is considered to be a kind of blessing by the Jews, for the Poles on the contrary, it's a curse. Others, however, justify the Jews, saying they cannot do otherwise, nor should they. However, after this incident they do not foresee anything good for the Jews.

For a long time rumors about the opening of a ghetto are heard in the city, that is a special Jewish district to which all the Jews will have to move. Naturally, they evoked terror among the Jews because the creation of the ghetto would be tantamount to a prison. Who knows if the spread of these rumors was not a kind of blackmail to extort money from the Jews which moreover often succeeded?

These rumors intensified in the second half of October. Jews in this case evaluated the situation as serious, because through their own information they learnt there were some preparations in this direction. Until...

23rd October 1940. The territory of the ghetto was marked, not being exclusively a Jewish neighborhood but beyond which Jews were not allowed to live except those who are 'quarters.'

The north eastern part of the city became the Jewish district, actually inhabited mostly by Jews even before the war. In the buildings at the Old Market, which was to be also somehow part of the ghetto, Jews could only live in areas facing the yard. Not from the front which was facing the market.

Implementation of the regulation is not yet ready, but the ghetto perimeter was marked by painting an X on walls, windows, doors and walls. It reminded people of the biblical Egypt. Jews are very depressed.

At this time, wives and children of 'Rzeszów officials,'

police and military, began to arrive in Rzeszów. Jews are not deluding themselves that the invaders are simply waiting for their still warm apartment. There are serious concerns that they will not be allowed to take furniture, so they secure hiding places with their Polish friends. It happens in several ways - some agree to the storage, others refuse. In general, however, Jews find a secure place.

DISCUSSIONS: ROOSEVELT AND MOLOTOV

30th October 1940. German newspapers reported that on provocation, the Italians have attacked Greece and were advancing. In short, a new war. Jews reacted in one way and the Poles in another at this news. If the Poles saw the prayer carried out, 'We pray, o Lord for the war of nations!,' the Jews looked at this fact from the world politics. Jews perceived the attack on Greece, legitimate or not, as a blow to the very sensitive position of England, which had to call out a corresponding opposition, perhaps Turkey, to come out against the Axis powers. This again would accelerate the declaration of war by Russia against Germany, maybe even now, in winter? Germans fear this because the preparatory work was going on at an incredible pace.

The German officers, especially the police, who live among Jews, are secretly saying that for some time many Ukrainians, as well as soldiers from the Soviet army, together with their officers, sometimes cross the San River. Civilians as well, armed with Polish weapons which remained after the hostilities in 1939, cross the San, often during a battle, and surrender to the Germans. They are deported immediately to the west where according to the expectations of German officers, they will be trained for special tasks. Now those refugees state that on 'the other side' there is an unprecedented anti-German propaganda preparing attitudes for war which will happen for sure.

These and similar news are greedily caught by Jews who tell one another with hope, 'Let tomorrow come!'

6th November 1940. The German press attacked America vehemently, the Democrats and Roosevelt who was supposed to give a pre-election war speech. German newspapers wrote explicitly that involvement of the U.S. in the war was not excluded.

That was enough. Gold immediately jumped from sixteen to twenty-two złoty per gram, and the dollar from thirty two to forty. Jews made it known that they were not suffocated and impoverished, that they are still there to think and to feel, that they are a dynamic underground force which at the right time could still cause a great impact.

'Roosevelt, he is concrete, a wall!' they shouted with all their might.

'Well, that is something to be happy about, isn't it?' a Pole asked an educated Jewish woman.

'What? Just to be happy?' exclaimed the Jewish woman, suddenly forgetting about her perfect Polish accent. 'It's not enough to be happy, we have to sing, shout and dance!' she cried.

The next day, that is, 7th November, the German newspapers announced that Roosevelt was in fact elected president for the third time. All were convinced that the Jews would be mad with joy, yet strangely they were silent. Indeed they were filled with joy so deep as to be speechless and dazed.

The Jews were already reading German newspapers very carefully in German, bought for them by Poles because they were forbidden to purchase them. Now they began to study the German press, and with Talmudic patience, they extracted messages from time to time, sweet raisins which fed their optimism.

This mood full of optimism and hope was suddenly interrupted by a brief message, so dreadful that the Jews froze; the Poles were also dumb with terror: Molotov was coming to Berlin. 'What for?' German press is silent. So from this emerged many suppositions and combinations. Jews put on a good face but you can see that they are worried.

Every following day brought some exciting and simply fantastic news that Molotov this, and Molotov that ... Germans want this, and they don't want to give that, and that a special English delegate has travelled to Russia...

Before the war, favorite places, for Jewish meetings and conversation, were certain squares and street corners. Was that still a past eastern tradition? After the prohibition of gathering on streets, of course meeting points spontaneously arose in Jewish homes and workshops where newspapers were read, commented on, and discussed. Poles also eagerly came to these houses just to listen or take part in the discussions. And while the Jews were perfectly informed of politics and generally accurately assessed the situation, they were totally inept in addressing Jewish issues in the context of general developments. There was in them still an exceptional belief in the power of Jewish influence in the world, and that attributed unintelligible or ambiguous events to the actions of Jews. Meanwhile, in the face of Molotov's visit to Berlin, they remained undecided. Many even supposed that Molotov had gained substantially.

One of the places for discussion was the flat of the goldsmith Singer, located in the Old Market Square, near Copernicus Street. Discussions were held in the workshop, and, in case of trouble, each of the participants had prepared some business with the host. Caution had to be maintained, the more so because the Gestapo in Rzeszów were obsessed with sending souvenirs from Poland to their families, mainly in the form of gold brooches and signet rings, ordering them en masse from Singer. For this reason the goldsmith felt to some extent safer than others, as he was exceptionally in demand.

After the departure of Molotov from Berlin, after the announcement from which nothing could be inferred at one of those occasional gatherings at Singer's, when everyone had heard all the latest rumors more or less disturbing, the host with a special smile on his face, as if possessing a secret, while playing with some gold signet ring, proclaimed while gesticulating:

"Gentlemen! If someone wants something from me, I do not go to him, but he comes to me. And when I want something from someone, then I go to him. If the Germans wanted that Russia in time of war would sit quietly with Poland, then Ribbentrop would go to Moscow. And now, when Molotov travelled to Berlin, he wants something, he will ask for something. And it seems to me that he will want a lot of, oh, a lot! And Germany will have to give, because they do not want war with Russia. They are afraid of this war. Have they written anything about the Soviet Army? No! They only talk about it, but with contempt and scorn. Until now. Today in 'Krakauer' there is a whole article describing the Soviet army, its training, weapons, spirit, strength, the largest power in the world. And now I ask myself: Why? ... Why right now? It is because if something will not succeed, they will have justified themselves in front of the community that it had to be so, that it was not worth to start a war with such a military power. For how long? How should I know?"

In general, Jews believe that there has been some agreement; like the Germans had wanted. And that would mean that for now there will be no war.

It seemed that the Poles, as a result of this peculiar atmosphere, turned to mysticism, like the Jews, to omens and prophecies. As the Poles begin to remember, or even create, different predictions and prophecies, so among the Jews circulate alleged mystical sayings of the rabbis. One foretold this, that one again something else ... In these predictions there were all sorts of endings as if the prophets were bidding at auction. Both communities prefer to listen to them rather than various actual news and logical considerations.

The more the Germans proceeded into these areas, the more the German authorities strove to create the least contact between themselves and the 'native' population. To this goal, different orders were issued continually, and finally, in late November, German soldiers were banned from frequenting small and out of the way taverns and inns. On the doors hung an official paper stating whether the admission for troops to this or other tavern was permitted or not.

Something is beginning to happen in the Balkans. Strange news are coming from there. Just now 29th November, Szupo (Schutzpolizei) are packing up and going in that direction.

December is already winter here. If something was really going to happen it was probably unlikely in winter. What the bolder and more far-sighted now count, is how many months until the spring. Jews with their mind trained in Talmudic scholasticism, endeavor to read something in the cards and letters coming from abroad. These letters are studied and treated like Kabbalistic riddles. The contents of the letters are analyzed meticulously. So one of the letters, written by a Jew beyond the San, who previously had contact with a Jew in England, became a kind of revelation to the Rzeszów Jews.

It said:

'Icek at one time was very weak, it was thought he would die. Then he recovered and now he is healthy and strong as a bull!'

In another letter someone else writes:

'Please do not send clothes from Rzeszów to Tyczyn, because I will need them soon.'

It seemed that he would soon return to Rzeszów.

When a Jew is in a good mood, he likes to tell complicated jokes. And that first winter, many Jewish jokes circulated and caused much laughter. But the full effect can only be expressed when told with a Jewish accent and Jewish gestures:

That winter, Icek wakes up, stretches deliciously, smiles happily, and finally turns to his wife sleeping next to him and says:

'Salta darling, I had a wonderful dream! It was a beautiful dream.'

'So dear Icek, tell me about that sweet dream!' asks his wife.

Icek relishes the words, licks his lips, swallows something, and then says:

'Salta, I dreamed about a wall, a long plastered wall.'

'A whaaat?' the wife asks dragging the 'a.' 'And you call that a good dream?' Then with a slight frown she looks at her blissfully smiling spouse.

'Salta! The wall is still nothing, but what was written on it, you can't imagine!' ... He is delighted.

'Darling Icek, what was written there?' asks the fascinated lady

'Hmm. It was ... it was written ... Many, many times ... beat up the Jew!'

'Icek a gawew!' exclaims Salta horrified. 'Fe! What are you talking about? That was a wonderful dream?'

'Bist du myszygen?' and she examines her husband closely, from whose face does not disappear a blissful smile. He lies there with eyes closed, as if entranced be some vision. Was he crazy?!

'Yes, Salciu, yes,' Icek drawls slowly with relish. 'It was a wonderful dream. Because it was all in Poland.'

Exceptional times are symbolized in various ways. And so the atmosphere of the occupation often crystallized in splendid jokes. The above joke illustrates superbly the Jewish view of some periods of the Jewish past. They noticed that the Polish anti-Semitism, so often decried by the world, was in fact a pastoral compared to Nazi Germans. So the Jews began to look at recent Poland quite differently. Instinctively, in many cases, they tried to be dual nationals, because as well as being Jewish they felt also Polish. This change in relation to Poland, drew them closer to the Poles, with whom relations in many ways became friendlier.

As a result of recent German regulations, Jewish life becomes difficult. Without Polish support it would have been harder. Poles are helping Jews. Here and there selflessly, for the sake of old acquaintance, but often Jews pay for help and services. Businessmen believe that it should be so as long as the recipient of the service had anything at all with which to pay.

The destitute now have to beg so as not to die of hunger. The adults cannot actually leave the ghetto, so a lot of children pass to the Aryan side asking for a piece of bread or a few potatoes. It varied at times but they always returned home with something.

Despite increasing difficulties, Jews did not abandon doing business. Without trade, it was hard to even imagine a Jew. Not being able to carry out many pursuits themselves, they enter into partnerships with the Poles. The latter become very capable students indeed and quickly master the disciplines which were once considered for Jewish heads only. It happened that in many cases the students surpassed the master. The outcome of all this was that probably there had never been such a good relationship between Poles and Jews as at this time. It gave rise to mutual understanding and rejection of divisions and differences.

From over the ocean blow ever friendlier winds. Gold and dollars have a constant upward trend. The Germans, who come directly from France, bring masses of looted stuff, they sell it and drink to excess. They prefer to sell to Jews because they can communicate with them more easily. Therefore, around the Jewish district, circulate a lot of soldiers.

In one matter, the Jewish solidarity is intact, and that is circulating news among themselves. In early December, news spread in a flash through the entire district that a well-known Gestapo in Rzeszów, Gawron, brought a portion of a letter to Singer from his fiancée, who mentioned she wished to have a brooch made from a Polish silver coin. Well, on the other side of the segment of this letter was a description of a terrible bombardment which had lasted all night. It was the worst since the beginning of the war. Singer got the task to find out where this bride lived.

At this time, nearly everyone knew that somewhere between Sanok and Dynów, Jews created a place of communication with the 'other side,' and even a transfer point. But it was interesting that people on both sides are not keen to come here or go there. And around this point, the insiders, and among them are Poles, do not want to reveal anything. There is a great and profitable trade. 'There' go clothes, underwear, watches, and from there dollars and gold. Now a certain Jew, who decided to return to Rzeszów, disclosed that on the other side one can see extreme war preparations, and it is conceivable that a war will break out even in winter.

Here too, preparations are increasing. To Jasło, and even to Zamosc, go trains filled with steel plates from the dismantled armaments at the Maginot Line in France. For a stroll? They throw people out of entire buildings and settle the army in them. In villages there are also a lot of military, there is also dreadfully overcrowded living conditions.

Branches of communication crisscross the whole area like over a broken pot. Everywhere, troops occupy schools, rectories and larger cottages.

In the second half of December, winter intensified. The army takes all the fuel. The civilian population has almost nothing. In the Jewish quarter it is even worse, there coal reaches unbelievable prices.

Suddenly, yet another plague fell on the Jews. Now in homes which the Jews were forced to leave in haste, some Germans found many valuable things hidden by the Jews in various places, in basements or attics. This aroused such greed in the Germans that mass searches are made. They tear up floors, pull down walls, dig, tear mattresses, and 'confiscate' countless things considered as illegally stored. Targets of special greed are new fabrics or clothing, jewelry, gold, precious items, etc. Jews are in despair because if the last of their capital is taken, hunger awaits them. Rumor goes that the anti-Jewish program will be exacerbated. Because of their hostile attitude towards the Germans, who wrongly ascribe it to Jewish propaganda, Ehaus issued a decree that one must not greet Jews in any way (to greet Poles only with a slight nod of the head but God forbid removing the hat) nor talk to them. This regulation was proof for Jews that the situation for Germans is working unsuccessfully.

Meanwhile, the saying, that misery always goes in pairs, was proven. Indeed since September 1939, it not only go in pairs but in crowds. Winter 1940 to 1941 was not only severe, but very snowy. At the end of December there were such heavy snowfalls which the oldest people could not remember. Drifts, mounds, mountains of snow. Cars sank on roads, trains were immobilized. Even newspapers did not arrive. So the Germans went into a frenzy. This winter! What if Russia strikes?

Masses of people are driven from villages. Some thousands of Jews are driven to roads and railroads from Rzeszów. The locals still can bear it so, but the deportees and the poor? In wind and frost, work people miserably clothed, and in flimsy shoes, poorly fed. Even if the poor man returns from work it will be to a cold room and cold food. Already, everyone knows that there is great mortality among the Jews, and it continues to increase.

Frost and snow gave the Germans an opportunity for new harassment. Now, German patrols and police circulated through the city, investigating whether the yards were cleared of snow. They carried out checks, especially scrupulously in the Jewish quarter. Here their 'careful' attention was brought to passages in the old quarter, mostly located in the courtyards or porches. And as a result of the cold and the high density of population, passages presented very unedifying sights. The patrols, depending on the degree of garbage, imposed on that house a fine usually of an average of fifty złoty, collected immediately. With the provision that the fine is to be contributed from all the tenants. These divisions of penalties again cause friction and strife which occur more easily.

5th January 1941. Something happened that no one can really remember. Snow poured as if from a million sacks and it blew incredibly. Communication stopped everywhere. And so again, thousands of people are forced into the fields to clear the roads. There is a terrible lack of coal. Jews cook 5-7 families on one stove.

The snow stopped, roads were dug out, and newspapers came again. In thoughts, they evoked no less a storm than that which recently raged in the world. German propaganda defends itself, then explains itself, then attacks the U.S.A. Roosevelt puts pressure on Stalin, he speaks of the need to raise Russia to her feet. Many people actually drink these messages like best vintages.

The Rzeszów Schupo, finally departed for the Balkans. There arrived another outfit in which many policemen know Polish. It is both better and worse. The Poles and Jews observe them closely. What can one expect from them?

Ehaus, having received a whole battalion of new people at his disposal, vigorously set about to remove snow from the streets which creates veritable mountains and tunnels. Civil servants, artisans, and merchants were appointed in turn to the job. The same system was applied to Jews.

10th January 1941. It was the turn of Jewish tradesmen who had to supply three hundred people. Early on that day, only a few people came to the meeting place, and it was those hired by rich businessmen. Ehaus, as often happened, flew into a rage. He sent a whole battalion of police into the city with orders to drive out all Jews from their homes, whoever was alive. Then women, with young children, were driven into one synagogue, and men to another synagogue. Several thousand people from each group were crammed together. It was the Day of Atonement for Jews, and hell at the same time. The mercilessly crammed people were kept in all day. Stench, confusion, people fainted, sobbed. The women were terrified that the synagogue would be set on fire with the men inside, and also that the men would be decimated. Everyone knew that one could expect anything from the Germans.

The women and children were only released first at night, and then all the men, with the Kahal at the head, were beaten, and all night they were herded to work on the snow.

Jews grow pale at the memory of that day.

This event caused a huge unrest in the Jewish community.

It looked like a real rebellion was possible. There was a sharp dividing line. The majority of displaced persons and the poor, often driven to work, had to suffer for the fact that several hundred well-dressed and fed people did not want to go to work. Hundreds of curses and condemnation fell on the Kahal, who would use the most severe measures for minor offenses by the poor, but on the activities of the rich they looked through their fingers.

14th January 1941. A new commissioner took over the city, Dr. Huller, a Viennese. Jews were happy. In any case he would be less harsh than the Prussian, Hahn.

The German press is ecstatic, that in spite of English activity, Germany has signed a trade contract with Russia. Not to mention Jews and Poles, the Germans themselves do not believe that it is good news. Actually they all believe in war.

Once again, airplanes are cruising in the skies, trailing behind them huge tails of smoke. People stop and observe this phenomenon. The Germans pretend that they know nothing and see nothing. However a Jew overheard a conversation of soldiers in airforce uniforms. 'So try to shoot them at that altitude.'

A new wave of depression, worse than previous ones, took hold of Jews. The policemen searched Jewish homes from attics to cellars. If they found any kind of goods in whatever quantity, and something would always fall into their hands, they took it away without pity. Jews are terrified. If they still have anything hidden, some stores of goods, they sell them. It is always easier to hide cash. Poles watched this in fear, because what will happen when these persecutions of Jews will cease?

After triumphal proclamations, silence. At the same time they whispered that in the region of Kolbushow, Majdan, Sokolow, there is a huge German encampment, and maneuvers take place there on a large scale. Soldiers in white helmets take part, and armaments and carriages are painted white. Are these tokens of friendship?

Ukrainians are saying that the Germans have ready, millions of anti-Soviet leaflets and brochures in Ukrainian, which they will disseminate after the takeover of Ukraine. It is also said that all Ukrainians in the GG will be resettled in the Ukraine.

A new battalion of police, no. 321, because on the headquarters an appropriate shield is hung, is a real God's punishment for Jews. They hound the Jews to snow work, day and night, in three shifts. The policemen beat them without mercy. Other groups constantly plunder homes, robbing according to their own judgment. The Jews, in order to save anything, sell whatever they can, below its worth and buy dollars. Those jumped to 47 złoty. Gold is sought more than dollars, but there is little of it on the market.

29th November 1941. In all sections of the military and police, a state of emergency was suddenly ordered, which lasted several days. Then everything was cancelled, but it could be seen at every step that readiness was still maintained. Some consolation for Jews that their hopes still receive some kind of sustenance.

Even more hope cause rumors that America will surely take part in spring. The Germans must also know about these rumors, because no one else but they disseminate them. They say that if America does come out it will be really bad for the Jews. And the Jews believe it. So America, which is a great hope, is at the same time cause for great distress.

As the Jews themselves say, and one can see it, some Jews are living superbly, since they do excellent business, especially in gold and dollars.

Germans try to harass the Jews wherever they can. Recently, they selected a Jewish school, which in December and January functioned perfectly, although the Polish schools were closed for lack of fuel. The children were learning only in Polish from 'Sterze' (the official handbook approved by Germans.) The Kahal was buying coal on spec, paying four hundred złoty per ton.

At the beginning of February the administration of the school was given the choice to teach in Hebrew or Yiddish, because teaching in Polish definitely was not to be used. Eventually, the school management chose 'jargon' because it could not find teachers of Hebrew. Anyway, what was the point?

As for the Jews, the bane is unceasing work in the city and the surrounding area, so for Poles it is the compulsory transport to work in Germany. The more Poles are transported, the more Jews are driven to work.

In 'Goniec Krakówski,' the official newspaper in the Polish language, popularly known as 'Podogoncem,' 21st February, appeared a regulation specifying the final structure of the General Government and its relation to Germany. The Polish state had been crossed out and removed, 25 million people were turned into a mass of slaves.

But no one took this seriously in the Polish community. More seriously, even of great concern, was a rumor suddenly released that in relation to the above, in spring will begin total and energetic action of Germanization, 'production' of Germans on a large scale. It was whispered, that anyone who had an ancestor with a German name would simply be forced to change nationality. For this reason, many people are in despair. But at every step they find people who comfort them that they should not worry prematurely.

For this reason Jews are also worried. What status will they have in a country where there will be no Poles?

DRANG NACH OSTEN

Until now, many signs indicated that the German-Soviet war is inevitable. However, one could always find a more or less strong story that questioned this certainty. There were not so many pessimists, but they were able to spread doubt. And now, suddenly on 5th February 1941, a new police decree closed the road from Rzeszów to Glogów for movement of horse carts, and on 6th February, from early morning, whole columns of German vehicles pulled up to the train in Staroniwa Station, where they unloaded different types of ammunition and delivered them to the new barracks in the woods behind Glogów. The strongest yet argument for war. This opinion was now often repeated. Additionally, whole convoys of ammunition sped to the east. They were transporting sections of works and other equipment.

Home-grown strategists now predict the course of possible actions. Accordingly, they say that there will be two strikes at the same time: at Russia and at the Balkans.

The Germans themselves do not conceal the possibility of a new war. Simultaneously they predict with certainty, that Russia in a few months would be 'kaput.'

Generally it is said that mobilization has been announced in Russia. Flights of mysterious aircraft are continuing.

Life in Rzeszów seems to be normal, only marches of troops with the transports of ammunition indicate that something is happening. Nothing is said that something extraordinary is cooking. In town, the new owners of shops are energetically rebuilding premises, renovating interiors and modernizing shop windows, removing ugly, sometimes truly frightful entrances. Therefore, tradesmen are earning well. And moreover, the city is improving in appearance.

However, the main topic of conversation is Russia and only Russia. This word fascinates people, delights the Jews.

12th February 1941. Finally it was decided to create a ghetto. Plans are accelerated. Acute terror took hold of Jews because it is not just rumors but a terrible reality. Nothing frightens them as much as starvation, because according to many, the ghetto is there specifically so that Jews would perish in this manner.

Economic terrorism is raging. Sudden inspections are carried out in restaurants, on the roads, on the streets. For failing to supply quotas they throw people in jail.

Prices have jumped up chaotically. There is already scarcity. It all acts on Jews worse than on the Poles.

At the end of February appeared columns of cars filled with SS troops going east. Usually they stopped at the market and the SS, armed with various types of cudgels, batons and whips, ran through city beating mercilessly any Jews they came upon. The same happens in each district, not only in Rzeszów, but in every larger city. It seems this was a specific type of sport which consists in finding the hidden, frightened people, and beating them with laughter and yelling.

Within a few days, a plan for the Rzeszów ghetto was drawn up. It would be surrounded with fences, walls, gates, etc. and it would cost more than a hundred thousand złoty. Of course, the Kahal has to cover the cost. It was even beginning to be implemented. Jews sank into real despair, they were well aware of what was in store for them. They sell off what they can, procuring food to survive until the autumn. All the troops still keep going and going east. There are even already some headquarters, and so many houses outside the city have been seized for the army. But maybe God will grant survival. Meanwhile, the more astute began to swap their housing with the Poles, transferring for the 'quiet time' for later, for tomorrow.

12th March 1941. Suddenly, the organizing of the ghetto was halted. It is widely believed that this was due to the opposition of Orstkommandant, because in Rzeszów there must be full freedom of circulation for strategic reasons and not various obstacles by building walls. It was whispered also that those strategic 'considerations' were only a pretext. In reality the Ortskommandant appears to be sympathetically disposed toward the Jews, and he did it for them, taking advantage of the situation.

The joy among the Jews that the establishment of the ghetto has been postponed was very short. Apparently, Ehaus proved to be stronger than the Ortskommandant. For several days, part of the city is being fenced in order to close it. High fences are built, outlets of the streets closed.

At the same time it is said that among the Jewish poor, there is great loss of life from starvation.

German soldiers drink unbelievably. Apparently from worry and bad premonitions.

In Malawie, on Mt. St. Magdalene, are being built great, mysterious constructions.

At the same time, Ehaus is building a truly lordly mansion, rebuilding a privately requisitioned villa at the expense of the Poles. A crowd of people work around it, among them many Jews. Despite the snow and rain they dig and level the garden. In the vicinity of the villa old houses are torn down so that the residence of 'Papa' Kreishauptmann should have a fitting environment. In the city, shops are still being renovated. Is this not in order to confirm to everyone the conviction that German victory was certain?

25th March 1941. The army occupied both synagogues even though they are completely ruined. Apparently out of necessity.

27th March 1941. Jewish residents, in twenty eight streets, received an order to vacate them within forty eight hours. The vacated apartments were to be exclusively for the army.

Suddenly a bombshell! Yugoslavia had rebelled against the Germans. The agreements have been torn up and a mobilization was announced. A new war? So at once arose the conviction that Germany will strike first at Yugoslavia, as of course they would not leave a hostile army at their rear.

An edict was issued, that families of the Reichsdeutch, must immediately travel to the Reich. The Germans are selling their possessions and buying food, especially fats. The Volksdeutsche have silly faces, because no one considers them.

31st March 1941. An instruction to prepare blackouts and clean out the attics was issued.

6th April 1941. German forces attacked Yugoslavia. What would Russia, a friend of the Slavs, do?

7th April, 1941. The movement east is enormous. News came that Germans had crushed the Yugoslav army, and Belgrade had been occupied.

8th April 1941. People's faces are sad. All speak only about the tragedy of Yugoslavia. And they now understand that it was an English ruse to gain time.

The Jews are continually working on the Ehaus mansion, even on the two days of Pesach.

Planes are continually flying. Since mid-April, German artillery fires at them relentlessly. The German authorities are bringing in drafted contingents. Simultaneously, transports full of commodities are transported to the west. Is this just in case?

Jews are completely consumed by anxiety, they walk in a daze. And no wonder. Before them is the threat of the ghetto, and they cannot wait to see the war with Russia and liberation here. They run and fantasize as if they want to speed it up. They speak of unbelievable rumors and combinations. A real hysteria has swept the exchange. Prices jump like fever in a typhus patient. These hysterical rumors and gossip have an effect on the price of gold and dollars.

30th April 1941. This morning was posted, a regulation for the mandatory preparation for darkening windows

For several days, rain is pouring down. The earth has become very sodden. Opinion has it that because of this, war has to be postponed, because in these conditions it is impossible.

6th May 1941. Kahal received an order to immediately obtain passports licences and documents of Russian nationality. There are many, especially women whose husbands are staying on the soviet side, were trying to obtain Soviet nationality for their families. It happened that some families did not accept these documents. Panic and despair, because the rumor mill declares of the confining of Soviet citizens into camps. Weeping.

8th May 1941. There was a special meeting of mayors and lawyers. They were advised in the case of foreign landings, peasants had to report immediately to the police or guards.

By night, move columns of tanks.

Around Rzeszów, heavy anti-aircraft guns are being installed. The desire and expectation of war is so strong that no one thinks that the war could spread near Rzeszów. But there could be a battle, a bombing of the city.

In Rzeszów, there is a huge continuous commotion, masses of officers. Streets are repaired, roads are cleaned and repaired. Lunacy and masses of Jews are doing the labor.

The most nervous and anxious are the Ukrainians. Despite this they have to renovate the shops.

Anti-aircraft defenses, 'OPEL,' are being organized, of course using Poles.

17ᵗʰ May 1941. The dollar has reached 90 złoty. The currency exchange is still in Jewish hands.

Air raid shelters are being built at breakneck speed in private buildings occupied by the Germans and in offices.

The endless columns of transports carry ammunition from Glogów, all to the East.

There is a great lack of food and it is very expensive. Among the Jews there is famine.

30ᵗʰ May 1941. What a terrifying military power is beating to the east! What quantities of artillery and of the most varied, and until now, unknown war equipment...

In the Jewish quarter, among the poor, there is a terrible famine. The rich, who are living well, are quite indifferent to it and do not give those dying of hunger any help.

Yesterday, that is 29ᵗʰ May, ninety Jewish families from Majdan, near Kolbuszowa, were brought to Rzeszów. That whole town will be deported and the houses destroyed. The Jews were put into vacant lodgings already prepared in advance in the ghetto terrain. The deportees were totally robbed. So a terrible poverty awaits them.

Near Strzyżow, two and a half thousand Warsaw Jews were brought to work. The Germans treat them dreadfully. They feed them very meagerly and drive them to work with beatings and abuse. But Jews are saying that these conditions are a paradise compared with the conditions prevailing in the Warsaw ghetto. Those trapped there were actually sentenced to death by starvation.

There has not been any official anti-Jewish propaganda for a long time. And suddenly in Rzeszów and its vicinity are stuck really tasteless posters insulting Jews, identifying them with typhus. The inscription reads, 'Jews - lice - typhus'. Its clear objective: To muddle up Polish-Jewish relations by scaring the Poles.

It was a fact that there is typhus among Jews. It would have been strange if it did not occur in such conditions, in such a concentration of people, in such misery. The Poles know this, so the poster did not achieve its goal.

In Glogów, a Jewish woman tore down the poster and was immediately shot.

Despite the numerous harassments and restrictions, many Jews especially women and children, steal out of the ghetto and go to the 'Aryan side' for food: for a piece of bread or a few potatoes. Jewish children are not required to wear armbands. Like all children, they easily smuggle out, and like every hungry child, arouse pity. No one pushes them away. So these children save many Jewish families from starvation. The women wrap themselves in shawls to conceal themselves. Some even pretend to be Catholic using a Catholic greeting. There was never a case that any such woman or child was denounced.

Jews use older children to trade with German soldiers. The soldiers sell whatever they can and buy food. Therefore it cannot not be cheerful in the German army. It is said loudly, moreover, that the main objective of the expedition to Russia was to obtain food, without which, Germany would also have to perish. So those boys who speak Yiddish, which is similar to German, buy all sorts of things from the Germans, which they later sell to the Poles. With the money, they buy food, mainly eggs, and all kinds of baked goods, and sell them to the soldiers. Again we could see that among the German population there is no anti-Jewish attitude. The soldiers can see clearly who they are dealing with.

One other thing is striking. Either for the soldiers going from west to east, the regulation of keeping away from the conquered population does not yet apply, or the soldiers themselves do not care. They not only do not avoid Jews and Poles, but seek contact with them and ask them about many things. Learning especially about the poverty, pillage, murder and maltreatment, they simply do not want to believe it. And when they finally believe it, they are sincerely outraged.

How bad the food situation had to be in Germany, was proved by the fact that the Polish people were not given bread, and in the newspapers it was announced that the population of the General Government relinquished it in favor of the army. This is absolute insolence! It was mitigated by the fact the information was not placed in the GG, but only in newspapers on German terrain in the 'Frankfurter Zeitung.'

3ʳᵈ June 1941. All night, somewhere far away, roared heavy cannons. All Rzeszów was on its feet. 'Already?' they asked one another. In the morning, the police seized a lot of young men and drove them to an unknown destination. Was it to dig trenches? Disappointment came quickly. This thunder was shooting on the military training ground.

Military divisions, which come straight from Yugoslavia, rush straight to the east. They boast that they will finish Russia within a few weeks. These troops bring a lot of looted things from Yugoslavia which they mainly prefer to exchange for food. The Germans give what they can for food. A real exchange is already taking place in Sokolow, where the Jews are doing fabulous business. The main trade product is sausage, supplied to Jews by smugglers from Sokolow. But all this create an even bigger shortage among the Polish and Jewish population.

Ever greater masses of troops are moving toward Sokolow. Now along the good road which was finished last year.

Despite the unprecedented penalties, trade in food is

flourishing. Interestingly, in large measure it is largely carried out by Jews from surrounding towns. There it is an easy matter to receive a pass to travel to Rzeszów. So they come and bring food to their coreligionists which they sell to them for hugely inflated prices.

10ᵗʰ June 1941. Polish rescue teams have been formed. Already on the nights of 10ᵗʰ to 11ᵗʰ, a trial blackout was conducted. The blackout did not concern Jews, nor were any other preventive measures ordered in case of war. All that provoked hysterical joy among Jews. The dollar jumped to 150 złoty,

There is no end of assumptions, rumors and gossip.

The Gestapo is furiously sniffing out Communists especially in villages which before the war were leaning to some extent toward communism.

16ᵗʰ June 1941. Cars driving east are camouflaged with branches. At the airport in Jasionka, dozens of bombers with bombs under the wings, are standing.

Nobody can count how many dates for war have already been predicted. This makes people anxious, especially Jews. If such a date does not eventuate they become dejected, and the dollar falls by more than a dozen złoty.

From the 'other side' still come very optimistic letters, mostly by Jews, regarding the outcome of the war, which is still to eventuate. Of course this consolation comes in the form of various communications.

A strong campaign against the Jews has again flared in the German press. It is obvious that the governing powers want to arouse anti-Semitism in the broad population. However the effects are not evident. In our area it was undertaken in another way.

16ᵗʰ June 1941. A whole squadron of Gestapo arrived in Rzeszów. They surrounded the house of a Jew and began to look through some plans, then to dig. They dug out a box of hand grenades and a packet of cartridges. Just at a Jew's. The home owner was arrested and taken to jail. They announced to all about finding the weapons, but no one doubted that the grenades and cartridges were deliberately planted by someone. An ordinary provocation.

Now the young people are being caught and sent to Germany to work. The 'hunt' for people is happening just like in Africa.

22ⁿᵈ June 1941. A great loss of tension and a deep breath. Dreams and prayers have begun. German-Soviet war is now a fact.

Jews are wild with joy.

Sunday afternoon, the first day of the war, and the first real alarm. When the war has become a reality, people are beginning to realize the horror of war, to remember the terrible September days. A real panic broke out among the Jews. There were those who looked to the sky, watching for Soviet machinery and the bombing of bridges, roads and railway stations. But nothing came of this.

24ᵗʰ June 1941. There are many rumors on the subject of the operations for the war. For Jews, it is a big, but hidden, disappointment that there are still no Soviet troops.

Posters were pasted, dated 22ⁿᵈ June 1941, with an appeal for 'citizens and women citizens of the General Government' with inflammatory content against Russia. But men and women turn away from it with irony.

There must to be a mighty battle, the wounded are continually being brought in. The main surgical ward is housed in the Jewish Hospital on Leszczynski Street. Many seriously injured are dying.

25ᵗʰ June 1941. It is already known that the Soviet army is withdrawing and the Germans are advancing. This has caused mourning, almost despair, among the Jews.

Today, a seriously wounded Soviet officer, a Jew, died

in hospital. Hospital authorities notified the Kahal to organize the funeral. The Kahal carried out the instruction. It is evident, that general sympathy and compassion are on the side of the deceased.

The exchange, which is of course run by Jews, is sensitive and alert. The dollar stands at 155-160 zł. The Jews say that surely things are going better for the Germans than the Soviets.

26th June 1941. A crowd of men in Polish uniforms and speaking Polish arrived in Rzeszów. These are Polish prisoners from Soviet captivity who had been employed digging fortifications and were absorbed by the Germans. They are happy to return home, mostly in the Rzeszów area.

Masses of the seriously injured are still being brought to Rzeszów. The lightly injured are sent directly to the west by trains. In Rzeszów every day die over ten Germans.

German authorities noticed that Jews practice trade in food on a large scale. In the last days of June dated 27th, posters, or more precisely a police order, were fixed, advising that Jews are only allowed to buy food in public markets during two hours from 11 to 1. Failure to comply with this order will be very severely punished. The order did not really touch them because the Jews have their regular suppliers who bring food to their homes or to an appointed place.

An interesting story spread through the city, certainly against the wishes of those concerned. One day in a transport from the east, they brought in a senior German officer, heavily wounded in the neck, to the hospital in Rzeszow. None of the German doctors wanted to undertake the operation and time was crucial. The life of the wounded man depended literally on minutes. And in this situation they called for a prominent specialist in diseases of the throat in Rzeszów, a Jew, Dr. Heller. What was he told? How did they persuade him? Hard to say. Suffice to say that the surgeon, after the deed, said he would have given half his life rather than to perform this operation. It succeeded, the officer recovered.

When the Germans began to advance, Rzeszów Jews became worried. What was happening to the Jews 'on the other side,' whom the Germans threatened as Soviet sympathizers? Soon contradictory and disturbing news began to emerge. That Jews went east together with soviet troops, also that Germans mass murder them, and that they also kill Soviet prisoners. At this time, the news also broke out that to the hospital were brought a few Rzeszów Jews, wounded as Soviet soldiers, one reportedly from Matysowka. They allegedly say that many Jews have been murdered. In fact no one knew for sure but the mood among the Jews was almost hysterical.

Another matter caused a lot of agitation. In Biazowa they arrested a few Jews and brought them to Rzeszów in connection with the alleged finding of a list containing the death sentences of more than eight hundred people by shooting or by hanging. Jews had to compile this list and give it into the hands of Soviet troops when they arrived to this area. On the list appear the Volsdeutsche. The news spread through the area of Rzeszów with lightning speed. Some Poles believed it, while others treated the disclosure with scepticism by rating it as the same sort as in Glogów with the grenades and ammunition story, and as German anti-Jewish provocation. Generally, after the 'bomb,' reprisals against the Jews are expected.

Germans have no consideration for anything. Polish peasants collected for labor are forced to transport ammunition to the front line. They are killed and wounded. Others escape, leaving horses and wagons behind.

Jews talk about (they do not want to provide surnames) that a German officer lived with a Jewish woman whose husband was in Lwów. He often saw his photograph. The officer found himself in Lwów and met this Jew from whom brought a letter to his wife. That would seem to prove that not all Germans are hostile to Jews. This Jew wrote that many of them were leaving to the east.

12th July 1941. Various rescue services have been established. The dollar and gold have plummeted. Perhaps the Germans are doing well because the Jews are very sad.

Mid July. Besides the war, two matters excite both Poles and Jews: the establishment of relations between Poland and Russia, also that Germans absolutely want to create in the GG a puppet Polish government, but they cannot achieve it.

18th July 1941. Today there was talk of posters, or rather large format announcements, with a sign 'V.' You can see them everywhere: at the railway station, in the windows of German shops, on fences. There were long debates on what it means. Finally it was explained that the 'V' was Viktoria, that Germany will obtain victory in the end.

Meanwhile, gold and the dollar jumped again. This was because of America, which at any moment is to enter the war.

From various signs, it seems that the Jews are destined to be the sacrificial goat, the consequences of such or other German failures will fall on them. In preparation, there were various provocative rumors. In the last issue of 'Das Reich' an anti-Jewish article appeared by Goebbels himself. The consequences of this article did not take long.

Today, that is 21st July, became doomsday for Jews. The immediate cause was the fact that the Germans caught replacements of Jewish laborers working instead of the rich. They are already so haggard and exhausted that they faint or even die at work. Many Jews were rounded up during the day and detained at the Arbeitsamt [Office of labor] without food until night. Finally they were released with a warning that no one should dare to send a substitute, and that even the richest must go to work himself. The rich however found a way out. A multitude of new functions were created at the Jewish council, and they got positions for themselves there.

On 20th July, a great uproar in Rzeszów was caused by the return from the 'other side' of the famous lawyer in Rzeszów, Dr. Braunfeld, along with his son in law. And this was after the article by Goebbels, and after his announcement that one must have special permission to return. The return of the two 'swallows' was all the more interesting because Dr. Braunfeld was known as an extremely smart lawyer who knew how to use loopholes and tricks. He returned, using just such a loophole.

And it happened like this: an important German officer lived with the wife and daughter of Braunfeld, who greatly enjoyed living in that house. Now this officer, having obtained a certificate from a German doctor that Mrs. Braunfeld is very ill and needs care, went to Lwów. The doctor and his family were no longer Jews but evangelists. On the basis of the medical certificate, evangelical birth certificates with German names and with the support of that officer, they got the pass to Rzeszów. Their arrival created much commotion, it reached the Gestapo which had excellent intelligence among the Jews. On 25th July they were both arrested. Since then, news about them have disappeared.

After this event, Jewish public opinion turned against the Kahal and the wife and daughter of Braunfeld, that they and the Kahal are guilty of the death of the husband and father.

At the very end of July some Jews, who had been deported in Spring to work, returned to Rzeszów in a deplorable state. About many however, there were no news at all.

Whole columns of vans are arriving from the front to ammunition depots both in Glogów and Sokolow. The Germans bring a lot of pillaged goods including plenty of food. Again the Jews through their children are buying them up and doing good business, especially in food. They sell to their own people in Rzeszów for considerable sums.

Ukrainians have met with disappointment. They had expected a proclamation of greater Ukraine, meanwhile, rumors appeared that Eastern Malopolska will be included in the GG. Despite this, many Ukrainians are planning to return to their own homeland.

In early August appeared a proclamation of the actual annexation 'District Galizien' GG. The community treats this as a joke. Among Jews, revived the hope to unite families separated for two years.

DEPRESSION

The conquests of the Germans and their rapid march to the east greatly depressed both Poles and Jews. But they did not destroy the belief in the eventual defeat of Germany. However, anxiety has grown because of another cause, and is compounded by a number of reports about the death of those deported to concentration camps. A deepening concern is that Germany, drunk on victories, will begin a fierce oppression of its most hated nations, the Poles and the Jews.

In different nations, different factors affect their resistance, their behavior, their attitudes or even their capacity for renewal. For Jews, one of these factors is the ability to trade, not only selling, but trading, even if it has to be amid the greatest difficulties. It is precisely this which generates a lot of spirit, and fuels their energy to live.

The situation of Rzeszów Jews compared with the situation of Jews in the provinces, in towns and in villages, is much worse. 'Provincials' have much more freedom and opportunities. Living in modest circumstances, generally poorer than urban dwellers, they were not in the eye of the German authorities and had not become the object of their greed. Often, even a friendly neighborly co-existence with the Polish people, made their lives easier. It is thanks to that, they can support the large cluster in Rzeszów in various ways.

Jews in Rzeszów are already stocking up on firewood with the help of their provincial co-religionists. Transactions take place only with the supply delivered in place.

At the front, after a long silence, it is announced that a third and final offensive had begun.

In mid-August, the Germans assumed a triumphant tone. Everywhere one reads huge red headlines: 'Die bolschewistische Armee zerschlagen! 895,000 Gefangene;

Panzerwagen 13,145, 10,388 Geschiitze, 9,082 Flugzeug vernichtet oder erbeutet!' *

* (The Bolshevik army is smashed! 895,000 prisoners, 13,145 armored vehicles, 10,388 guns, 9,082 aircraft destroyed or captured!)

Terror seized people but it soon dissipated. Diligent readers of the German newspaper, and especially Jews with their minds educated in the Talmud, found large discrepancies in the descriptions of events from previous and recent times. Victory seemed to be only on paper, propaganda to support the German spirit for war. From all this it follows that the defeat of the Soviet army is not so drastic, and that the army was not beaten but dispersed. This was clearly understood by the discerning Polish and Jewish minds.

Did the German minds understand? There are many indications that in Germany there is great anxiety. Among the Ukrainians there is disappointment and bitterness towards the Germans. One hears of numerous arrests especially among the leaders.

The Germans enlist even young boys into the army. There seems to be disagreements between Hitler and Brauchits, because Hitler was to make a peace offer to the British. This all gives hope, but also evokes fear of some German fury.

13th August 1941. All night from 12 to 1 motorized divisions raced east. Maybe the English declaration is close?

16th August 1941. News came of Roosevelt's signing a declaration. Actually, it signifies American entry into the war. Foreheads become smoother.

An announcement, allegedly by Hitler, has been circulating for a long time, eagerly confirmed by the Germans that the Soviet campaign would not last longer than 72 days. Why exactly 72 days? Superstition. . . Kabbala . . . Magic?

72 days are actually at an end but one cannot say the same about the German campaign. And since this is not just about, 'schadenfreude' (pleasure from another's misfortune,) but actually about life, joy albeit having to be hidden is great. And again jokes appeared, signs of a brighter mood:

A Jew is walking back from work, black eye, swollen cheek, slightly limping.

'What happened?' asks a friend aghast.

'Everything is just fine.' replied the man.

According to the opinion of Germans themselves, Hitler is superstitious. He surrounds himself with soothsayers, clairvoyants, naturopaths, especially since the start of the war with Russia. Once he heard about a famous Jewish clairvoyant. He summoned him and asked in an imperious tone:

'Who will win the war?'

'Achse (the Axis') responds the Rebbe without hesitation.

'And who will lose the most?'

'Jud (The Jew') falls the immediate response.

'You can go!' shouted the jubilant Hitler, and the Jew leaning and bowing went out.

He comes back to his coreligionists who are dying of curiosity and anxiety and tells them what was asked and what he said.

'Rebbe! Rebbe!' they raised desperate moans and screams. 'You said this? You?! Rebbe! The Achse will win and the Jew lose! Rebbe!!!'

'Sha-Sha!' the Rebbe calmed the crowd smiling.

'This will happen like I said. The Achse-Ch-S-E, that is: America, China, the Soviet Union and England, and Jud will lose: Italien und Deutschland.'

In fact Jewish jokes are very popular and repeated with enthusiasm.

72 days passed and the defeat of the Soviets seems still far away. Or maybe something opposite has begun? Again a feverish atmosphere.

2nd September 1941. Today, 'Krakówski Messenger,' the German daily, issued in Polish language, had an article in it:

'It would be a mistake to predict the final outcome of the struggle between armies of millions, because until now, the course of the war brought us so many surprises that all prognoses for the future become unpredictable.' Typical! After so much fanfare!

Concerning compulsory contributions, the Germans are in a veritable frenzy and seize them in without mercy, while on the roads they carry outright robbery. Naturally, the Poles have reacted accordingly. And, because they tower over Germans in cunning, they avoid many traps and snares. They invent so many ways to dodge the Germans who are furious and helpless.

Jokes appear in increasing numbers, which means that the mood is lifting. And this is in September, the third anniversary of the German attack on Poland. And the Germans also seem to leave Jews in peace, apart from driving them to work. In this matter, the Jews are also able to manage, because the Germans are increasingly eager to take bribes. But this cannot last.

Jewish jokes are still the most popular. God knows whether they are made up by Jews. And even if not, then this particular Jewish joke against the Germans is most suitable.

There was lot of noise, conjecture and speculation in connection with the meeting of Hitler and Mussolini.

'Nu, what do you think about this meeting, Mr. Luft?'
One Jew asks another.

'You don't know?' replies Luft, with a question to a question. 'When partners come together, business is sure to come to nothing.'

Hitler again ordered to call in 'his' rabbi. He engages him in a friendly chat in which he moves slowly to the topic of the 'rod of Moses.' He asks, as if in passing, what were its properties. But the Rebbe caught on and begins talking about its real miracles, how it can divide the water in the sea to cross by on dry land to the other side, that ...

'And where is it now?' asks Hitler seeming casually, actually trembling with excitement.

'Nu, it is currently in London in the British Museum,' with a half-smile the Rebbe explained.

After that response, Hitler changed the subject. At one point, trying to find out what opinion the Jews had about him, he asked the rabbi for a loan of a thousand złoty. Rebe willingly took the note out of his pocket and gave to the Führer.

'How is it?' Hitler was surprised. 'You slander me so much, and you're not afraid to lend me so much money? Are not you afraid that I will not repay you?'

'Why should I be afraid? You have taken Poland, France, Belgium, Netherlands, Norway, Yugoslavia, Greece and you will give it all back, so wouldn't you give back this stupid one thousand złoty to a poor Jew?' replied the Rebbe with a question to question.

The third year of the war. According to pre-war opinion, a modern war cannot last long. But what has happened? It is already two years and its end cannot be foreseen.

Jews are living in various conditions, some well, and there are even quite a number of them, and others are living in terrible poverty. One sees real human skeletons wrapped in rags. Only now one can see Jewish 'aristocracy' of the Judenrat and various functionaries of the Board of the Jewish community. They have almost unlimited power which they actually received from the hands of the Gestapo, whom they serve completely. This is also one of the German methods, giving such power to those who never had it and allowing them to use it without limits. Germans knew that a sudden seizure of power often corrupts, so they corrupted the Judenrat completely. They are in the hands of the Gestapo and have to serve their purpose. And one such is the moral degradation of the Jews. The Judenrat at all cost are determined to remain on top regardless of the fate of the masses, and the fact they are hated more than the Gestapo is completely of no importance for them. The Judenrat fleeces their fellow Jews unmercifully. This is supposedly for gifts for the Gestapo and for their parties. If by some miracle at this point all obtained freedom, the fate of the Judenrat would be terrible: a lynching. If here and there appear any signs of reaction against what is happening, the Judenrat quashes it decisively, not being fussy about the means. It allows some charitable operation, which is managed by young people, brought up in a different spirit.

In mid-September came absolutely fantastic news that the Germans in the east are in trouble. It is true that paint recently washed down from the windows in the Polish Aviation Factory is again hastily reapplied. There is a prevailing psychosis that war might even come to these parts. This terrifies the Germans and the 'native' population in GG very little.

Close to Raniżow, in the area of the town, part of which was a German colony from the late eighteenth century, in the vicinity of the secret terrain for training SS troops, it is planned to create some large German colony. This is spoken in connection with the displacement of entire villages. Firstly went Jewish farmers, living in relatively large numbers in Razinow itself as well as neighboring villages Staniszewski, Zielonka, Masuria. They were allowed to take with them everything except cattle. They established themselves in Głogów and Sokolow.

It is already an open secret that the German authorities treat Soviet prisoners brutally. They feed them poorly and beat them. This is something unheard of. There are even whispers about shooting of prisoners. This is terrible!

23rd September 1941. Rumors more and more optimistic. Many believe increasingly that the war might be over this year and at latest next spring, as in 1813 after Napoleon's defeat in Russia.

In the German army, perhaps not for all, hunger now reigns. The soldiers who guard huge stockpiles of ammunition in Glogów get disgusting food. They steal cabbages and potatoes from the fields, they kill with bayonets poultry that wander away from houses. They plunder sheds and stables for eggs and openly rob the Jews. They take their clothes which they then sell, but mostly they prefer to swap them for food. If the aggrieved Jew goes to complain he gets such a beating that he comes out barely alive. The officers concerned have no proper control over the soldiers.

Unprecedented restrictions have been introduced for food and others things, 'everything for victory.'

24th September 1941. In addition to repression and economic deprivation, came reports about new successes of the Germans in the east. A new wave of depression fell among the Jews, the deeper because their lot is so hard.

The morale of the Poles was influenced by news of the formation of a large Polish army in Russia which will take part in battles against the Germans.

At the end of September, news began to arrive of

increased very heavy bombing on Germany. Whether or not in connection with these news, a rumor spread that a large, most orderly part of the city because it was modern, that is the streets Jagiellońska, May and Castle would be completely 'cleansed' of Poles, who will be moved to homes in the current Jewish quarter, and Jews will be housed in barracks somewhere outside the city. As rumors often come true, the Jews were almost out of their minds. They sense what is menacing them.

Many Hungarians arrived in Rzeszów having stopped on the way to the front. They salute all Germans. This is very distasteful. Their relation to the Polish and Jewish population is quite friendly. Especially the Jews, with whom they develop trade relations.

In early October, appeared great loads of barbed wire moving to the east. The wire is already very rusty, probably removed from fortifications in the west. Did the Germans want to wire themselves off for the winter? Was it possible that the announcement of the imminent beating of Russia was a flop?

3rd October 1941. Between hours 9 and 10, some companies of soldiers who had arrived only yesterday from the front to rest, surrounded the whole suburb so tightly that even a mouse could not squeeze through.

Irrespective of that, every street and alley, all the lanes, tenements and gates were shut also. There was no room to move. Fear fell on those trapped, people struggled like birds in nets.

At one point, many German policemen and guards rolled into the surrounded district. A seeming scrutiny of documents began, but in fact, of goods and food. Finally the main purpose was revealed: to plunder the Jews. The policemen and guards broke into Jewish homes where without pity they took away cash, jewelry, materials, furs, shoes, bed linen and bedding. The loot was driven away in trucks. Jews who tried in some way to defend their possessions were beaten.

The soldiers behaved with dignity and quietly. Apparently they believed that it was not fitting for a soldier to participate in such 'bedlam.'

4th October 1941. In the town, no one is talking about anything but of yesterday's operation. The reason for it has also become clear. Actually the Hungarians had robbed a military store and sold a lot of goods to Jews, hence this inspection. During the search for those goods, other possessions were taken away, and where something stolen was actually found, nothing was left. They even took white flour dough, butter and any fat.

The trade of Jews with Hungarians began almost from the first hours of their arrival. Hungarians look and behave like a 'civilian' group. Only officers carry guns. They hate the Germans, who in turn despise them. Between the allies occur incidents and brawls. Hungarians openly provoke the Germans. One can now see what friendship there is between them.

The battle for Moscow has begun. Unprecedented movement of cargo aircraft. Is it not in relation to that battle?

The friendship between Poles and Hungarians is blooming. The Hungarians curse the Germans dreadfully, they loathe them. It was revealed that among the troops, ran anti-Nazi leaflets.

8th October 1941. Three degrees of frost. How is it, near Moscow and Leningrad?

10th October 1941. 'Der Krieg im Osten ist entschieden!' (The war in the east is settled!)

Such headlines appeared in German newspapers today. Was it really? It would be terrible. Many people break down, but there are optimists who mock this.

11ᵗʰ October 1941. Today the Hungarian battalion in Rzeszów moved out. 'Well, they have stolen enough!' say the Jews. 'More such battalions, and war would soon be over

Already, since one week ago, mass transports of German troops are going from east to west. What is the meaning of this?

12ᵗʰ October 1941. In Rzeszów it is already the usual winter.

14ᵗʰ October 1941. Today, warm bedding was again taken from the Jews. Apparently everything was for the soldiers in the east where there is already a severe winter.

Jews are being robbed at every step. If a Jew stops in the street or buys something a few minutes before eleven, or looks out onto the street on Sunday, he is at once grabbed by a German or Polish policeman who immediately imposes a penalty of 5 to 100 złoty. They give a receipt for small fines, but not for big ones. Pure business. Food prices are rising but wages remain the same.

Jews from the area Kolbuszowa are being settled in Glogów; from Glogów, formerly displaced people from the west are transferred to the barracks in Rzeszów. The fate of these people will be worse than terrible. They are threatened with starvation.

15ᵗʰ to 16ᵗʰ October 1941. During the night, throughout the city, someone with a sword and on empty buckets beat out many times: 'Nieder mit dem Hitler!' (Down with Hitler) Mostly in Jagiellonski Street where the Gestapo is located. Will there be reprisals? People are quaking.

The ghostly spectre of the ghetto is materializing. Only now, the Jews admit that for a long time they did not take it quite seriously, and they considered the issue of the ghetto a bogey and a means of blackmail, because the Germans have already drawn out a lot of money from the Jews, just scaring them with the ghetto. Now the Germans themselves say nothing about the ghetto and do not demand money. Despite the inconvenient season, bricklayers are working feverishly, they close off various passages and entries, naturally at the expense of the Jewish community. And how it costs!!

Mortality among the Jewish poor is high from starvation of course.

Great depression. The dollar is 50 złoty, gold 40 złoty per gram. Food is very expensive.

Poles are returning from the east where the Germans had taken them, either as laborers or as drivers of horse wagons. It is dreadful to listen to them, to what they tell. A horrible butchery, piles of corpses from both sides. The retreating Soviets are destroying everything. Over there will be real destruction. This year the Germans do not gain anything there.

21ˢᵗ October 1941. After several months of illness, Ehaus returned to Rzeszów. The street quickly tidies up the area of Dombrowski Street, where he resides in the palace, or rather an estate decorated at great expense and labor. New sidewalks are installed, hedges planted, roads repaired ... Once again crowds of Jewish young men and women are driven to work. They work in mud and rain, dirty, shrivelled, not resembling humans. Some of them, especially the pious ones, say it is God's punishment, because the Jews never wanted to work physically.

It was well known that Ehaus is a pervert, a sex maniac. If he notices a young Jewish woman, he either orders her to be beaten for a fictitious offense or even does it himself. They are very afraid to go to work there.

With the arrival of Ehaus, preparations for the closure of the ghetto are in full swing. At the same time, it is said that the Jews once again paid a large sum, and the deadline of the ghetto was postponed. For how long? To live constantly in the shadow of this nightmare is to be in the vestibule of hell.

In late October, rumors began to arrive that near Moscow and Leningrad, terrible battles are raging. Could Germany conclude the war before winter? ... Would they acquire these key cities?

A dollar is 40 złoty, gold 28. The supply is large and demand relatively small. Both come from Jewish reserves.

Although it is already November, work on tidying up 'the district Ehaus' is in full swing. Even shops and apartment buildings are being painted in the area. The poorest beggars are still doing the work, the rich just send them in.

Someone pointed out to some important German, that if Jews are really a danger to Reich it is above all the rich, the capitalists, not the poor. Meanwhile, they stay at home doing very well, and the poorest, the least dangerous, are dying. The German then replied: 'They too will get their turn.'

Depressing news are coming from the east. Masses of Jews are murdered for alleged cooperation with the Soviets. In Stanislaw, many Jews were shot for the murder of a German officer: they say twelve thousand, in Kolomyl two thousand were murdered. News of deaths of many Rzeszów Jews have also arrived. Weeping, moaning, grief. Among Jews there is a deathly atmosphere and the worst forebodings.

A few days ago, a neatly dressed man was driven into the forest in Babicy and was shot. Above the corpse they nailed a note to a tree saying: 'Jew, lawyer, a criminal.' Was it not perhaps Dr. Braunfeld who recently returned home illegally from Lwów to Rzeszów?

Autumn. A typical late autumn, soggy, cold, mud up to the ears. Right now the Germans want, or more precisely Ehaus wants, a series of works, and those on a large scale. Throughout the beautiful summer actually nothing was done. The Poles had a high opinion of German organization of work, and now? They curse and now they see it differently.

In the summer, Hetmanska Street was dug over. It was turned 'upside down.' Now in the winter, work has started again. What torture for people. It seems that it is done deliberately to harass people. There must be a lot more perverts like Ehaus among the Germans.

There is now loud talk about a complete collapse of the German offensive on Moscow and that America is just about to enter the war.

11th November 1941. This morning, the whole town was plastered with flyers on which was the Polish eagle and the inscription: 'Poland will win.' The community is both glad and sad, what if there are to be new repressions?...

Concerning the ghetto, a new hell. Recently, after the seizure of many Jewish homes in the city centre, many Jewish families were moved into Orzeszkowa Street, into the north eastern outskirts of the city. Actually, Jews felt better, because they had moved away from the eyes of their persecutors and found excellent opportunities for contacts for food trading. But soon, the Germans sniffed it out, or maybe someone drew their attention to it? So these people are again moved back into town to the Jewish quarter. The 'Kahalniks' make good business out of this, taking huge bribes for housing, which is so difficult to get. For this reason, there is great discord among the Jews. Large numbers accuse the Kahal point blank, that it is they who want the ghetto because then they will have unlimited power. But maybe it is just bitterness speaking through the lips of tormented people?

A few weeks before, still during the absence of Ehaus, some department managers took from the Jews 30,000 złoty to postpone the closing of the ghetto until spring. Ehaus crossed all that off. He speeds up the work and announces its early conclusion.

The myth of Jewish solidarity, their tribal power, their discretion, has vanished completely. All the dirty tricks, and there are many, are already well known to everyone. Now it turns out how, by their abnormal life, this people is undermined. And not only Poles, but also many Germans, who not so long ago had compassion for the Jews, begin to feel distaste towards them. Progressive Jewish youth, who suffer, especially looking at the fall of their own people, say out loud, that their nation, who recently had succumbed to the worship of the golden calf, has to be fundamentally transformed. These young people judge the Kahal still more severely, accusing them directly of collusion with the Germans and the sharing of property ripped out from their coreligionists.

Coming back from work today, the Polish brigade sang with all the breath in their lungs: 'My rosemary' ... and about the sabre. People were crying with emotion and happiness.

14th November 1941. What a winter! People are simply freezing, they complain.

'And what would you do if you were at this moment near Moscow?' someone asks a shivering man.

Actually, from Moscow come wonderful news. Germans have received a monstrous beating. Russians were helped by this terrible winter for them too. People rub their hands from the cold and from satisfaction.

Trains arrive with the frostbitten. Jews cannot enjoy these events, because the nightmare of the ghetto, which has threatened for a long time is rushing at great speed toward the terrified people. Now there is no way for them to protect themselves against it.

Houses in the Old Market were divided into two parts: the Jewish and the Aryan. Through the middle of the walls of houses they built a wall and a second staircase. The ghetto is being surrounded more and more tightly with high fences. Only here and there are built some gates. The overcrowding is unbelievable. Into one apartment, even into a single room, a few families are pushed in together. The fight for a corner is simply terrible. For many it is lucky if they can at least put down a bed. Thus a lot of furniture is sold for a song, or given in pledge for a loan. Whoever cannot sell it now or has nowhere to place it, he just leaves it. The municipality takes it. It is obvious that the purpose of this action is the destruction of the Jews, and even prior to that to apply sophisticated and sadistic torments. Apparently the torture of others is necessary for the German soul.

Jews with desperate determination pray to God to survive till spring. In spring, disaster for Germany will surely occur and deliverance for the Jews will come. 'But who will survive to see this?' they sadly end every discussion.

Misfortunes always come in pairs. It's not enough that Germans seize the food, but this year a lot of potatoes were not harvested in the fields. And those that were already collected as a contingency and temporarily only lightly covered, froze. Hunger.

Trains are still running with a healthy army to the west.

Conditions in the camps of Soviet prisoners are dreadful. Hunger and cold ... They say the seriously ill are killed to get some rags sooner.

In America, the statute of neutrality had been cancelled. Another ray of hope.

17th November 1941. The fate of the ghetto is in balance and the same is for the Jews themselves. Once again they want to save themselves with bribery. Only now it appears that the Jews have a protector, who is the city Commissioner, Dr. Huller, a Viennese. He definitely did not submit to government authorities, he is neither a Nazi nor an anti-Semite. As a Viennese, he likes a carefree life and to have fun. The Jews found a way to him and to his sympathetic ear. It seems that Ehaus became aware of this, and he is an implacable enemy of the Jews. As a result of his efforts, Dr. Huller has to leave Rzeszów. Even the Ortskommandant can do nothing to help, though the main communication artery to the east would pass through the ghetto. Ehaus is implacable. Already those Jews who have supplied military quarters received orders to leave their homes and to move to the Jewish quarter. Widespread panic. The threatened Jews buy food at any cost so there is a crazy hike in prices.

At the entrance to the Old Market- in Mickiewicz Street and New Tow- huge gates are constructed in Galezowski Street which, however, will have to be open during the day and night for the movement of military vehicles. For this reason, the creation of the ghetto was opposed by the Orstkommandant and the Executive Board of the city, and actually the deputy commandant, because the commandant was on leave. And also Soltner, in charge of Jewish Affairs. The Chief ordered absolute opposition to the first, while the deputy was well 'lubricated.' Between Ehaus and the deputy commander occurred a hellish row. Ehaus has to be very important and have great influence, because the deputy captain, Dr. Huller, and Soltner, have already received a transfer. It is said that the same fate will meet the Commander as soon as he gets back from leave. For now, the only Jew in Rzeszów living outside the ghetto is the Commander's hostess. He had commissioned her to guard the responsibility. On 18th November is announced the great final meeting concerning the ghetto. All Jews are waiting for the outcome with great anxiety, like an accused for a judgment: acquittal or death.

20th November 1941. The meeting took place, and now everyone knew there was a big fight, they almost punched one another. The Jews know this through their protectors, but this is small consolation for them, compared to the date set for closing the ghetto. This is to be 29th November, that is the following Saturday. Jews sell everything not essential and buy food.

23rd November 1941. The Germans are strangely nervous and agitated. Their attitude to the Poles has suddenly hardened. It is simply intolerable. Is it due to the participation of Polish pilots in the bombing of Germany? And what will be their attitude to Jews?

German planes are flying east.

The Germans' rage about the defeat, falls primarily on the Soviet prisoners. They are driven, standing in open cars, in rain and snow, fulfilling their physical needs where they stand. They are starved, beaten, shot for a hand stretched out for a piece of bread. It is common to speak of cases of cannibalism among the Soviet prisoners of war ... Terrible!

24th November 1941. In the town hall, there was a ceremonial farewell for Drs. Huller and Soltner. Ehaus was at the farewell, undoubtedly to keep up appearances. He praised the merits of the Commissioner for the city, especially in the setting up of the ghetto. Ehaus' speech was full of unconcealed irony. Those present, sensed that Dr. Hüller was actually being censured. In response, he found at the end a few warm sentences for Polish officials. This was so characteristic of the man, proof of his culture and courage.

13 degrees of frost. Work on the road in the Hetmańska Street goes full steam ahead. When striking the frozen ground, sparks are flying. How is it outside Moscow or Leningrad?

Train are arriving full of frost bitten soldiers. There is talk of the tragedy of the German army, from the Polish side, with insane joy.

29th November 1941. Saturday. The ghetto has not been closed yet. There is talk that between Ehaus and the Orstkommandant, who came back from leave, took place a furious row, and almost came to blows. And what would be the result? Is there a connection between this row and the delay in closing of the ghetto?

The through traffic from west to east, which ran across Kosciuszko Street, Old Market, the streets Mickiewicz and Galçzowski to Lwów Street, will be changed. From Kosciuszko Street, it will be directed to Grunwald and Sobieski Streets. Across Kosciuszko Street, next to the outlet of Grunwald Street, they are digging in huge posts, a sign that the traffic in this direction will be barred.

The situation for Germans who found themselves in the Soviet territories is supposed to be very difficult. They found no furniture nor bedding. Once again the Jews are to be responsible. They are looted of their bedding in an inhuman manner, especially featherbeds and pillows. But in the ghetto, hygiene conditions are deplorable, the bedding is indescribably filthy. This does not seem to disgust the 'cultured nation of the masters.'

6th December 1941. Poles talk of nothing other than the visit of Gen. Sikorski to Moscow.

The date of the ghetto closure is again not decided. There are whispers that the Jews delayed it for a few months with a big sum, maybe even until spring. And moreover, it whispered that Ehaus is leaving, following this famous row. It is difficult to confirm these rumors.

The latest speech by Churchill, that the war will drag on until 1943, greatly depressed people. Dollar fell to 60 złoty. America would only be ready by that time. Terrible!

7th December 1941. Today, a large squad of young Jewish women came from the ghetto to remove snow from the streets. Many of them well dressed. Chic, moving gracefully, they attract the attention of the Germans. They stop, smile, and say something. You can see that any of them would have been happy to engage in flirting or maybe even a romance?

8th December 1941. Japan has attacked America. And so the whole world is on fire. The Germans have sad faces. Why? Everyone is talking of a Soviet offensive. Behind the German army, partisan units are forming.

15th December 1941. GG government wants to send Ukrainians back to the east, to the Ukraine, to compensate them for the harm done to them by the Polish government, but Ukrainian nationals are terribly afraid and opposed to it. Where would they be better off than here? After all, they have plenty of everything. It is also loudly said that 'teasing' of the Poles will soon begin.

16th December 1941. In the morning, a German policeman stopped a cart going to Tyczyn. On the cart was a Jewish woman, who was carrying some food. The policeman calmly shot the woman. Is that human?

In the afternoon, the same day, a German soldier crosses the Wisłok with a goose which he bought in Drabiniance. Probably going on leave, he wanted to take it home. The boat capsized and the soldier drowned. Excitement among the Jews. They consider the death of the soldier to be a clear punishment from God.

There are more frequent cases of enteric typhoid fever. In the German army, typhus is raging. In Rzeszów, there is a whole area of barracks belonging to the hospital for infectious diseases.

18th December 1941. Today, a rumor spread that the ghetto would be closed, but only for the Jews. Entrance to the ghetto would be allowed for non-Jews. Already, a security group is formed, in German Ordnungsdienst. But generally, it is called 'Jewish police.'

21st December 1941. The rumors proved true: tonight the ghetto was closed, but really, only for Jews. Aryans are issued with special passes to the ghetto.

GHETTO

Ehaus had nevertheless stood his ground.

On the night of 20th to 21st December 1941, the ghetto was closed. It became Judgement Day in there. Indeed, it is actually shutting thousands of people in jail. In the evening, the closing of the ghetto was announced by sirens, something like an air raid siren. It was only a rehearsal. A typically German joke.

23rd December 1941. In the morning, on the city walls, various posters were pasted and printed on them, firstly was a regulation from the governor General Frank dated: Warsaw, 15th October 1941, which reads:

1) Jews who leave their designated quarter without a permit will be subject to the death penalty. The same penalty shall apply to persons who knowingly provide such Jews with a hiding place.

2) The instigators and helpers are subject to the same punishment as the perpetrator.

3) The decision will be settled by special courts.

This Regulation enters into force on the day of the announcement.

Based on the above basic regulation, Ehaus issues a 'police order' to create Jewish neighborhoods in the territory of Reichshof (Rzeszów.) In Rzeszów itself, Jews were allotted 24 streets and two squares.

Paragraph 5 says that this regulation comes into force on 10th January 1942 in Rzeszów, and on 1st February in the country.

Some Jews did not wait for this moment. The more courageous, possessing few Semitic features, having some capital resources and good Polish friends, risk leaving Rzeszów, first providing for themselves with false papers. They travelled mostly to big cities like Warsaw or Kraków, where it is easier to lose oneself in the crowd. Some others came to Rzeszów from other cities, took up some jobs, and various occupations.

A sensation and a revelation for everyone, is the resignation of General Brauchitsch. This event is variously discussed. It is certain there had been a division of opinion with Hitler.

Germans want to reach the hearts of Poles by way of the stomach. For the holidays, they gave extraordinary rations, simultaneously with the announcement of the closure of the ghetto. Interesting methods: Polish officials were given leave from 24th December 1941 until 2nd January 1942, and offices were closed for that period. It is not without significance.

During the holidays, many German women came to visit the men serving in the military. Such couples were assigned, for this time, extra rooms with furniture and bedding robbed from Jews of course. It is hard to believe that these couples did not know it.

Hungarians are retreating, that is from west to east.

Large numbers of typhoid patients and frostbitten soldiers are brought to Rzeszów. Daily 6 to 10 people die. There is worry about what is happening in the east. Therefore, some Jews, even under the spectre of the ghetto, are optimistic that this could soon end.

27th December 1941. Saturday. At dawn, all gates leading to the ghetto were closed. Navy-blue police stood by them and German ones went inside. They went from house to house, from apartment to apartment, and announced that, under the penalty of immediate death, all furs, even cuts and scraps, have to be surrendered. They went along without taking anything. Just behind them marched in the members of the Kahal, repeated the order and designated the collection place for furs, namely the building of the Kahal.

Throughout the district, there were frantic searches, tearing out, and cutting up. More than a dozen sacks were brought in. And what kinds of furs! Many millions in value. The Jewish passion for the beautiful furs of martens, polecats, silver foxes, otters, beavers was well known.

Collection is collection, but did this action need to be marked in blood? Several Hasidic Jews, though it was strictly forbidden, gathered in one of the houses on Copernicus Street for the Sabbath prayer. The German police found them, and began to beat them. After the beating was finished, one of the Jews wanted to leave, but the policeman took out his pistol and shot him dead on the spot. Then he delivered a few extra shots to the fallen man. It was probably an act of rage.

In another place, a Jewish furrier did not want to give up the fur, explaining that it was not his but that of a Polish client. The policeman shot him, and again a corpse. The Jewish woman in the house was left unharmed. An older man, at the time of the shooting and the screams, died of heart attack.

The closure of the ghetto, the swarm of police, the shooting, distressed all the locked up people terribly. Presumably some will begin to run away again.

The next day in the 'Krakauer' appeared a warning from Hitler, that if anyone dared to take just one piece of fur from these 'voluntary' requisitions, he would be immediately shot. This mostly related to 'their own.'

The dollar was again 75 złoty.

On railway stations, even on the streets, it often happens that soldiers take furs from civilians by force.

31st December 1941. That morning, the Schupo Battalion 313, which gave such grief to Jews, departed from Rzeszów. So in Rzeszów, there is only very little police left. Today, elegantly dressed, Jewish women, again cleared the streets of snow. The Germans plainly enjoy this.

2nd January 1942. Who would have thought that the war would drag until this time! 26 degrees of frost. And near Moscow? There is no coal, food is poor. People pray God for few more degrees. It is from 'love' for the Germans, champions of Christian culture.

Churchill made another speech where he predicted the end of the war in 1944. People comment, ask each other whether perhaps the old man has gone crazy.

Rzeszów is one big hospital, only for typhus victims and frostbite. The daily mortality rate has risen to ten people.

Ehaus called in Jewish doctors to investigate if there was any typhus in the ghetto. He warned them, that concealing even one case of typhus, was on their head. They guaranteed there was none and invited a German committee to investigate. Indeed it was a miracle that in such difficult conditions, there is no contagion.

5th January 1942. According to the regulation of Ehaus, in three days the ghetto is to be definitively closed. To this end, at the inlet and outlet of the road running through the ghetto, powerful gates have been installed. Jews are no longer counting days, but hours. But that day at 1pm, a group of workers came to both gates and began to demolish them. Unable to dig up the posts because of the frozen solid earth, they cut them down right to the ground. These same workers removed the bollards blocking entry to Kosciuszko Street. After these works, made in rapid succession, the first military car traversed the Market, by Galęzowska and Mickiewicz streets to New Town, welcomed by the Jews with a sense of relief, as a harbinger of life. Once again hope flowed into many hearts.

The removal of these gates is one of the manifestations, invisible to the Poles and Jews, of the struggle between Ehaus and the Ortskommandant. Whether this action of the latter is motivated in respect to the Jews, concern for the convenience of military transports, or personal reasons and ambition, is hard to know. Enough that victory is on his side.

The landlady of the commander, in accordance with the order of the administration, had to move out to the ghetto, leaving the apartment to a well-disposed tenant. He also gave her a pass. With this, she leaves the ghetto every morning, and returns in the evening, housekeeping all day in her own apartment.

But Ehaus is really a fiercely stubborn item. It seems, that at any price, he decided to stand his ground. He plans to demolish several houses and to cut straight through Kosciuszko Street to the Kraków Street right next to the Bernardine church. And to show it was not a baseless threat, they have already begun to demolish the pillars near the Bernardine church from Bernardine Street and from Kraków Street. This is called war.

In the meantime, a 'police order' dated 5th January, 1942, and signed by Ehaus, was again pasted on the city walls. It said:

"Due to sanitary security, it is prohibited for German, and German Aryan population, to enter into established Jewish neighborhoods, in Rzeszów and Kolbuszow. In exceptional cases, it is acceptable to enter Jewish neighborhoods with a written permission."

Next, followed more criminal penalties, and that this order will take effect on 10th January. So Ehaus is also stubborn. There may not be gates, there may be traffic through the ghetto, but the Jews have to be locked up and separate.

9th January 1942. That evening, they finally shut in the Jews. Many Poles were witnesses when the gates were nailed, with the exception of Mickiewicz and Galezowskie streets, where police stations have been set up, namely German, Polish and Jewish police. Faces of witnesses froze with terror. Total annihilation. It seemed as if live people are shut in a monstrous coffin. Some people remembered a painting by Matejko, 'The Descent to the cellar of Maciek Borkowic, to a certain and horrible death from starvation.'

10ᵗʰ January 1942. Plague is spreading through the whole district. It is spread by Soviet prisoners who escaped from German captivity and whom the Polish population take under their roof. The prisoners are covered in lice. In Rzeszów itself there have been three cases of the disease. From 12ᵗʰ January, which is from Monday, Polish schools, cinemas and even churches will be closed.

It is becoming increasingly evident that the East German army is experiencing a disaster. So, among many soldiers, one can observe despair. Incredible news circulate among them.

The attitude of Ukrainians to the Germans is unfriendly or even hostile. Naturally, they do not show it openly. Now one hears about a Ukrainian underground, and at the same time, about arrests and repression. Belief in the imminent defeat of Germany is rife. Here there are notions, how it would be? Many assumptions ... Human brains have an occupation.

18ᵗʰ January 1942. Supposedly, the ghetto is closed, but not enough according the idea of Ehaus. The closure is watched by Polish and Jewish policemen, under the supervision of the German police, but smuggling into the ghetto and out of the ghetto is happening almost openly, with the difference, that it costs even more, and new people, not excluding the German police, are doing good business.

Near the gates of through traffic, palaver of Jews with Poles is taking place freely. They discuss various matters that will be carried out at dusk or at a fixed location. There are already a lot of suitable places for doing business.

The fate of the poor is becoming more dreadful. From the ghetto, Jewish children cross to the Aryan side in different ways, go from house to house and ask for food. They complain about the great heartlessness of rich Jews.

Apparently, between Ehaus and the commander, a bitter war is continuing. The commander said to his hostess, who it did not fail to disseminate it, that once the typhus is controlled, the ghetto will be opened.

Hungarians and Slovaks are returning home. At the same time, large transports with all sorts of ordinance are going east, but if soldiers are going, they are largely old men and children.

Food and fuel prices are very high.

19th January 1942. Today, Ehaus introduced the new Commissioner, Albert Pavlu, brother of the Commissioner of Kraków. Apparently, they are both greatly favored by Hitler, because they had taken an active part in the assassination of Dollfuss. Ehaus, with his characteristic impudence, stated that this land for centuries was German and it flourishes only under German management. Pavlu confirmed this, and added that Rzeszów is extremely dear to him, because his father served here in the Austrian army. And so the harmony between Pavlu and Ehaus promises to be cordial.

It certainly will not be favorable for the Jews.

The third day of the ghetto has arrived. And, what was to be something tragic, is until now, ridiculous. Perhaps Ehaus is proud of his work and revels in the belief that he has actually sentenced the Jews to death by starvation. It is hard to imagine what would have happened to him with his hot tempered nature, if he knew the real situation.

The Germans have many innate and valuable characteristics, but they cannot boast about being quick witted. If it were not for the wild terrorism on their part, and the shameless shooting of people so ... Jews and Poles in the German rear could become very dangerous. Germans undoubtedly feel it, and are aware of this situation, and hence such a hatred for both Poles and Jews.

Between the ghetto and the Aryan side, there are so many passages through attics, basements and chimneys, that in fact, the ghetto is fiction. Ironically, in fact, is that in the ghetto, it is easier to obtain food than in the city. Indeed the food there is even cheaper. One just needs money. And in the ghetto there is money. There is even a lot of money. The various dealers now have an ideal setting to show off their skills. The ghetto deals only in wholesale, while on the Aryan side, they usually deal in retail, and so the ghetto gets all the goods and pays a lot of money. Therefore, traders prefer doing business with the ghetto, rather than with the Poles. As a result of supplying the ghetto, prices in the city have gone up markedly.

Smuggling of food is fully understandable. But would Ehaus believe that into the ghetto at night enter several ladies, refined elegant women, for whom only a dress, sewn by a Jewish seamstress, is a 'model?' There are fittings, quirks, whims, just as in the good old times. And again the work is usually paid with food.

At the open gates of the crossings, incessant communication between Jews with Poles takes place. Here is where business usually takes place. These gates are in fact money markets. Polish policemen pretended not to see it. They have moreover the order, above all, not to let anyone in or out. But talking?

The Jewish policemen are grotesque figures. You can see that power and importance have gone to their heads. They simply revel in their status. They walk so puffed up and so important that they look like characters in a comedy.

Jewish policemen have a round dark blue cap with white binding, whereas on the Polish design, distinction of rank is marked with shining buttons, from one to three. The mark for a Jewish policeman, is a round white badge with an engraved Star of David, and the inscription, 'Judische Ordnungsdienst' (The Jewish service.) And finally, the highest symbol of power, a rubber truncheon. They have no uniforms, they walk in civilian clothes. They wear belts.

According to Jews, the Kahal chose the worst gallows birds for policemen, to have them as faithful praetorians. They imitate the Germans in screaming and shoving people, and they take bribes, brazenly. The Jewish community call them a real plague and curse them mercilessly.

31ˢᵗ January 1942. Today Italians are wandering around the city the whole day. Their transports go one by one to the east. They wait for a locomotive but there is now a lack of these. The majority of Italians sit in the ghetto and there is great trade going on. Strange, the Germans did not forbid them entry.

The next day 1ˢᵗ February, the deadline for the return of all women and children to the Reich expires. Mrs. Ehaus has already left. What is the reason?

In place of the previous battalion of Schupo, a 111 reserve has arrived. Where from? No one knew. The police are going simply crazy. They carry out searches on their own initiative and plunder whatever falls into their hands. Because, among the Germans, the soldiers at the front, as well as civilians in the Reich, there is poverty and even starvation.

In connection with the robbery of fur, the perfect Jewish joke is going around:

'Hitler got dressed, as was his custom, in a new civilian suit and an elegant fur coat and went out into the street along with an aide. But from the very beginning, the aide noted that instead of adoring eyes and bows, people, with concealed smiles, jostled one another with elbows and walked quickly away, looking moreover back several times. Hitler noticed it also. Upset, he examined himself, looking for possible causes for laughter, and only then noticed with dismay on his right shoulder ... an armband with the Star of David.'

2nd February 1942. Hitler again gave one of his 'big speeches.' He announced that the war will drag on until 1943. And because for a long time now people take his words in reverse, because he had just announced the imminent end of it, they are glad that now they can talk about a quick German defeat. And what was most interesting, Hitler suddenly appealed to providence. Perhaps someone taught him the Polish proverb 'as the death nears the arse, so the soul runs to repentance?' *[This rhymes in Polish. ed.]*

Concurrent with Hitler's speech, in which there was again strong anti-Jewish propaganda, a big colorful poster in Polish, stupid and distasteful is put up. Do they think that Poles will believe it? The absence of a German text suggests that the designer did not believe in the naivety of the Germans.

And so, on the poster, a Jew is grinding a rat in a meat mincer which is supposed to be food for the Poles, while the second kneads dough on which crawl cockroaches. Brrr! Only Germans could create such a joke. Underneath is the inscription: 'The Jew is your only enemy.'

Who is the only enemy of the Poles? They themselves know very well. After the speech of the Führer, illustrated by the above poster, one could expect a really stricter policy against the Jews. In the city, rumors have spread that German police in the fields near Kolbuszowa shot two Jews carrying bags of potatoes, which they had bought or maybe begged for somewhere.

Whoever remembers World War I, also remembers a word coined by Austrian and German wonderworkers, said to have magical properties and bring victory. It was the word 'Durchhalten' 'endure to the end.' And here today, 5th February 1942, in the 'Krakauer,' in capital letters, stands out: 'Durchhalten!' Is this not the beginning of the end?

In the area, and in Rzeszów itself, they are again preparing buildings for the military. And the Italians are returning. This is called economy of time and equipment. Among the poor in the ghetto there is dreadful poverty, hunger and death by starvation. Those working on the streets beg for a piece of bread. Others who still have money buy. Polish boys are engaged in the sales, traders of everything, especially cigarettes. How terrible must conditions be when in spite of the danger of death, the Jews leave the ghetto to beg for something, buy it or maybe get it out of hiding. Yesterday they caught a Jew, death awaits him.

6th February 1942. At noon in the alley, Under Kasztanami, a German policeman challenged some woman who did not want to stop. He shot her on the spot. The victim turned out to be Jewish. These are the visible effects, echoes of Hitler's speech.

Days of February are passing quickly ... The Germans are preparing for some huge offensive in the spring. Generally it is thought that the German successes are not excluded, but eventually it has to come to disaster. Only when?

11th February 1942. Today again, Hitler passed through Rzeszów and already, well known warnings were repeated again.

Many squads of police ferociously loot and pillage villages. In small towns and villages exists terrible poverty. People get sick, tuberculosis is widespread. If this continues for a year ... People look into the future in despair.

The Germans are a monster nation. Without thinking, on orders, they kill and murder! Totally uncritically! After another speech by Hitler, the minor 'führers' again interpreted it according to their own ideas. A truly Germanic fury arose against the Jews, the Germans were seized by a killing frenzy.

They once shot seven Jews for crossing the border of the ghetto. With this news was combined the sight of the hearse driving through the city, where on the box next to a Jewish coachman, with the air of a condemned man, sat a Polish policeman with a rifle. For a long time, already dead Jews are no longer transported to the cemetery, according to religious ritual, but they are taken out in a hearse, a black covered wagon on whose walls is painted the Star of David.

In the past that the same hearse was seen more often on the streets but with a cross on the sides driving out of prison or the Gestapo.

Life in the ghetto is a living hell for another reason. In the conditions in which Jews live the worst instincts awaken in people. Jews denounce one another to the Germans, write anonymous notes, and denounce those who have illegally returned from Lwów because even more mouths have arrived to eat.

Still the bane of the ghetto are the Jewish police. Authority has made them insane fanatics. They are insolent and brutal. Jews praise Polish policemen to the skies and cast their most terrible curses on their own.

Jewish policemen are ruled by a strict procedure. So passing by any German in uniform, they are obliged to honor him, not by saluting, but by standing to attention and turning the head towards the honored one. By contrast they have to salute the Polish police force the Polish way, with two fingers to the cap, and Poles salute the German way, with the whole hand. Such are the provisions because they are under the command of Germans. This is also not accidental but deliberate.

The Germans seize upon all manner of means to subjugate a conquered nation. They seek out from the Jewish as well as Polish community the worst types and the vilest characters, giving them in return either authority or Judas's pieces of silver. Among these types, they select their informers and helpers.

They also use anonymous denunciations. Out of this flourish vindictiveness and the settling of personal scores. And as a consequence, there is growing mutual distrust and suspicion, a demoralization of society. How many tragedies are brought about by these anonymous denunciations?

24th February 1942. A thaw. For the ghetto, it is really a turning point. In the ghetto, they burned everything possible that was not essential, floors, doors, rafter parts of the attic, sheds, fences. Many people have died from hunger and cold. Every night they take away full hearses. The Germans, on the other hand, rob Jews at every opportunity. In prison are two Jews and a few Jewish women sentenced to death for leaving the ghetto. One of them poked fun at the court and judgment. She prefers a bullet than slowly dying of hunger. The prisoners await authorization for the judgment.

The prison in Rzeszów is overcrowded with peasants accused of not fulfilling the quota. They did not give it because they had nothing. The wealthier buy and hand it over, and the poor do not even have anything for themselves. It is increasingly difficult to buy food even for big money.

Great anguish was caused by rumor that the GG was to be incorporated into the Reich, and that Poles were to be enlisted into the army. Already, 'Ostbahn' (Eastern train) had been renamed 'Reichsbahn' (Reich train,) and Polish railroad staff got German hats and coats with German buttons. They are hence, German railroad staff.

Ukrainians do not want to be driven out to the east! Just as in the past, they disparaged the Poles, now they do not want to return to their own. They are peaceful down here, they sit quietly and rake in money.

Among the Germans, that is the police and gendarmerie, there are urgent preparations. Barracks are heavily fortified, and the German civilians had reportedly received weapons. They go to the city only in pairs. What are they so afraid of?

2nd March 1942. In the ghetto there is menacing hell. Ehaus himself went there accompanied by his 'puppies.' He examined the matter of stores of preserved eggs destined for the army and for export to Germany. There will be bad goings on! But if anyone had taken them, it was just the hungry ones.

Typhus seems to abate. Schools are to be opened where the buildings are not occupied by the army.

In early spring, a German construction company, Ahag, is to complete houses begun in 1939. Among them are several Jewish ones.

Actually, in spring there is to be significant activity. They are supposed to build entire neighborhoods of barracks and also something in the east. Even youths were enlisted for this purpose. It is said that a lot of Jews are deported to work in Kiev.

7th March 1942. Winter snow fell, it was -20 degrees. And near Moscow and Leningrad? The Germans are reportedly walking in padded uniforms from captured Soviets. If captured from stores, it is still acceptable, though shameful. But if torn off the prisoners?

Several Rzeszów schools are being rebuilt into hospitals. Will they be needed in spring?

The Germans have some trouble with the ghetto. Whichever passage to the Aryan side they liquidate, the

Jews make two new ones in their place. In the ghetto there is a lot of food but expensive. The poorest cannot not afford it. So en masse they seek assignment for work outside the ghetto, especially in rural areas, in Jasionki or Slociny. Only, for such an assignment, the Kahal has to be well paid. Such out-of-towners bring an amount food into the ghetto and do business with it. While work on the streets is considered bad luck.

Also progressively, the German district is being organized, which is intended to include streets May 3, Zamkowa, Jagiellonian, Sigismund, Prince Joseph and Kraszewski, the most modern part of town. Already Poles are being removed.

The so called 'profiteers,' who not so long ago were judged without honor and faith, now increasingly are looked at with longing. Because without them ... you better not think about it. Only those who are enterprising and clever take this on, but they also sometimes risk their lives. What ideas they invent ... The Germans have much trouble with them.

TERROR

14th March 1942. Yesterday's rumor became reality today. The premonitions of the Jews are fulfilled. Blood starts to pour in streams.

In Mielec, for some real or imagined offense, Jews were decimated. Several hundred victims fell. A Polish policeman who witnessed this terrible scene became insane.

The cause of this massacre is given, because of the failure by Mielec Jews to leave the city as ordered. Therefore, in the Rzeszów ghetto, a rumor spread that the Jews would have to leave Rzeszów. This city in fact has to play an important role in connection with the spring campaign in the east. It is to be one great hospital. For that space was needed to be obtained at the expense of the deportation of Jews. And because anguished minds are prone to all the rumors, this caused great distress.

Many Poles near Rzeszów are arrested. Those arrested are transported to the overcrowded prison. Therefore, from time to time, transports leave for Auschwitz, and from there come news of death.

There is still talk about some lists, rosters. Is it not by chance for the Gestapo to terrorize people in this way?

The shooting of Jews for leaving the ghetto is on the daily agenda. What misery has to be there, since people are still risking their lives?

Even in this horror, people find relief. 'If so much worse, so much the better,' is often heard. So the Germans are behaving so furiously because they can see ahead of them the spectre of defeat. Even in the official newspapers, one reads that the Germans are aware of the Soviet danger.

21st March 1942. First day of spring and yet in the east it is 13 degrees below zero. As is said, 'for the poor, wind is in his eyes.'

Passive resistance by the Poles is becoming active. One

hears about killing of Germans, about the theft of weapons, also of the shooting of hostages. Germans are afraid of some Polish uprising.

28th March 1942. From the ghetto keep coming increasingly horrible revelations. Some Jews seem to leave it deliberately to find a certain death. Better from a bullet than from hunger. Others take the risk in case they succeed. Police carry out special manhunts and raids for them. The prey, when caught, is 'finished.'

In the villages and small towns, Jews have been, until now, almost free. But now, they drive them out of villages into larger towns, and in the towns there are preparations to establish Jewish districts.

From time to time the German police go on bloody expeditions. Last week, they rolled into Niebylc and Glogów. They summoned someone from the Jewish community and issued a command that within a few minutes they had to provide so many pre-war stockings and soaps. Before the Jews agreed, before they pulled the goods from hidden storage, the appointed time had passed. Consequently, in Niebylc, seven corpses, and in Glogów, five.

"The Jewish hearse repeatedly drives from prison to the cemetery on Czekaj. We know for whom and what it carries."

The following story is circulating:

Somewhere, near Tarnow, a German policeman caught a Jew. He drags him along, and meets an old farmer supporting himself on a thick pole. The policeman stopped him and told him to kill the Jew with this pole. The peasant begged him to stop, finally declaring that in his life he had not even killed chicken let alone a man. 'If you do not kill him then I will shoot you,' threatened the German. 'I have not much time left,' insisted the peasant. 'I will not kill.'

Then the German gave the truncheon to the Jew and told him to kill the peasant. The Jew at first refused, but when the police officer threatened him with a revolver, the Jew raised the truncheon to strike. The German grabbed it back and said, 'This man chose to die rather than to kill you, and this is how you want him to repay him?' And he shot the Jew.

Many people believed this story. Those, more thoughtful, saw in it only one of the methods to provoke feelings of anti-Semitism in Poles. Of course this work was 'sewn with a thick thread.'

Lately, there have been air raid sirens during the night. What kind of aircraft?

Recently, a Soviet professor of chemistry, being transported to the west, was temporarily detained in prison. When asked by the guards about the war, he bragged, in a propaganda speech, that Russia was strong and would definitely win this war.

5th April 1942. German brutality becomes increasingly dreadful. In a more distant district of Rzeszów, arrests are still going on. Yesterday, eight men and one woman were brought to the Gestapo, so beaten and ragged that passers wept at the sight of them. They will get their 'Christmas Holidays.' From this nation, everything human has been blown away, leaving only unnatural beasts.

Jews from the villages are constantly driven into towns or to Rzeszów. Black despair has overcome these people. Because until now they could live, but what awaits them in lock up?

Many young Jewish people, the rural ones especially, living close to field and forest, and having friends and acquaintances in villages, are hiding in the villages or in forests. What will happen to these people? Will they survive?

Once a group of Soviet prisoners of war was escorted

through the city. They walked proudly, boldly. This was admired by all. It must be a matter of upbringing. Endurance? They work somewhere nearby. Their situation has much improved since the Soviets began to take German prisoners.

11th April 1942. Yesterday there was an incident which upset the whole city, of course once again, concerning the ghetto. Nobody knew the real cause, hence various conjectures. Namely, numerous branches of the German police, auxiliary police made up of Ukrainians, and Polish police made an official inspection in the ghetto, coupled with a sacking of Jewish belongings. How this was done is not yet known, but after the event, many wagons of all kinds of goods were taken from there straight to the Gestapo. It was said there was a lot of gold and silver, whole bales of the finest fabrics, jewelry, lingerie, bedding, accessories, etc. They robbed the remaining shops. The value of the loot was estimated at three million złoty! And so many people have died of hunger ... One has to admire the Jews, how they had so far managed to protect and hide so many things, in spite of so much looting. It could be explained that the Jews, used to living within the city walls, could become almost invisible. The poor consider this as a divine punishment of the rich.

Today, when the Jews came to work as usual to their posts, the matter was explained. In Rzeszów, there was a well-known and wealthy jeweller, Zucker. Like many others, he fled to the east. His wife, with the help of the caretaker of the building, buried all the gold and silver in the ground. The Jewish woman was resettled into the ghetto, to another building. Of course the caretaker remained outside the ghetto. Mrs. Zucker paid the caretaker a certain sum for his help and silence. When the ghetto was closed, the treasure was within its territory. Mrs. Zucker did not want, or could not actually pay, the caretaker for this silence. When she did not respond to his reminders, the caretaker took his revenge and reported this to the Gestapo. The Gestapo came with this caretaker, removed the treasure, and also did a search at Mrs. Zucker's and found two furs. Mrs. Zucker was arrested and probably will see no more of God's world. Finding the furs was the direct cause of this whole great inspection in the ghetto.

It did not end there. Even Jews, in whose home some things were still found, were arrested. The fate of these people seems to be a foregone conclusion as the Germans are only looking for an excuse and a most trivial one. In addition to Mrs. Zucker and those arrested, 24 hostages were taken including two women.

In the city there is huge outcry against the caretaker, and in the ghetto against Mrs. Zucker. The caretaker was cursed for his collaboration with the Gestapo and for the procurement of such a fortune to the Germans.

The Jews claim they saw with their own eyes how the German police, in addition to official recording of things, did not forget about themselves. They hid the finer and more valuable items in their own pockets.

And it did not end only in Rzeszów, the action was carried out throughout the whole 'Kreishauptmannschaft.' In Rzeszów there were no casualties on the spot, but in Sokolow, during the investigation, they shot three men and a woman who wanted to hide themselves or something of theirs.

The situation of the Jews is beyond belief. They go to work for which they were poorly paid or not at all. The Germans give them nothing to eat and carry out more and more brutal beatings and treatment. And there is such a demand for work that soon only women and children will remain in the ghetto.

Laxity in the German army can already clearly be

seen. The soldiers sell what they can, even military things, though such trade is forbidden by strict regulation. It is said that in Lwów, Germans, for a fee, allow Poles to listen to the radio, but they do not trust the Ukrainians.

12ᵗʰ April 1942. Today in Rzeszów something happened that people had never dreamed of, though the basis of it is characteristic.

It is well known that Ehaus is a pervert and a sadist and the Jews mostly bear the brunt of it. Like every sadist, he is also a coward. So in the house in which he lives he has hung heavy curtains, and the windows to the south, which after all provide the most light and sun, he had bricked up. Most probably because opposite, though at a great distance, stands a multi storied house from which he could possibly be shot at. That house must have worried him greatly, because he decided to enter it under the guise of his concern about how Poles lived. He made the inspection on the same day as the holiday. He entered apartments, looked into pantries, raised lids of pots. He was angry that Poles live better than Germans. At the sight of a ham he was actually shaking.

He was not just visiting the neighbors, but other homes in the city. Everywhere, he found 'holiday' supplies plentiful. People were afraid of the consequences and subsequent inspections. There was a hasty hiding and taking of many things out of houses.

One day after the holidays in Rzeszów, a very popular Jew was arrested (perhaps he has already been shot,) Joseph Heilblum, generally liked by Jews and Poles. This type is very rare among the Jews. Tall and broad-shouldered, handsome, athletic, he did not even look like a Jew. A little of a cowboy type, with a flourish, with a gesture, a bit adventurous, in a word, real man. He liked risk and danger, he was brave, and with that, a good comrade and companion.

He had money, helped people without discrimination, be it a Pole or a Jew.

Heilblum was the leader of a group of people who kept in touch with Lwów. They took food and things over there for Rzeszów Jews, and from there smuggled people who wanted to return. The group had a car at its disposal. Together, with Heilblum, they arrested more people. It is expected to be a great affair.

Jews who did not leave with the Soviet army and remained in the general area of Lwów, east of Małopolska, lived there in great poverty.

Wrenched from their homes, whatever they had was long since exhausted. Legally, only a few individuals were able to return, and that with great favoritism, such as relatives of the housekeeper of the Ortskommandant. Before the closure of the ghetto, contact with families was maintained through Kraków, and more recently through Heilblum. He did not stay in the ghetto at all. He was at large in the vicinity of Rzeszów. He kept contact with the ghetto through secret passages.

14th April 1942. The case of Heilblum is a real affair to say the least. Poles played in it a relatively small role, only one was arrested. One Jew escaped. Heilblum was not shot, just slaughtered during the hearings. Surely he died without denouncing anyone. A hero.

The juiciest is, that German policemen are involved in the affair, who, of course, for a suitable fee, conveyed Jews from Lwów. A very pretty and very seductive Jewess won over a policeman, who once again forced a certain Jew, with the help of these German policemen, to marry her. The Germans are furious in connection with this affair. Not so long ago it was a Ukrainian and a Jewess, now again the German police and the Jews ...

As it turns out, during the recent inspection, the hostages

taken were mostly watchmakers and jewellers. A ransom in gold was expected as happened in Sokolow. The Jews were not able to pay this 'gold' ransom and paid with their life.

Hans Gawron, a Gestapo, has a bad reputation among the Jews. Reportedly he is Silesian, because he knows Polish. He is also a kind of pervert. He carries out the death sentences against the Jews and the Poles. Execution of the sentence is his pleasure.

Well yesterday, this same Gawron clashed with another Gestapo. At one point he pulled out a pistol and shot the other one on the spot. That such people are killing each other is quite pleasant to hear.

Sunday visits by Ehaus seem to be in connection with plans to create a German district. The first one will be the Ehaus district, because he would not tolerate Poles in his environment. Also he may be afraid.

18ᵗʰ April 1942. The Gestapo-Gawron affair is quite spicy. The Gestapo, who quarrelled, was one of the ones who had murdered Heilblum. It is difficult to say why they argued. The one who was shot was the first to raise his pistol, but Gawron was faster and hit the opponent in the stomach. Then he pretended that the other had committed suicide. Gawron was arrested, but he sent a wreath to the funeral. SS dignitaries arrived for the inquest from Kraków.

Human life has become very cheap. A worker from PZL was killed, also a Jewish woman near Dabrowski Street. There are further arrests of Jews.

Some German, reportedly proposed a project to create a special concentration camp for men somewhere outside of Rzeszów, the Glogów Buda is mentioned. From this camp would be drawn a labor force where and when it was needed. Execution of this project would be a further step towards the destruction of the Jews.

A large group of Hungarians has arrived in with heavy

anti-aircraft artillery. The traffic in the streets is regulated by the Hungarians. They wander in the streets in 'Polish fiats', which were interned in 1939 by the Hungarians. It hurts the heart.

25th April 1942. It is very bad for the Jews. The workers outside the town, beg in tears for a piece of bread. They are shot in the prison every day, a few at a time. And in the ghetto, they kill them even with axes. Nothing evokes in the captives any thought which could change their attitude. They behave passively, waiting for death, or for some pity from God. Such resigned attitude cannot evoke great pity or sympathy. Can one give them help if so many do not help themselves and do nothing to save themselves!? Once, Jews believed in the power of money, but it misled them. Now, they are broken and helpless.

The arrangements to organise Jewish districts in small towns, also are proceeding. This will upset the Polish community, who, after all, have businesses inventories and commercial buildings. In the past week, seventy Jewish families were transported from Sokolow to Glogów.

In the former district of Kolbuszow, now joined to the Rzeszów district, governs a certain Walentyn Twardon, who is the Landrat. A humble man, who was a lowly officer in the council. Grabbing onto power he became a real Satan. It is fearful what he is doing to the Jews.

28th April 1942. This morning, Jews going to work have unseeing crazy eyes. They shiver in fear. They say that in the ghetto there is hell, a pogrom, shooting, bodies in the streets. For some time, the town heard gunshots coming from the closed district. Poles realize that when the Germans will finish with the Jews, they will get busy with them. There was a lot of gun and rifle shooting. By their quantity, it is estimated that there will be many killed. Many, many, killed.

Rumors are circulating that the Germans came to the ghetto with a list, on which were communists avoiding work, mainly arrivals from the east. Many of those hid themselves, and instead, they are killing accidental passers-by. Most often the victims fall who flee in panic.

Who had organized this list? Whispers came to me that in the ghetto, there are lot of denouncements. Not even for money, simply it is a way to curry favor, to obtain good will, saving one's life. To this behavior, inclined mostly those who convinced themselves that money really has no value. Can they save themselves in this way?

30th April 1942. Today it is known that the pogrom took place, not only in Rzeszów, but in all GG. The worst was in Lublin, where it is said many thousands were murdered. The massacres have their source in the speech of Hitler, who again has attacked the Jews. But it is true, that mainly many leftist elements were lost.

Many leftists from the surrounding area are brought to prison in Rzeszów, most likely before May 1st. In Rzeszów itself, 26 people from the labor section were arrested. So even here, the Germans have their informers, who for Judas pieces of silver sell their brethren.

Poles, living near the Castle (Kreisburg,) have to move. Only the Germans can live there. Again Ehaus's hysteria.

Yesterday, four hundred German policemen arrived to Rzeszów from Lwów. What for?

3rd May 1942. This day was 'celebrated' in large numbers, but by the German police. 'Solemnly,' and in important groups, they circulated in the whole city. Besides that, it was very quiet.

In the south of the city circled eight German fighters. Apparently a raid on the PZL was expected.

5th May 1942. Today, the District Governor, Dr. Wédler, was in Rzeszów. He was accompanied by Ehaus and Pavlu.

They inspected the city, then held a conference. Rzeszówian Germans were asking the governor to not install a German district. The Governor admonished them, that this was an order and must be executed. Ehaus and Pavlu, taking leave for a few weeks, inspect houses, actually apartments, which are located in the district set in their sights as the Deutsches Wohnviertel [German residential district.] At the same time, they do thorough searches, look inside the cupboards and pantries and become furious and swear when they find a quantity of food somewhere. And in one of the houses, they went completely crazy at the sight of a huge store of the best specialties. All this was confiscated and a suit was brought against the owner.

And the Germans do not want a special quarter. They are afraid of the bombing, which they could escape if they lived among Poles. But the authorities do not take this into account.

Food prices continued to rise. This is scarcity.

7th May 1942. Suddenly, German police drove out of Rzeszów. So suddenly, that they took away their dirty or wet clothes from the washerwomen. In all, fifty men are left. They reportedly went to the east to fight the Soviet partisans.

The population of Rzeszów lives in great excitement, so many various news and rumors are circulating. They all say that something is brewing, that action against the Germans is proceeding. What will be the effect?

The Germans are afraid of something. Perhaps of the Soviet landings, about which one hears, which are occurring, but as yet in small quantities. Maybe Polish rebellion? In important buildings, windows are barred, posts are strengthened.

13th May 1942. The Hungarians have left Rzeszów. Their attitude to the Polish population was rather friendly. Only, it was difficult to communicate with them. Sometimes, they gave the poor some soup or other food.

One Hungarian officer gave a Jew half a loaf of bread for carrying his suitcases. A Gestapo saw this and transferred the Jew to another man. The Hungarian officer took out his revolver and fired. The German, seeing the determined attitude of the other, left with his tail between his legs.

15ᵗʰ May 1942. Fighting has intensified in the east. People await its outcome with bated breath. Since so much depends on it, after all...

23ʳᵈ May 1942. German forces are going to the east! There will certainly be a 'party' there. And so many hospitals are being prepared in Rzeszów ... On German orders, strong units of fire brigades are organized in the villages, and trained at a frantic pace. Will there be air strikes?

The end of May is as hot as July. Wisłok is full of people bathing. In the ghetto, hell, hot, stuffy air, bad smell, lack of water. People do not even have anywhere to wash after work.

30ᵗʰ May 1942. The radio and the press go wild with joy in connection with the victory at Kharkov. But neither the civilians nor the military show enthusiasm.

In the Jewish Arbeitsamt, since several days, they are working quickly on the census of the Jews, on statistics, where someone works, how many are working in their place of employment. From hints of the Germans, one can conclude that something imminent threatens Jews. Would it be a massive deportation to the east to those still half-empty areas where there is a lack of manpower?

Many Jews are quite resigned. They even wonder whether it will be better there than in the ghetto, which resembles a coffin. The Kahal and the police, who are still doing very well, are afraid of deportation.

In various work locations there are different treatments of Jews. In the Polish companies it is paradise compared to some in the German ones, where they are beaten, tormented and injured. Often one sees how after work his fellows in misery carry somebody totally weakened, half-dead. And those walking, look like spectres.

Those in the ghetto, who allocate Jews to various individual work locations, have a gold mine. Because Jews draw out the rest of their clothes to obtain a tolerable placing where no beating threatens them and where they can get some food. The Municipal Museum is considered such an ideal institution where there is the quietest work, under shelter, with the possibility to buy food.

Many German women with children arrived again to Rzeszów to the husbands' leave. They often live with Polish families. The women cook in the kitchen along with the Polish women. If the Polish woman knows German, there comes a lively exchange of opinions. About this terrible terror in Poland they know nothing there, but in Germany it is similar. The Germans have bad premonitions. There is no joy and certainty of victory among them.

Somewhere, in the beginning of June, began some great British air offensive. People's hearts are lightened. Already, the German press itself, writes about it. It admits to unpleasant consequences. Germany is beginning a total war. From June 10th all non-military work will cease. Therefore, what was begun, is being finished as fast as possible.

Reportedly, at night full trains of Jews from Kraków are being sent to the east. In the Rzeszów ghetto at night, inspections take place of where someone is employed, and they record those who do not work anywhere. It is believed that they will be deported, so one can observe intense searching for a job, the offering of hefty bribes, as it was until recently, not to go to work at all.

All the time you can hear of flights of Soviet aircraft that are carrying out landing operations and dropping weapons. In the Lublin area there are already whole units executing sabotage in the rear.

There is very thorough checking on the trains.

*7th **June 1942.*** Again, a Jewish man and woman were shot. Despite this, they take the risk. They go to the countryside looking for food. They say they prefer death from a bullet than from starvation.

Groups of escapees, Soviet prisoners, and German deserters, drift through villages looking for food.

Wounded German soldiers are brought to Rzeszów hospitals.

Ehaus was in Berlin on some official matters, and returned angry like a hornet's nest. This morning, he rushed out of the house like a mad dog and whipped Jewish women working in a city park, who were in his opinion too lazy. Pavlu is just as angry, and lashing out. What does this mean?

In the ghetto, the situation is frightful. Many people are dying of hunger, Germans shoot many rounded on the street. It is a situation with no exit. On 9th June, Ehaus summoned the whole Judenrat of the district. It is known that he requested clothes, underwear, bedding and textiles, because as a result of the bombing in Germany, a lot of these things are lost.

Unprecedented anxiety in the ghetto. It is increased by the fact that Jews from Kraków are taken east in closed wagons. When the train stops at the station, the locked up inmates beg for a drop of water. They offer to pay the 50 złoty for a bottle of water. Some Bahnschutz (station guard) took the money and then hit a woman with a bottle in the head, from which blood flowed.

In Kraków, the ghetto no longer exists. A part of Jews

were shot on the spot, a part were deported. Only a few are still left for a time as a work force. Poles are pushed into the abandoned Jewish houses. This is what the Rzeszów Jews fear. Many Poles are aware that they will follow the Jews, according to the plans of annihilation of nations. The reason the Germans' frenzy, is the bombing. Jews most commonly fall victim to their barbarity. The Germans themselves are saying so.

Even girls of fourteen years are harnessed to work. And it is to hard labor, digging with pick and shovel for example, near the Castle. Pavlu rides near them secretly, and when he sees the girls standing, condemns them to 25 lashes, which to cause even more pain, Jewish policemen administer after work. And the police, fearing for their own skins, beat them without mercy.

10th June 1942. They have drawn up a list of all Jews not from Rzeszów and children up to ten years old. A terrible panic, people go out of their minds, out of fear for their children.

These last days, fifteen hundred sets of bedding were again ripped off the Jews. And again, this plague has become a source of hope, because if the Germans were intending to kill them, after death they would have taken everything.

When it comes to spiritual attitude, a Jewish community can be roughly divided into three groups, with many factions. The largest group are those terrified, pursued and set upon individuals, whose main purpose, as the main engine of behavior, is the survival instinct. This governs the behavior of the many individuals who form a group, just because they are enclosed on one area, driven together, beaten, murdered. But at the same time, everyone in the group is thinking firstly about himself, and in a broader sense, that of his family. And surely one could observe something similar in any other nation, but perhaps not to such an intense degree. Among Jews, a specific Jewish individualism is manifested very clearly, which even under normal conditions, was made explicit. It is this individualism, enhanced with a high intelligence and life wisdom, which is perfectly suited only to urban conditions, and helped many Jews in attaining fortunes; but on the other hand, it did not allow Jews to find and activate a group spirit, and through it, to create a common front for an active defense.

German tactics against the Jews were developed by good psychologists. One way, is the German means of giving individuals false hope, that if he is humble, surrender, pay, he can save his life. This method created the Judenrat and the Jewish police, institutions which were the most striking example of this. And through the fictitious and fictional hopes of saving oneself, the Germans caused a reciprocal control among the Jews, amounting to spying and informing. Not for material gain, but in order to save one's own life. Powerful blows so stunned Jews that they could not understand reality. Is not this the result of centuries of abnormal life?

The second group, no smaller, is a block of the Jewish people. In this group are included Jewish peasants, Jewish workers, who were most in contact with other nationalities. They looked at the world more realistically, took better notice of what was happening, and had no illusion that the German goal was the destruction of the Jewish nation. In this group, most took strong action to save their lives with their own efforts. It is among these people that were those, who to save life, were not afraid to risk their life.

To this group should be included deeply religious Jews. Not these bigots and devotees, Talmudists, religious professionals, but the truly religious. These, simply said, that Jews will die for the sins which the Jewish people have committed, because they valued the gold and wealth over God.

They even prayed not for mercy, because in their opinion the judgments of God are irrevocable, but to beg the angry God that not all Jews should fall victims of his wrath.

At the opposite end was a group of mostly young people, whose special characteristic was revolt, pathetic and powerless rebellion against German barbarism, against the debasement and passivity of their own people, against those who calmly and resignedly waited for the execution of divine judgment. This group, not having anything to do with the concept of a social or ideological group, was actually people with similar emotional responses. This included young people ranging from communists to the extreme nationalists. The latter, provided the time and conditions allowed and learned Hebrew, with the thought of Palestine.

Among these people, in certain conditions, it came to vicious, violent and ruthless discussions in which was highlighted the tragedy of this.

STORM CLOUDS

10th June 1942. They have drawn up a list of all Jews not from Rzeszów, and children up to ten years old. A terrible panic, people go out of their minds fearing for their children.

Among these people in certain conditions it came to bitter violent and ruthless discussions which highlighted the tragedy of this nation, its hopeless position.

Soviet prisoners were being moved into cattle cars. In that heat! Through the window one could see that they were naked.

Recently, one of the Rzeszów teachers, who knew German very well, accidentally overheard a conversation in the street between two Gernab women: 'It is really terrible how the Poles are tormented. They are given very little food, are poorly paid, driven to work. Would it not be better to shoot them at once?' A classic gem of German mercy.

Yesterday, 10th June 1942, a meeting took place between Ehaus and the Judenrat. And actually it was a kind of meeting in which the Jews were not allowed to open their mouths. It lasted barely a few minutes. The Judenrat, standing at attention, listened to the orders of Ehaus. The Jewish Kahal, up to 17th June, which is until Wednesday of the following week, were to put together a million złoty. If they failed to collect it, they had to report, not to him, but to the German police. The small towns in the area were to supply from one hundred to two hundred thousand złoty.

In the Rzeszów ghetto arose a terrible lament. This was above all by the rich, who claim that, among the Jews, such a large sum could not possibly be collected. The poor remain calm. Some can hardly conceal their joy that finally to the soulless rich had come divine punishment. They say the money will be collected for sure. They will gather even more, and ahead of the deadline. In connection with this contribution, it is expected there will be a great supply of different commodities and falling prices in the market.

Jews breathed sigh of relief. Many said: 'Thank God that is all. It could have been something worse. Let them take everything, just let us live.' Jews are hopeful that those persecutions were against the resistance to giving money. They comfort themselves, they are in good spirits. They see a solution as they want to see it. They explain to themselves that things are surely bad, and that is why the Germans are becoming increasingly enraged. And they need the money, since they are looking for it, from the Jews.

12th June 1942. Money suddenly has become very expensive and sought after. Goods became cheaper. Jews started to collect the money resolutely. Hundreds and thousands of rivulets flowed to the Judenrat in gold and złoty. The Jewish zeal for collecting money was influenced by the rumor about the emerging second front. So it was better not to annoy the devil. At the same time, circulate rumors that the Germans are counting on the fact that the Jews will not collect such a sum. And they wanted this as an excuse to apply the most severe repressions.

13th June 1942. A new nightmare. Someone spread the rumor that the million was to cover the costs of the transport of Jews to the east. This had occurred in Tarnow. There they collected one and a half million, and after receiving the money, the German preparations for deportation began.

In those days, where even a finger could be squeezed into the ghetto, hundreds of Jewish craftsmen with families, mainly tailors and shoemakers, were brought in from the surrounding towns. Where are they all to be accommodated?

A cooperative was formed in the ghetto where Jewish tailors and shoemakers would work. They have to sew and repair uniforms and shoes for the military. In relation with this, again run rumors that in the ghetto only craftsmen will remain and all unqualified people will be deported.

14ᵗʰ June 1942. Yesterday, in the afternoon, about a hundred SS arrived in Rzeszów. Around the town drove a car with the flag, 'SS-Gruppenführer.' This caused great fear among the Jews. Nobody slept that night, there were cries, moans, prayers, there was even expectation that something would begin that night. That night was frightfully long, after which arrived morning and with it a slight relief.

Jews have to report daily about how much money has been collected. Despite the poor population being sure that the sum will be collected before the deadline, there are some difficulties. The Judenrat, while collecting the money, encountered resistance from the wealthy, who avoid giving it if they possibly can. Until yesterday they collected only 250,000 złoty. What will happen if they do not raise it? And, that they will not raise it, is certain.

The whole German press, followed by the German Polish press, reports a speech by Goering that the Jews are courting death during the current war in a most irresponsible manner. So they will have to pay with the extermination of their race in Europe, and perhaps far beyond its borders as well. What honesty! Can one still have any illusions?

General opinion is that the arrival of the SS branch is connected with the words of Goering. Have they come to liquidate the Jews? How resilient is man! It is a miracle that the Jews have not yet gone insane.

The terrible war machine has lurched eastward. Today, dense squadrons of aircraft. It was predicted that a gigantic battle will take place. What will be the outcome?

16ᵗʰ June 1942. The dominant feeling in the ghetto is fear. They dread that they will meet the same fate as the Jews of Tarnów. There mainly businessmen, traders and factory owners were murdered. Workers were left alone. So again there is fighting for a job or to get a position in the Kahal. So far only the proletariat was working, the 'upper class' had bought themselves out. Now they pay large sums to get work. Some profit from this business. Even highly educated Jewish women apply willingly to sweep the streets. Mostly, however, they prefer to go to work in the countryside in a village, in the estates. So estates have plenty of workers. This is costing Jews heavily, and they will not manage to make it last long.

17th June 1942. Yesterday evening the Jews had gathered 750 thousand złoty. Would they extract in another 250 thousand złoty by the next evening? The Kahal draws money by draconian measures. It concerns their own heads. With the help of the police they cast opponents into cellars, beat them, forcibly take away property and sell it at auction. Jews curse the Kahal that this is unjust. It protects some and destroys others. The Jews themselves say that power in the hands of Jews is a sword in the hands of a madman.

Jewish policemen behave worse than the Gestapo. They take bribes, used blackmail, grab people, allegedly for work, in order to obtain a ransom, steal under the pretext of inspection or control. After that, they drink and organise orgies.

Some Jews still do not want to sell their more valuable possessions. They give them as collateral to the Poles as loans in złoty, but calculated in dollars. Germans pretend they do not see Jewish dealings with the Poles.

Today it is pouring rain. An actual flood. And in such a downpour they brought in a mass of Jewish families from Kolbuszow. It was pitiful to look at these drenched people, children, and chattels. Once more they were shoved into the ghetto. They are still there in the afternoon under a ceaseless downpour. This crowding, the Germans certainly organized on purpose.

At the last moment the Kahal paid the full million złoty into the KKO.

18ᵗʰ June 1942. The Judenrat was again summoned the next day to Mister Kreishauptmann. Another nightmare.

19ᵗʰ June 1942. Friday. The Judenrat from the whole district was convened, to whom Ehaus announced, that until Wednesday, that is, up to 24ᵗʰ June, all the Jews without exception have to pay back taxes, debts to banks and building societies, and even private debts owing to Aryan persons. For those absent from the Rzeszów area, relatives have to pay, and if they are absent, the Kahal. The Kahal has to draw from those present to pay the amounts due by the Silber family and other financial giants whose debts mount into hundreds of thousands.

The community dropped their hands. Resignation to the inability to achieve something like this overcame nearly the whole ghetto. They realized increasingly, and convinced one another, that the end was coming. They were warned that they have to pay under penalty of death.

20ᵗʰ June 1942. Can a man who has himself not experienced the ghetto with all its horrors describe the mood that prevailed in those terrible days? Never! One may know the terrible facts, one can sympathize, but to describe the gehenna of tormented people...

Many Jews buy vodka. They say that on that black Wednesday they will get drunk and wait for the end. They believe that even if they pay, Ehaus will come up with something new. Until it reaches the point that the Jews will become helpless and so 'stubborn.' The vision of Tarnow is becoming increasingly real.

In the villages it was announced that on 27ᵗʰ June, that peasants were to prepare horses, carts and food, both for themselves and for the horses. Jews believe that the purpose of the emergency is the deportation of the non-working Jewish element. Where to? They shrug their shoulders and their eyes become sad.

A mass of Jewish children, older women wrapped beyond recognition in shawls, also girls working on the roads and in the park, wander through the city, but it is absolutely impossible to help them all.

The more so because they haunt only certain districts, namely outside the centre and near the work stations. Is it possible to feed daily an additional dozen, or even dozens, of people?

The Jews themselves admit that from the Poles they get a lot of support, much more when compared to the Jews. And would the Jews be so merciful if something similar happened to the Poles?

From Africa come news of the successes of Rommel. It has a very bad effect on everyone.

Waves of soldiers and equipment are going east again. Italians and Hungarians are arriving on trains from the Poznan area, people who speak Polish. Lots of wounded German soldiers wander around the city. In addition, a German district is being created at speed.

Ehaus is in his element, he wallows in his hatred of Jews and Poles. He is achieving a 'Reichshof.' Finally, they proceeded to remove the Polish eagle from the castle tower. Jewish tinsmiths are doing this work, to whom he gave the impression that he will let them live. Will he keep his word?

24th June 1942. By tomorrow the Jews have to settle all debts under penalty of death. The debts, mostly fictional, amount to three million. Among the Jews, almost at the last moment, awoke a desperate will to live. They collect what they can, put aside gold, but without any faith and conviction. In the ghetto reigns unbelievable terror. The closer the spectre of death the stronger the instinct for life. That is so human. Actually, those resigned to die are few. They are those for whom death would be a deliverance. For them, the preparation of the wagons is a comfort.

Jews have gradually less gold, dollars and jewelry, and so more and more they fanatically cling to those possessions. The very devout say that this golden calf destroys the Jews. Even in the face of death they do not want to give it up.

The eagle is no longer on the castle tower.

The German hospitals have requested 500 towels and furniture in good repair. Jews provided this at once, in the hope in this way they could appease the German hydra.

At the same time, from somewhere, came the news that the world has now learned about the Tarnow pogrom. An uproar was raised against the Germans, and allegedly came orders not to repeat that in the future. Did not the Germans themselves announce this intentionally to extract the towels and furniture?

Before six o'clock in the evening, the whole Judenrat lead by Dr. Kleinmann as chairman went to the Castle, a total of 24 people. Next to them walked policemen carrying briefcases. Behind them in silence came the Judenrat of the whole area, all as if condemned to the scaffold. Terrified looks followed them: Would they return?

Somewhat later, rumors spread that some of the Judenrat were detained as hostages, and even that they had already been shot. Or is it just a rumor?

23ʳᵈ night. During the previous hour, many shots came from the castle. Distant and closer ... Were they murdering Jews? People shudder in terror.

25ᵗʰ June 1942. Yes, it was mass murder in Under the Chestnuts Street. Fifteen Jews were shot. And it happened like this:

The Judenrat came to Kreishauptmannschaft and their members lined up in the hallway in threes. They had to wait a long time for the arrival of Ehaus. Finally he appeared in the doorway and learned that despite their greatest efforts they were not able to assemble the designated amount. Instead, they gathered what he did not request, that was five kilograms of gold. The Jews gave up wedding rings and other rings. In addition, they gathered several kilograms of silver. Ehaus took note of this statement. He ordered the gold to be taken to the bank, he did not accept the silver. However, because his command was not actually carried out, from the Rzeszów Judenrat, six leaders of the most important departments had to remain. From the provincial ones, one each, a total of seven. Among the Rzeszów hostages were two most hated. Dr. B. Kahane and Dr. Reich. However Pavlu saved them selecting others in their place. Late in the evening, between the hours of 22.30 and 23.15 all were shot. Then they telephoned the Kahal for two policemen. Kahal sent the worst thugs, called by the Jews, 'Jewish Gestapo,' especially popular with the Germans for their ruthlessness, merciless beatings and rape of girls. They were also shot. This demonstrated the value of German fellow feeling.

26ᵗʰ June 1942. In the ghetto reigns the blackest mood. Again pessimism had taken over the people. Some pray with resignation, others blaspheme. The human impulse, in the form of rebellion, which appeared, is blaming publicly the disgraceful men who allow themselves to be slaughtered like sheep. It is found only among young women. Some already do not care at all, they even behave provocatively.

Ehaus extended to Jews, the payment for the rest of money until July 8ᵗʰ. They began again to sell up. Will this save them?

Besides the shooting of members of the Judenrat, the German police stations took it upon themselves to organise pogroms in several small towns. In Sokolow they shot 26 infirm elderly men. It was similar in other towns.

The purpose for the preparation of the carts became clear. Today from early morning, enter the ghetto, convoys of peasant carts on which sit women, the elderly and children next to the remains of their possessions. One sees almost no fit men and young people. Perhaps they are working somewhere else? The Germans are liquidating ghettos in small towns, and bringing the people to Rzeszów. And how will they all fit in?

Once again it is raining from the sky in torrents. They were all soaked and frozen ... Polish and Christian consciences shudder. Polish women, at the sight of this hopeless misery, wept and begged God for pity and punishment for the barbarian German nation.

At the same time, they felt their helplessness in the face of it.

Here and there one pointed out this crime to the Germans. They calmly reply, 'Germany is dying, others must die also.' From all sides, come news of arrests and executions of Poles.

Increasingly, one hears of partisans or insurgent units. Of what origin? Soviet landings or maybe Polish partisans? Here and there they burn a sawmill, blow up a bridge, rectories and manor houses are plundered, but without killing anyone. It seems that people pursued by the Gestapo, flee to these units, preferring to die in battle from a bullet than to rot in a dungeon.

Germans from the provinces, flock to Rzeszów. Are they running away?

For two days, Jews are driven in from everywhere. Mud everywhere, or rather a fetid bog. People are camped out in squares, sit in attics and basements, a dozen people crammed in one hovel. Crying of children, screaming, curses, added to this smoke from fires, shooting here and there. In such a situation a person is capable of anything. Would Dante have invented something like this?

No one was allowed to move into abandoned houses in towns nor even to take back one's own, or approach them, and this on pain of death. Of course the Germans are concerned about the things left inside. This is vulgar robbery.

Jews in the ghetto, seen from the Aryan side, have blank resigned faces. Looking at this misery, on these beggars' belongings, on this degradation, breaks one's heart.

During the resettlement of Jews again, there is robbery of anything that is any good, which has any value. In the ghetto stores are liquidated, the remaining goods are taken away to make room for displaced persons.

In the future, the German district, hundreds of Polish families received an almost immediate notice to vacate But there is no housing. So families are shoved together anyhow.

German women with children are arriving. Almost with nothing because, there everything is lost in the rubble, hence such looting of Jews to give the refugees something for a new household.

People from nearby towns where Jews, even at the end, at least in the majority, were doing well, say that despite so many robberies, Jews still have a lot of all sorts of goods. Some sold them off for a song, others gave them to Polish acquaintances for safekeeping, saying; 'You will give them back when we return. And if we don't come back it's better you should have them than the Germans.' But there were also those who hid the remains of their textiles or other goods in their homes, sighing with hope: 'If only we could come back, even to bare walls. From America they will send us so many dollars that we'll manage.'

Something must have happened in the world because the Germans suddenly decided to liquidate the Jews. By creating ghettos in towns they did not have some determined final deadline.

Rzeszów was not alone. The same action is happening in the whole GG.

Dante's Inferno is an idyll compared to the reality of the ghetto. So say the young educated Jewish women who had read 'The Divine Comedy,' and the main feeling is a desperate and powerless rebellion. The Kahal has washed its hands about housing the new arrivals, leaving the problem to them. But they are absolutely determined to get the rest of the contributions. Their priority is saving their own heads. They are afraid, and no doubt rightly, that if on the 8th July they do not provide the desired amount they will be the first to get the bullet. They give a free hand to their praetorians who torment those whom they suspect to still have something. Parents in front of children, children in front of their parents. They extort worse than the Germans.

The tension of the Jews rises to its zenith. Mass hysteria attacks cause scenes worthy of a hospital for the insane.

It is not known whether the Jews are already aware of rumors relating to those deported from Kraków and Tarnow. The transports were sent to Belzec where are installed huge gas or electric chambers. In them, people are killed en masse, and then burnt to ashes without a trace. How this marks German ingenuity.

German police are driving around the area doing searches, because in recent days in the vicinity of Rzeszów, numerous Soviet landings have occurred.

28th June 1942. In the ghetto, the Jewish police have unlimited power. They do not shoot, only because they have no weapons. They ravage their fellow coreligionists without mercy. They take hundreds of dollars in bribes for placing families which camp in the street with another family. At night they eat and drink themselves to death. In the ghetto, fights and rows, because hysteria is reaching a climax. Rebellious girls spit in the face of men for not being able to summon any male courage, that they only want to redeem their life with money. Even those who until recently had a rebellious attitude.

One German official from Starostwo approached with a threat one of the Poles working in the District Office asking what unites some Germans with Jews. Will this Pole explain? It is very doubtful. In fact, many Germans look at one another with suspicion, for they do not sympathize with the campaign against the Jews, even the Stadtinspektor Goer. Not only he, but many others, believe in the defeat of Germany and do not want to affect their 'mortgage.' But perhaps his attitude comes from a purely human feeling? After all some Germans lived among the Jews for two years and they lacked only 'bird's milk.' Certainly many personal feelings were or have been established.

Ehaus holds all the lines of the campaigns against the Jews, acting in close collaboration with the Gestapo. Or rather, with a special group in the Gestapo, which has a Jewish department headed by a certain Dannenberg. To this company belong also Pavlu and the head of the Gestapo, Mack.

30th June 1942. There is silence in the surrounding towns, an eerie calm as after the funeral. Because, during the deportations once again, a large number of victims died. The Germans, almost for fun, without anger or orders, as if for practice, shot at people, aiming at the victims and they joked making fun of each other after they missed. They encouraged those leaving to take with them as many things as they could, providing them with the appropriate number of peasant carts. Peasants driving the Jews had stone faces as if they were driving the dead to the cemetery. People whisper that a lot of Jewish youth escaped into the woods and fields to save their lives.

Suddenly the Jews, who worked as laborers in the surrounding area, are taken to Rzeszów. They come on foot with bundles on their backs. They are placed, not with families, but separately in barracks. Some had walked many miles. Whenever one of them weakened and fell on the way, the guards killed him on the spot.

A terrible famine reigns in the ghetto because now little food is brought in. The newcomers actually have some reserves but they really conserve them.

From the region come constantly news of the Soviet landings. Germans arrange manhunts, but to no avail because the Poles are on the side of those wanted, and warn them in time.

In the ghetto, people are dying en masse. Simply from starvation. The German guards purposely do not allow food in from outside, so as to starve the people.

1ˢᵗ July 1942. Today, the Jews have paid the outstanding one million and 250 thousand złoty to the account of bank debts and tax. The poor have to pay for the rich, who themselves sit safely abroad. Kahal lowered the 'bar' for the ration of bread and jam. They were now pulling in a second allocation in the same fashion as before.

Ehaus, on receiving the money, behaved to the Judenrat very graciously. He changed his position somewhat, until recently so absolute: he said that now each one was personally responsible for his own debt, not the entire community. The Judenrat felt a big relief.

The Germans, referring to the ongoing war, push a new slogan, not the same as last year, 'Deutschland siegt an allen Fronten' (Germany is victorious on all fronts) but 'Sieg um jeden Preiss' (Victory at any price.) And that is a great difference. In this price, are Jews also included?

Slowly to Rzeszów come news of events that took place in nearby towns. Dreadful to hear!

In Glogów, a brother and sister were sentenced to death. The girl confessed first then begged to spare the life of her brother. In vain. She asked therefore that they could die together. They were both shot in the cemetery. Meanwhile, the brother was only wounded, he got up and walked blindly on without purpose. And where to? He got to Stobierna. There a Polish policeman found him totally weakened and took him to Rzeszów.

And a second tragedy in Glogów. In the small town, there lived a wealthy family of bakers called Birnfeld.

In July 1942 it consisted of only five people. Among them was a young and very attractive girl whom I knew very well. A local lad, Wladyslaw Piechowski, fell madly in love with her. He found a shelter for the family Birnfeld with an older childless couple in a house in Polna Street, while he hid the girl in a neighboring village, High Głogowska. He himself delivered food to her there, or through a good friend in Glogów. What happened later to the Birnfeld family? I do not know.

Everything was fine until the autumn of 1942. One day, the girl was walking along the road. Suddenly a carriage appeared, full of Germans. Surprised, the girl turned her head and covered her face with her shawl. The German police stopped and recognized the girl as Jewish. They drove her to the village administrator. What happened there was hard to know, enough to say that the girl began to show houses in High Glogów in which she hid. The five policemen shot the hosts, including one woman. The terrified village head, who knew German extremely well, advised them that the girl was insane and did not know what she was saying, and that because of her, they were shooting half the village. Then they shot the girl. On the basis of her testimony in Glogów, they shot four people: the elderly couple, Piechowski, and the woman who brought food to the Birnfeld girl. All this news spread around a wide area.

In Sokolow, older and infirm Jews begged for death before going to Rzeszów. What did they have to survive for? The Germans 'graciously' acceded to their request.

In Kolbuszow, Twardon allowed himself special barbarity with the help of a young, maybe seventeen year old, Jew. Twardon arranged for himself a special 'sport.' He would stop Jews released from work in Mielec and walking to Rzeszów. After taking away their passes, he let them go. A little further, a German policeman stopped them and as escapees without a pass he shot them.

One hears about resignation, generosity, solidarity, also of escapes, but one does not hear about men's revolt. Don't the Jews see that the Germans are playing with their death for fun?

The Germans continue to boast of their victories.

5th July 1942. Today, from early morning, pairs of German and Polish policemen circulate densely as never before in the streets. And interestingly, in addition to guns, they are also armed with rifles. Something will happen. Are they afraid of something?

6th July 1942. Something will happen. Just yesterday in the evening, the ghetto was densely surrounded by German and Polish police. This coincided with the already widespread news that for a few days, prisoners are digging huge pits in the woods near Głogów.

Today, not a single Jew left the ghetto to go to work. On the streets, almost a dead silence, as if waiting for something extraordinary and dangerous.

Speculations and rumors, drifting in whispers, rustled like the wind. In the Glogów forest, a pit has been dug fifty meters long, four meters wide and three deep. In this place, between the hours of 12 at night and 5 am, shots were heard in volleys and singly. In the morning, four trucks left the forest and drove to Rzeszów.

Who was shot? Jews? Poles?

Again, one hears ominous rumors and speculations. Everywhere numb faces trembling with fear.

In the afternoon, everything became clear, thanks to the guards of the prisoners. In the night, 150 Jews were taken from the prison, those sentenced and those who were still under investigation. They even took a mother with a baby several months old. Some saw the cars going in the direction of Glogów. The rest is known ... They are certainly not among the living. In prison, from among the Jews, remained five American citizens of Jewish origin, three men and two women. Among them was a 'Cossack,' who with calm, balance, and even humor, made his companions feel better.

Was that a giant pit for only 150 people? Such a pit can hold a lot more victims.

ACTION 6TH JULY

Movement in the city is only by the Germans.

In the morning, first entered into the ghetto, a strong detachment of police followed by the SS, and finally Ehaus, Pavlu and a lot of German city officials. Everyone in uniform. Nobody could leave the ghetto. The Chairman of the Judenrat, Dr. Kleinmann, accompanied by two police officers, was led outside the gates of the ghetto by Ehaus himself. During the day, at intervals, two German policemen with full briefcases marched in the direction of the council and returned after a short time. They took away the money and gold which the Jews were giving away with silent pleading for life.

In a few rooms in the building of the Ghetto, beds were installed. The SS would be sleeping in them. The most efficient telephone operator was at the phone.

Through the windows of the Aryan part of the marketplace you can see what is happening there. The ghetto is like a cage surrounded by ruthless hunters, in which struggle trapped animals. Jews are running about half conscious, half mad with fear. It is obvious that this was without purpose or meaning. Some sit passively and still others are praying desperately.

One is moved by old ladies with glasses on their nose repairing torn clothing with thick needles, mothers cooking some food for children in the backyards. Seeing the latter playing carelessly and not knowing what awaited them, clutches at the heart. So many of them playing and defenseless. Against them, armed with official hatred and guns, burn the German warriors.

In the ghetto, inspection is taking place. Excluded are the young and the healthy craftsmen approved by doctors, police and the Gestapo, a total of about six thousand people. And in the ghetto there are probably more than twenty thousand. What was to happen to the rest? Again there is talk of Belzec.

By late afternoon, the streets and squares of the ghetto are completely empty. Incredible emptiness and silence ... The silence of death?

Polish women workers were released early from work from some offices near the ghetto. German officials, usually stern, are today excited and cheerful urging them to go home quickly because there is to be a massacre in the ghetto.

Under escort of German policemen, boys from the Baudienst entered the ghetto.

In the evening, from the ghetto, began the sounds of machine guns and occasionally stronger explosions. Are grenades being thrown into basements? The Poles hearing them, shudder with sorrow and horror.

The Germans surrounded the fences and looked through gaps between the boards at what was happening inside. And also from the balconies, civilians as well as soldiers. This is reminiscent of the days of Nero, which were soon followed by the fall of Rome. And the Jews thought that with gold they would save their lives! How naive. Had they not read 'Grazyna?'

Between Poles and Jews, in some particular cases, occurred sincere sympathy and even cordial friendship. But the Jews, as a whole, did their utmost to preserve their separation and to resemble as little as possible the people among whom they lived. At the same time, they guarded that as little as possible of that nation penetrated into their world. They put great effort to being as different as possible. They considered themselves as a group much more worthy than the Poles. They often treated Polish people with mild contempt. Today, they can see that their otherness, especially in speech, prevents them from saving themselves, by mixing into the local, but so different a group. Despite this, the Polish majority has compassion for the tormented and the murdered, taking pity on them as human beings, helping them, and even making sacrifices in cases of a cordial friendship, forgetting that this nation tried hard to remain strangers to Poles. On the other hand, the Poles, on seeing how passively with such resignation men even in the prime of life are going to their death, feel something like contempt. They expect that people should risk their life for them, but none of them risks his own life to save himself. They prefer to have someone else risk his life. These and similar comments were often heard in recent days when storm clouds whirl over the ghetto.

'Can one worry so much today about other peoples' fate,' said someone else, 'when perhaps in a few weeks our fate will become similar? Nothing will help those others any more, better to think of oneself.' From this terrible example, one must extract life's lessons.

There were even those extreme materialists who wondered how economic life will look like without Jews.

In the late evening, the following notice was pasted throughout the city:

'Pursuant to Regulation of SS und Polizeifuhr in Cracow, on 7th inst., Jews will be deported from the city of Rzeszów. If any Pole will in any way interfere with, or obstruct the action by hiding a Jew, or giving him assistance, etc., he will be shot.'

7th July 1942. Today, from early morning, in the vicinity of the Castle, or the Wislok, one could hear shooting. Later it transpired that once again, 15 Jews were shot for wanting to hide or escape.

In the morning, the whole town already knew that in the ghetto, Jews were being prepared for deportation. It was true. Into the square near the cemetery in Zerornski and

Copernicus Streets, some thousands were driven, old men, old women, variously disabled and the sick. All around them police and German gendarmes, a few Polish ones. Germans with rifles and helmets. Beside them, a crowd of youths, boys from the Baudienst. From this crowd of paupers flows continuously a small stream of people who come to be standing before the committee. And the committee is composed of two brutes with rifles at ease and truncheons in their hands (all Germans had truncheons in their hands.) In front of this committee, every old man or child had to give up their bundle, even the smallest. What could be inside them? A little food, a water bottle, a small pot, a few wretched rags. And that is not all. They grabbed the better shawls from women, and coats from the men; they were left only in their suits. Whoever was slow at giving up their property, or asked something, got a beating from the young knights. The one who had been stripped, crossed to another group.

On the sidelines stands another group. Only old men and old women. From time to time, a police truck arrives, crowds them in like bags and rushes off somewhere to the north. To the forest in Glogów?

Another truck pulls up from time to time into the square. The youths throw in the bundles, which had belonged to the Jews, and take them to the unfinished Stationmasters house, standing next to this square (the construction had started in 1939.) They throw the bundles through the window into the building.

The unfortunate people had illusions that they were going somewhere to the east, therefore they took the remnants of their things. The observers understood that this was not deportation, this was death! And did they also understand?

All this crowd sat in the open square from four o'clock

in the morning. Then came the infernal summer heat reaching up to forty degrees. In its breath, the old and children. Without any food at all. Only water was allowed to be brought. When someone opened an umbrella over the kids, or the elderly, the guard immediately destroyed the umbrella by hitting it with his truncheon.

Waiting to die in such agony!

Around the square wander many of Jewish policemen. Maybe in the crowd there is a mother or grandmother of one of them? Will there be even one who will in some way protest?

In the Old Market, on the south side, and therefore in the shadow, is a long row of rifles arranged in stands. Around the market wander their owners, the soldiers of the SS. Small young fellows. They are certainly not Prussians. Their faces are still childish, often pleasant. Under the council arcades stand benches on which they can relax. Some are sitting. Some girls pass nearby. They talk and laugh with them, they flirt. It is almost idyllic. Others are buying blueberries, strawberries, and drink lemonade. They did not go to the ghetto. Perhaps they stand as a reserve against a possible Jewish revolt?

The general headquarters, the source of the action, is in the town hall. Phones were deployed, and guards, as if during a battle. On the balcony sit policemen and gendarmes, supposedly an additional guard, held for the decisive blow. And the enemy is the exhausted, starved, bunch of old men women and children parched by the sun. Is this not a parody of war?

One German policeman, a Volksdeutsch, comes to an inn. He comes from Jarosław, and speaks Polish. He complains publicly that they, that is the military police, arrived hoping to do some shooting for themselves too, and meanwhile they met with disappointment. They are being sent back to Yaroslavl. The shooting will only be enjoyed by the SS.

Finally, 'deportation.' At three o'clock, a squad of the SS, consisting of those pleasant young fellows, entered the ghetto and surrounded the terrified and bewildered crowd, numbering about two and a half thousand people. The gate from Kopernik Street was opened and those 'nice' boys suddenly changed into veritable fiends. On command they raised a terrible yelling and began to beat the defenseless human mass. The macabre procession moved, running from the square to Grunwald, Matejko, then past the parish church, the new post office on Moniuszko, now with a clear direction: Staroniwa Station.

Still the yelling and beating ... The stupefied crowd, tortured by more than ten hours of sitting in the square in the heat, dumps everything now, some remnants of rags, pots, caps.

In the vicinity of the parish church, an older woman falls to the ground. A quick shot in the head, that is all. She remained in Rzeszów.

Among the driven, however, awakens an instinct for life ... it compels to hide, to flee. Hence the chaos, attempts to escape. Shots ring out. Randomly fired bullets plough the air. Brave witnesses, civilians, German officers and soldiers run away, hide in gateways of houses. Some just stand, appalled, with fright. A German woman gets convulsions.

The terrible convoy rushes on. Screams of children, yelling of 'nice' SS men, now in a state of complete beastly rage. Growing numbers of shots are becoming more distant. They come from Pulaski Street. It is a crossroad covered by many corpses. Behind the convoy, drive cars, not military, but from the fire department 'Feueramt,' manned by Jewish policemen, who collect the dead bodies and cover the pools of blood with sand. The police are dirtied in blood.

There are already five full wagons and one, two horse cart. Because order, so German, must be there.

At the junction of Moniuszko and Pulaski, stand terrified German women returning from a walk. Next to them, in front of their eyes, one of those 'nice' boys, perhaps to show off, with a sharp steel baton, hits a screaming, maybe one year old, child carried by his mother in her arms and cuts it almost in half. One of the German women faints, others shout hysterically, cursing the 'hero.' Another propels a father, carrying in his arms two children, to march faster, beating him on the head with his baton with all his strength. He cannot quicken his steps, he takes no notice of the blows ... he is rescuing his children.

But there was probably an even more dreadful deed yet. Here a mother, seeing what was happening to other children, takes her baby by the legs and swings it hard against the wall of a house. The little head cracks. The mother throws the little corpse on the road and continues to run, driven by blows.

At last, the station and cattle wagons. Into each are stuffed fifty people. It is obvious that in this scorching heat and no water they will be a real gas chambers.

The 'heroic victors' came back to town before six, singing, smiling pleasantly again. They went to the town hall, where soon the sounds of a waltz emerged, played on the piano.

At seven in the evening, the men who that afternoon had been driven to work in some rural outpost, returned to the ghetto. How many of them found their wives and children?

Passing witnesses, who had not been driven away, cannot shake off the horror. People ask themselves: what is the purpose of such a bloody spectacle? Is it in order to ingratiate themselves to Poles? Or rather to show how people, whom the Germans regard as their enemies, end up? Memento?

The murdered victims were taken to the Jewish cemetery on Czekaj and thrown into a heap there. From the ghetto, carts are still bringing those killed at night. A mountain of corpses.

Corpses lay there all night. Those living next to it, said that from the cemetery came moans, so some were still alive. Someone made this known. Policemen came and finished off the wounded.

8ᵗʰ July 1942. The entire city is under the impact of yesterday's gruesome day. Witnesses were not able to return to normal. One hears a lot of details.

Before leaving for the action, the SS unit received forty liters of vodka, purchased from the factory in Rzeszów 'Alko,' at the expense of the city. Many of the SS had special steel bars, whose blows split skulls like egg shells.

The Jews were shot not only by the SS and police. All those who were inside the ghetto were firing, namely the Gestapo, the Commissioner Pavlu, a high dignitary of Kreishauptmannschaft, Dr. Schneidehalter, dressed for this 'fete' in party uniform. He excelled in finishing off the wounded and shooting at young Jewish women. Shooting the Jews, they considered simply, as a final test of the Germanic being, of fidelity to the Führer and his ideas, of solidarity, of good taste. Others also fired.

Of the municipal officials, Inspector Goer was not in the ghetto terrain. An older man, an excellent officer, but having little power.

Before the wagons were closed, the condemned were given water brought in a fire tanker. A real battle erupted about the water. The train departed into the unknown at seven in the evening.

Yet still this afternoon, groups of Jews, for whom came

representatives of several posts, went to work. Human spectra in rags. These are the experts who remained. They are used for any job but their expertise is somehow in reserve.

Some companies which employed hundreds of Jewish workers are left with a few or a dozen. They demand to have some people assigned to them. Otherwise they will reduce the work or even stop. Among those remaining, mainly men, you see also women, mostly young girls. From them, one can actually learn something, but many cannot yet speak, from terror. They had lost their parents, siblings, fiancés.

From 6th to 7th July, in the night, the entire southern part of the ghetto was emptied. All residents were driven to the square near the cemetery. During this round up several hundred people were shot. Grenades were thrown into cellars where people were hiding.

Yesterday, in the ghetto, were posted announcements of a new organization of the district. Characteristically, in German only. It is to be substantially reduced. The new ghetto is divided into two parts, the larger for those who are destined for deportation and the lesser for those remaining. The latter received red stamps in their Kennkarte from the Gestapo. They remain together with their wives and children. Only the Gestapo decides, in consultation with representatives from Arbeitsamt, about the ones who are to remain. They were directed by what was written there. Other factors had absolutely no influence. Intellectuals, merchants, people without a specific skills, off they went!

According to the announcement the route from the selected streets of the new district will be in the morning between four and six, and through a single gate. Everyone can bring with them only a fifteen kilo package. Communication between the two parts of the ghetto was forbidden under pain of death. With this separation, again terrible atmosphere. Because Jews realize that deportation means death. And among those were mothers, sisters, fathers.

The Judenrat was dissolved, but Judenrat members remained as Ordnungsdienst. They even wear police hats. Perhaps, as a reward for squeezing such a fortune from the victims. Jews today, still give money.

In the ghetto, the abandoned dwellings are already being cleaned. What fortunes are taken from there! At today's prices, the Germans obtained even a billion. An opinion grows that this destruction of Jews is not the result of inborn hatred, but simply out of greed and the desire to gain Jewish goods, and means, to continue the war.

The Jews themselves said that many of them have buried gold in the ground. They also buried jewels and other valuables. One day they will emerge as treasures.

The next transport will depart on Friday, the 10th of this month. Jewish policemen organise it. They behave no better than the SS. They hit just like the others, but these blows are undoubtedly more painful.

From the behavior of the Germans, it seems that any rightful follower of Hitler would consider it a stain on his honor, if his hand touched a Jew. To hit, kick, and shoot the Jew, was an honor, only not to touch them. Hence the employment of Baudienst boys and Jewish policemen.

The German press is boasting about the successes on the Eastern Front. Whom will this happiness serve?

9ᵗʰ July 1942. Thursday. The Jewish question comes to a head. Women, who saw Tuesday's occurrence, are still crying today. Already, it was commonly understood, that the whole nation is to be murdered.

New details continue to emerge about this terrible massacre. One mother dropped her child. An SS man skewered it on a steel rod. A passing German woman got convulsions. A witness to the incident, a German officer, rebuked the murderer with severe words.

Throughout yesterday corpses are taken out of the ghetto, which often have to be found through attics and basements. In the cemetery, there are now three big heaps. A stench. This is July. Some cemetery hyenas have mangled many corpses. Only today, a detachment of Jews was sent to bury the bodies.

The train, which went into the unknown, came back. The interiors of cars, attest to the terrible agony of those people. The Jews cleaned them because tomorrow another transport is to leave. It is a fact that the SS Führer has arrived from Kraków. With a detachment? Will they again perform this monstrous spectacle? Some German delegation was supposed to visit Ehaus about Tuesday's massacre.

Transports of Jews are announced from Frysztak, and somewhere else. In Wielopole, all were killed on the spot in the night.

It seems that the noise made by different companies, had an effect. Yesterday afternoon, in addition to those remaining, an additional five hundred people were registered. Anyone who even accidentally found himself near the Jewish Labor Office, adjacent to the ghetto, got a red stamp. When this word got around, it created such a rush, that they almost smashed the building. Fevered people, red, dishevelled, like the ghosts ... Terrible.

Whoever came to the Labor Office from a company, which previously employed Jews, and by a miracle, got into his hand a Kennkarte from his former employer, went to the main office. The infamous killer Pfeifer was absent on business, and from his successor, a member of the SS, one acquired the red stamp without too much difficulty. Following this, you had to deliver the Kennkarte to the relevant person. A number of Poles undertook this service who, even with the outlay of large sums at the Labor Office, gained by trading on life and death, saved many Jews from deportation in this way. When the Gestapo released from their hand this red stamp, presumably many frauds were committed, especially by the Germans. The Kahal and the police are doing great business requesting for themselves generous payments for such favors, as to find someone and delivering the letter or card.

Jews accuse the Kahal of another crime. Those who have worked hard over the years, found themselves behind barbed wire for resettlement. But others, who always loafed about as functionaries doing good business thanks to the money gained previously, are included with the professionals, if they go to work, they will stay.

Many Germans running companies eagerly look for Jewish labor. There are even some who do it really just out of a humane spirit. They provide money, putting themselves at risk of the Gestapo. And that is also true.

Few women have actually remained. During the action, that Tuesday, some Jews however managed to escape. As they moved through Pulaski next to the priest's fields, one or another fled into the field of wheat and, despite shots, escaped with his life. Several also ran away during this terrible night, but police are already catching them. Yesterday, they were leading a mother and daughter. A brute was kicking the staggering older woman with a hobnailed boot. Six or seven people committed suicide that night by taking poison.

10th July 1942. It was similar, yet unlike that terrible Tuesday. Again at dawn, thousands of people were driven to the square near the cemetery. The same terrible heat. Today the Germans do not hit, do not shout. There is calm and almost silence. In contrast to the previous transport, all were allowed to take a bundle of ten kilograms per person. An SS unit entered the ghetto again and meticulously searched empty homes in the evacuated area. They shot several 'hyenas,' who came there to scavenge. Again, a 'procession' was formed, which moved towards the Staroniwa Station after two o'clock. This was 'Versailles,' compared to Tuesday. Ehaus himself, took care of everything, riding next to it in a buggy, and politely encouraging them to walk more slowly.:

"Langsam bitte, bitte langsam. Sie haben Zeit!" (Slowly please, slowly, you have time.) He repeated over and over.

Close behind the convoy drove several cars. Not for the dead however, but those weakened by the march, and mothers with young children were taken into them. What humanity!! At the station, any amount of water was delivered to them. Nevertheless, it did not occur without casualties. But a few succeeded to escape.

At five in the afternoon, the SS escort returned to the market, singing. Then they went back to the ghetto.

The entire city was asking this question: 'When were the Germans honest and sincere? Maybe once, but today?' The answer was clear: They were true once, but today's 'civilized' (?) behavior was the outcome of a command issued by Ehaus, as a result of an intervention by the Germans themselves. After the horrendous murders of children under the eyes of the German women, two of them got a nervous breakdown and are in hospital, and one grabbed a child to save it, but it was too late. She was holding a little corpse.

There is great indignation among the Germans. One can hear words of sincere sympathy. Nevertheless, the Poles realize that Germans, neither at the previous time, nor now, were honest. Both performances were done at an order, according to a pre prepared script. Only a callous German seems true.

As on that terrible Tuesday, so today from early morning, seven trucks, not police vehicles, but temporarily requisitioned from various companies, carried the elderly, infirm and exhausted into the woods in Glogów, where new pits had already been dug. One truck took an average of sixty people. The truck from the Agricultural Depot did seven round trips.

It was repeated in whispers that the doomed are told to strip completely before they are killed. The shooting would damage the clothes. This fact is confirmed by the workers employed not far from the place of execution, to whom came a Jew, running demented with fear, in rags of underwear. He begged for clothing. So the belief is confirmed, that the Germans are just after robbery.

It was also generally said that the Germans deport Jews to Belzec where they kill them with gas or electricity. The engineer, who drove that first train, said that he came to a small station near Rawa Ruska. There, the engine was disconnected and he was told to leave. When he returned after a few hours the wagons were empty.

There is an additional registration, due to the intervention of companies working directly for the military. Even the Gestapo have to give in. The decision is based on a list of personnel in the Arbeitsamt. For someone who is qualified to remain, a Jewish policeman runs for a Kennkart, on which the Gestapo put a red stamp. Policemen take advantage of this situation asking big bribes, and a man who wants to save his life will pay everything. And then the cards have to be delivered to those concerned. Recently, due to sluggishness of the police, many people, qualified to remain, were deported because they did not receive the card in time. It even happened that cards were delivered at the last moment to those already standing in line.

Again they separated families. So much tragedy! Tragedy deepens indifference, it is an animal struggle for life. Selfishness is seen at every turn.

In the east, terrible battles. Germans seem to advance but Soviet resistance hardens. And England has time. How many curses fall on her head ... She too cares only about herself. So many people have been killed, so much suffering enforced, and for the world it is as if nothing has happened. The sun is shining, people run about their concerns, they eat, drink, sleep ... What a powerful force life is!

Near Głogów, there is shooting in the woods from nine in the morning until one in the afternoon. Moans, cries and supplications were interspersed with volleys, and could be heard far in the fields.

The Germans forcibly took the youth brigade to help with the killing. They did not know where and why they were going.

On Friday there was an unusual event in the square. When the 'procession' was already fully formed, and the Jews were ready to march, Ehaus drove up in a carriage, in company with someone. They drove around the column as if doing a comprehensive overview, then once again and suddenly stopped. Ehaus turned to one girl, a very attractive blonde incidentally, one had to admit not resembling a Jewess, and says to her imperiously:

'You are Aryan, you are not going!'

The girl shuddered, quickly denied she was Aryan, saying she was Jewish. But Ehaus again, firmly and emphatically, repeated that she was Aryan and that she would not go anywhere. The girl recovered from her surprise and announced that she would stay if her parents would also stay and indicated two older people standing next to her. Then they too were ordered to step out from the column. The column immediately left. The parents of the girl went back to the ghetto, she herself was taken to some restaurant there. Soon the committee arrived. The girl had to undress completely. She was examined, according to a particular system, and it was judged that she was definitely Aryan. For the time being, she received a referral to the officers' mess. The girl was called Katz, she came from Swilcy. In 1939 she had matriculated in Rzeszów.

Rzeszów is talking more about this case than about the transports themselves. Much commentary, speculation, conjecture.

The 'large' ghetto has shrunk, the 'small' one actually grew. Those who qualified to work are arriving there. Aside from these, are a few who managed to escape from the big ghetto and hide there. They would wait for favorable circumstances to receive the red seal.

Many Germans try in different ways to save Jews, especially young Jewish women, who knew how to be attractive and arouse pity. You can hear of even deeper feelings, though platonic. Some Germans are using different means to carry out their schemes.

11ᵗʰ July 1942. After the recent events, many Poles walk around dejected and depressed. Not in fear for themselves, but at the sight of a rebirth of some apocalyptic beast in man, which wallows in blood and poisons many souls with venom.

There are rumors, causing apprehension, that in the countryside, lists of Polish intelligentsia were being drawn up, that Kraków would be emptied of Poles, some of whom would come to Rzeszów.

If, until the bestial deportations, the Poles felt only hatred for the Germans, from that Friday they feel revulsion and disgust. All bow their heads before Sienkiewicz, who so brilliantly was sensitive to, and presented the full horror of the German soul. On Friday, when they staged this monstrous comedy, more disgusting than Tuesday's massacre, when they led Jews to the station, a la Versailles, in wagons, they took away from them everything: bundles, outer garments, all the food, money and valuables. The search took all night. The train departed on Saturday. Everyone was given only one eighth of a loaf of bread (20 grams) and a little water for the road.

Only after this was revealed the meaning of, very low flying aircraft over the convoy. It is certain they photographed ranks of people walking calmly, loaded with bundles and behind them cars carrying the weak and mothers with children. In case of condemnation, these pictures would be shown to the world as a document of German humanity. Monstrous vile abomination! Planes were not flying over Tuesday's column!

In the Glogów forest, more than a thousand people were murdered. The murder lasted all night. Naked Jews approached the edge of the pit, where they saw still quivering bodies. If anyone was unable to approach, the boys of the Baudienst lead them to it. The Gestapo shoot the back of the head then with a kick pushed the body down. The shot victims got an additional bullet when in the pit. Only the Gestapo did the shooting, while the policemen stood as guards.

From some parts on the Aryan side, one can observe life in the large ghetto. There it is quiet and peaceful, death. As if one is not looking at Jews. Even children play quietly, as if afraid of scaring something. The elders pray, other women in white shawls on their heads silently do something. Looking at this, one does not have the courage to say a loud word.

One interesting phenomenon can be observed among the Jews: as if suddenly, the worship of money and attachment to wealth, has disappeared.

It would seem that they have nothing left anymore. Yet somehow, they still drag out hidden gold, some small jewel or some clothing, and trade them for food. And bringing it to the ghetto is a real art, and the risks great. Now, as there is no more bargaining, both parties are usually satisfied with the transaction.

In Rzeszów, about six thousand people are to remain, mainly locals. There are few newcomers, only craftsmen. It was easier for locals to save themselves somehow. They have remnants of wealth, knowledge, relationships. Finally, many had been powerful. What methods are used there, deceptions, subterfuges? It would be worth to collect them all.

It seems that the famous Italian-German offensive in Africa has collapsed.

After the hot weather, storms and rains have arrived. Potatoes are rotting. You pay 60 zł for one kilogram. How is one to eat?

14th July 1942. Today was the third deportation of Jews. Actually it was the same as on Friday, 10th July, the only difference being that, instead of heat, it was raining and really cold. In addition to the old people, any who were still alive in the Jewish hospital, were taken to Glogów.

Today, one side of Kopernik Street and Tannenbaum Street was being deported. Again this separation of families. You hear of suicides. In contrast to Friday's deportation, during which passers-by were moved or even driven away, now it was permitted to watch the procession from nearby. The cars that drove the weak people soon returned bringing mountains of bundles and packages. Once again these people were allowed nothing. Was it not about taking possession of the bundles?

This time a few, maybe a dozen people did not obey

the order and did not leave the ghetto. They hid. After the departure of the convoy, the police and the SS spread out running to find them, it was treated as a sport. Whoever was found, a corpse. In total, more than a dozen corpses. But this does not make any impression. For Jews' death is already commonplace.

You can stop and wonder how the Jews clasp the thinnest thread of hope, they count on some chance, luck, something extraordinary. With what kind of faith and stubbornness they try different tricks and loopholes. And always money. They feel most secure in the city, even in its ruins. They prefer to die there, than to risk life in the field or in the woods.

There was a wave of bogus marriages, because generally they do not separate married couples. The newly married do not take it seriously, but they treat marriage as one of the loopholes before deportation.

The girls run after the men who remained. This leads to a real auction. The one who can give more, becomes a wife. Naturally, without an obligation, to meet the duties of marriage. And it is not enough to have money to buy a husband, you still needed to pay the writer of the certificate very generously. The Germans already discovered it ... Or rather did someone report it to gain favor? Recent weddings were cancelled as fictitious, and the wives were moved to the 'big' ghetto. And that means that they are destined for deportation.

Last night, the Jewish police carried out raids and caught many hiding in the 'small,' as well as in the 'big,' ghetto. All those caught were destined for transport.

It was always thought that Jews had great wealth. These two years of occupation fully confirmed it. So many robberies, contributions, high cost of living, even the Jews themselves thought that everything was already exhausted.

Meanwhile, some still have treasure in gold and valuables. They are extracted only on really darkest days. One pays a fortune for the little stamp.

Some thought in this black hour, this or that Gestapo would relent, would help. A disappointment. The Gestapo are cunning and deceitful people, cold and ruthless, unyielding. One needs to use an indirect way, and that costs money.

The Gestapo have probably some reason to suspect the red stamps because they say that after the action there would be another inspection of the Kennkarte. This would be an idea of Ehaus. He must have seen older respectable men at work who did not look like workers at all.

How much corruption is taking place in connection with the red stamp, what base tricks to extort money and not just any money? The smallest favor is not without payment. Money has become God, or rather gold, gold!

Ehaus seemed to suddenly remember that the Jews still owed him something towards those two and a half million. He told the Kahal that if they did not contribute the rest of the sum, they would pay with life. Kahal reacted vigorously. They announced that for gold, dollars and other valuables, they would help with the red stamp. How much treasure they still gathered up! The Kahal saved their heads but the promise was not kept. Not only were the promised stamps not delivered, but they lost the documents somewhere, so that there was nothing to which apply such stamps. How many curses, how many wishes, for the most miserable end fell on the Kahal ...

Eventually it was revealed, that in place of the legal documents, those of people who paid more, were submitted. The legitimate holders were deported, the crooks stayed. Even complaints to the Germans did not help. Besides, Germans like to see how the Jews eat each other up. Some sigh that if there was more time they would make a false stamp.

During this terrible tragedy, the Germans seemed to burn with desire for young, pretty Jewish women. Ehaus himself, a known degenerate and pervert, without any requests, enrolled some fine looking girls into the cooperatives and so into the safest places.

Once, Pavlu was driving through the ghetto, and saw in the window a beautiful Jewess. He stopped and talked to her then drove to the Kahal and also enrolled her in the cooperatives. How to explain this?

July 15ᵗʰ 1942. Yesterday, again Jews were deported to an unknown destination and to Glogów. There, they not only murder old people, but people in their prime, both men and women. At one point, five men jumped out the van. One old man killed himself on the spot, another who could not flee, was killed, but three ran into the wheat field and disappeared.

Several young Jewish women, the defiant ones, voluntarily registered for Glogów, so as not to leave their parents. Their sacrifice was graciously accepted. Two of these girls, seeing what was happening, with sudden instinct of self-preservation, already naked, rushed into the woods to escape. One was caught, the other escaped. What will be her fate?

In this tragedy there is another one, very painful for Poles. Despite assurances from Germans, Poles from the Baudienst were forced to assist in this crime. They were ordered to dig the pits. Later they were plied with vodka to kill, a humane reaction. Intoxicated with alcohol, they are forced to undress infirm Jews, to pour lime over the corpses, then load the bodies into trucks. Polish women, who have sons in the Baudienst, are wild with despair.

On Tuesday, after a search through the city, Jewish

policemen carried out corpses. From one house, the body of a two-year old child was brought out. The policeman seizing it by the leg, threw it like a parcel into the truck. In these men, only bestiality remains.

The commander of the Jewish police was Biesuch, a professional photographer. A skunk of last resort. He strutted bloated, with a lecherous smile. He was shot yesterday. Apparently, through the efforts of Kleinmann himself. He knew too much and therefore had to disappear.

A few Jews have fled by various means from the ghetto. The Gestapo knows about it and is certainly planning how to catch and eradicate this fraternity. And they have subtle ways. This is a story being told:

In Babica, a Jew came to a peasant, who lived near the woods, and begged him to hide him for three months. The peasant was indignant and did not want to hear about it. The Jew pulled out a lot of money and shoved it at the peasant. But he threatened the Jew to leave immediately. Then the alleged Jew turned into a Gestapo officer, praised the farmer, and gave him a reward of several packets of tobacco and 200 złoty as well.

This news spreads like lightning. It is sure that the story was circulated by the Gestapo through their agents in order to create suspicion and fear.

19th July 1942. On Friday took place a rail transport. It was the same as before, except relatively few people were taken to Glogów. It is estimated that in two gigantic graves there are about two and a half thousand people lying in eternal sleep.

According to probable calculations, of a total of more than twenty thousand Jews, about six thousand remain, of whom almost four thousand are in the 'small' ghetto, the rest are scattered around the area in various branches of work.

Beside that, a few hundred are hiding somewhere in the area, but mostly in the ghetto, because a Jew feels safest among walls. How many are hiding in the area, God only knows! Inside, the ghetto atmosphere is like after a funeral. In fact after many funerals.

<table>
<tr><td>

AUFRUF
an die jüdische Bevölkerung

Im Auftrage der höheren Behörde hat die jüdische Kultusgemeinde die namentliche Registrierung der jüdischen Bevölkerung durchzuführen.

Zu diesem Behufe haben sich alle hier wohnenden Juden beiderlei Geschlechtes im Lokale der jüdischen Volksküche Matejkigasse 2. II. Stock, an den nachstehenden Tagen zwischen 8–12 u. 14–18 zu melden:

Sonntag	den 19 November	A – C
Montag	den 20 „	D – F
Dienstag	den 21 „	G – J
Mittwoch	den 22 „	K – L
Donnerstag	den 23 „	M – N
Freitag	den 24 „	O – R
Samstag	den 25 „	S – U
Sonntag	den 26 „	W – Z

Zur Registrierung ist erforderlich:

1) Name und Vorname
2) Geburtsdatum und Geburtsort
3) Stand (ledig, verheiratet, Witwer, geschieden)
4) Beruf
5) Genaue Wohnungsadresse
6) Genaue Geschäfts (Werkstätte) Adresse.

Für die richtige Registrierung der Kinder unter 16 Jahren sind die Eltern, beziehungsweise Vormunde verantwortlich.

Auf die genaue und pünktliche Einhaltung der obigen Termine und Anmeldung sämtlicher Familienmitglieder wird aufmerksam gemacht! Im widrigen Falle werden strengste Strafen angewendet.

DIE JÜD. KULTUS-GEMEINDE.

</td><td>

ODEZWA
do ludności żydowskiej

Z polecenia wyższej Władzy ma Gmina żydowska przeprowadzić rejestrację ludności żydowskiej.

W tym celu winni zgłosić się wszyscy zamieszkali tutaj żydzi obojga płci w lokalu żydowskiej kuchni ludowej przy ulicy Matejki 2. II. piętro w godzinach od 8–12 i 14–18 w dniach następujących:

W niedzielę	dnia 19 listopada litery	A – C
poniedziałek	dnia 20 „	D – F
wtorek	dnia 21 „	G – J
środę	dnia 22 „	K – L
czwartek	dnia 23 „	M – N
piątek	dnia 24 „	O – R
sobotę	dnia 25 „	S – U
niedzielę	dnia 26 „	W – Z

Przy rejestracji należy zapodać:

1) Nazwisko i imię
2) Data i miejsce urodzenia
3) Stan (wolny, żonaty, wdowiec, separowany)
4) Zawód
5) Dokładny adres mieszkania
6) Dokładny adres sklepu (warsztatu)

Za dokładną rejestrację dzieci poniżej 16 lat odpowiadają rodzice, względnie osoby, na których utrzymaniu dzieci te się znajdują.

Należy bezwarunkowo przestrzegać powyższych terminów i dokładnego zgłaszania wszystkich członków rodziny pod rygorem najsurowszych kar.

ŻYD. GMINA WYZNANIOWA.

</td></tr>
</table>

Zarządzenia Kahału o rejestracji ludności żydowskiej Rzeszowa oraz obowiązku noszenia opasek z gwiazdą Dawida.

<table>
<tr><td>

an die
Jüdische Bevölkerung !

Der Gouverneur für den Distrikt Krakau hat angeordnet, dass alle Juden im Alter über 12 Jahre, mit Wirkung vom 1. Dezember 1939 ausserhalb ihrer eigenen Wohnung ein sichtbares Kennzeichen zu tragen haben.

Als Jude im Sinne dieser Anordnung gilt:

1) Wer der mosaischen Glaubensgemeinschaft angehört, oder angehört hat.
2) Jeder, dessen Vater oder Mutter der mosaischen Glaubensgemeinschaft angehört, oder angehört hat.

Als Kennzeichen ist am rechten Oberarm der Kleidung und der Überkleidung eine Armbinde zu tragen, die auf weissem Grunde an der Aussenzeite einen blauen Zions-Stern zeigt. Der weisse Grund muss die Breite von mindestens 10 cm haben, der Zions-Stern muss so gross sein, dass die gegenüber liegende Spitzen mindestes 8 cm entfernt sind.

Dieser Anordnung unterliegen auch nur vorübergehend im Distriktbereich anwesende Juden für die Dauer ihres Aufenthaltes.

Juden, die dieser Verpflichtung nicht nachkommen haben strenge Bestrafung zu gewärtigen.

Die Armbinden sind in der Jüdischen Kultusgemeinde, Rzeszow, Ring 21, zum Preise vom 50 Pf. resp. 1 zl. pro Stück erhältlich.

JÜDISCHE KULTUSGEMEINDE.

</td><td>

do
ludności żydowskiej !

Gubernator Okręgu Krakowskiego zarządził, by wszyscy żydzi ponad lat 12 nosili od dnia 1-go grudnia 1939 r. począwszy poza obrębem swego mieszkania widoczne odznaki.

Za żyda uważany jest w myśl powyższego zarządzenia:

1) Ten, który należy lub należał do żydowskiej społeczności wyznaniowej.
2) Każda osoba, której ojciec lub matka należy lub należała do żydowskiej społeczności wyznaniowej.

Odznaką przynależności do żydostwa jest biała opaska z błękitną gwiazdą syjońską umieszczoną na zewnętrznej stronie opaski noszona na prawym ramieniu ubrania lub płaszcza.

Opaska ma być szeroka conajmniej 10 cm., gwiazda syjońska 8 x 8 cm.

Rozporządzeniu temu podlegają również i ci żydzi, którzy przybywają na teren Okręgu krakowskiego celem załatwienia sprawunków i t. p.

Żydzi, którzy nie poddadzą się temu zarządzeniu będą surowo karani.

Opaski są do nabycia w lokalu Gminy żydowskiej w Rzeszowie, Rynek 21, w cenie po 50 Pf. względnie 1 Zł za sztukę.

ŻYDOWSKA GMINA WYZNANIOWA.

</td></tr>
</table>

Order of Kahal for registration of the Jewish population of Rzeszów, and the wearing of armbands with the Star of David

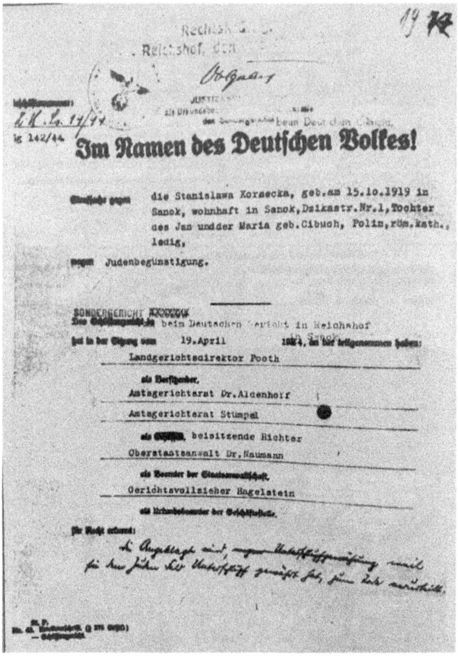

Im Namen des Deutschen Volkes!

die Stanislawa Korzecka, geb. am 15.10.1919 in Sanok, wohnhaft in Sanok, Dzikastr. Nr. 1, Tochter des Jan undder Maria geb. Cibuch, Polin, röm. kath., ledig,

wegen Judenbegünstigung.

SONDERGERICHT ... beim Deutschen ... in Reichshof

... in der Sitzung vom 19. April 1944, ...

Landgerichtsdirektor Pooth

als Vorsitzender,
Amtsgerichtsrat Dr. Aldenhoff
Amtsgerichtsrat Stümpel
als ..., beisitzende Richter
Oberstaatsanwalt Dr. Naumann

als Beamter der Staatsanwaltschaft,
Gerichtsvollzieher Hagelstein

als Urkundsbeamter der Geschäftsstelle,

Death warrant for assisting a Jew

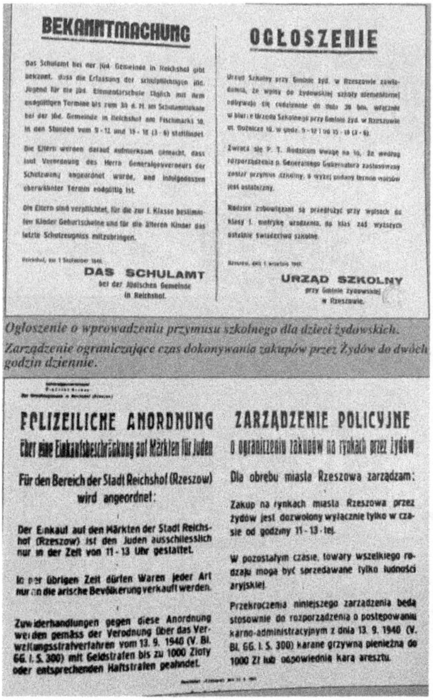

BEKANNTMACHUNG

Das Schulamt bei der jüd. Gemeinde in Reichshof gibt bekannt, dass die Erfassung der schulpflichtigen jüd. Jugend für die jüd. Elementarschule täglich mit dem endgültigen Termine bis zum 30 d. M. im Schulamtlokale bei der jüd. Gemeinde in Reichshof am Fischmarkt 10, in den Stunden vom 9 - 12 und 15 - 18 (3 - 6) stattfindet.

Die Eltern werden darauf aufmerksam gemacht, dass laut Verordnung des Herrn Generalgouverneurs der Schulzwang angeordnet wurde, und infolgedessen obererwähnter Termin endgültig ist.

Die Eltern sind verpflichtet, für die zur I. Klasse bestimmten Kinder Geburtscheine und für die älteren Kinder das letzte Schulzeugniss mitzubringen.

Reichshof, am 1 September 1940.

DAS SCHULAMT
bei der Jüdischen Gemeinde
in Reichshof.

OGŁOSZENIE

Urząd Szkolny przy Gminie żyd. w Rzeszowie zawiadamia, że wpisy do żydowskiej szkoły elementarnej odbywają się codziennie do dnia 30 bm. włącznie w biurze Urzędu Szkolnego przy Gminie żyd. w Rzeszowie ul. Bożnicza 10, w godz. 9 - 12 i od 15 - 18 (3 - 6).

Zwraca się P. T. Rodzicom uwagę na to, że według rozporządzenia p. Generalnego Gubernatora zastosowany został przymus szkolny, o wyżej podany termin wpisów jest ostateczny.

Rodzice zobowiązani są przedłożyć przy wpisach do klasy I. metrykę urodzenia, do klas zaś wyższych ostatnie świadectwa szkolne.

Rzeszów, dnia 1 września 1940.

URZĄD SZKOLNY
przy Gminie żydowskiej
w Rzeszowie.

Ogłoszenie o wprowadzeniu przymusu szkolnego dla dzieci żydowskich.
Zarządzenie ograniczające czas dokonywania zakupów przez Żydów do dwóch godzin dziennie.

POLIZEILICHE ANORDNUNG
Über neue Einkaufsbeschränkung auf Märkten für Juden

Für den Bereich der Stadt Reichshof (Rzeszow) wird angeordnet:

Der Einkauf auf den Märkten der Stadt Reichshof (Rzeszow) ist den Juden ausschliesslich nur in der Zeit von 11 - 13 Uhr gestattet.

In der übrigen Zeit dürfen Waren jeder Art nur an die arische Bevölkerung verkauft werden.

Zuwiderhandlungen gegen diese Anordnung werden gemäss der Verordnung über das Verwaltungsstrafverfahren vom 13. 9. 1940 (V. Bl. 66. I. S. 300) mit Geldstrafen bis zu 1000 Zloty oder entsprechenden Haftstrafen geahndet.

ZARZĄDZENIE POLICYJNE
o ograniczeniu zakupów na rynkach przez żydów

Dla obrębu miasta Rzeszowa zarządzam:

Zakup na rynkach miasta Rzeszowa przez żydów jest dozwolony wyłącznie tylko w czasie od godziny 11 - 13 - tej.

W pozostałym czasie, towary wszelkiego rodzaju mogą być sprzedawane tylko ludności aryjskiej.

Przekroczenia niniejszego zarządzenia będą stosownie do rozporządzenia o postępowaniu karno-administracyjnym z dnia 13. 9. 1940 (V. Bl. 66. I. S. 300) karane grzywną pieniężna do 1000 Zł lub odpowiednia karą aresztu.

Instructions regarding schooling for Jewish children

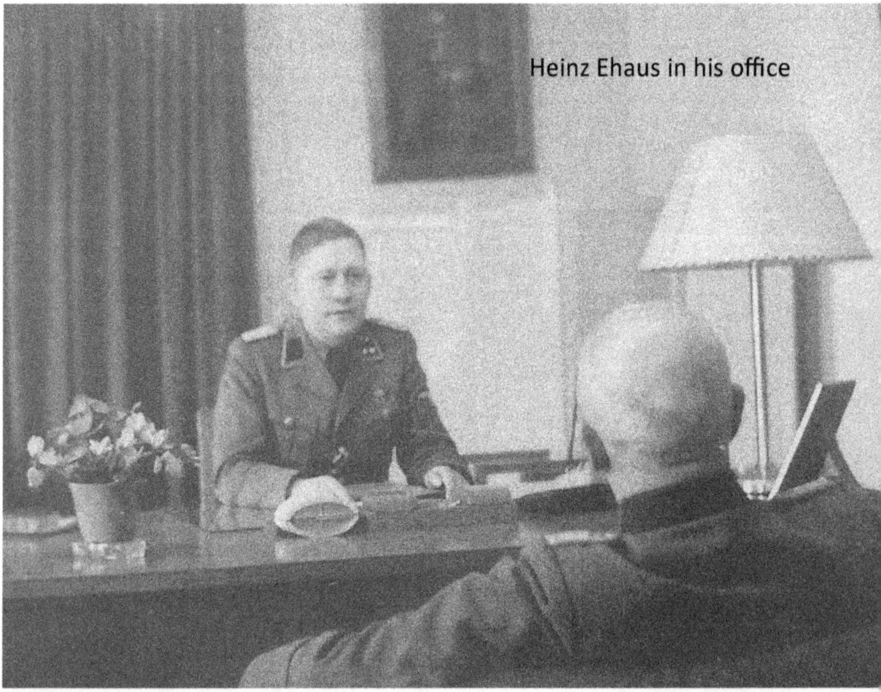

Heinz Ehaus in his office

Life in the ghetto in 1939 took place mainly on the street

Opposite & above: Jews chatting on the streets

Jews forced to sweep
the streets

Jewish women gathered to sweep the street.
A Jewish "policeman" poses behind them

Jews from outer districts brought to the ghetto

Men going to work

16th century synagogue burning in July 1944

New synagogue changed to military depot.

On the street near the Synagogues

Area of destroyed cemetery

Area of the old cemetery where they assembled Jews for deportation

Assembly of Schupo Battalion before the action in the ghetto

After the action

Deportation assembly of men to a labor camp

Assembly on past cemetery area before deportation 1942

Death road: Deportation march to the trains

Mass murders of old and sick Jews at the pits near Głogów.

Victims were forced to strip naked before shooting.

Anti-Jewish exhibition named 'Judische Weltpest' ('Jewish world plague'.)

Germans visit the exhibition.

1944: One of the last Jews.
The ghetto gate is open

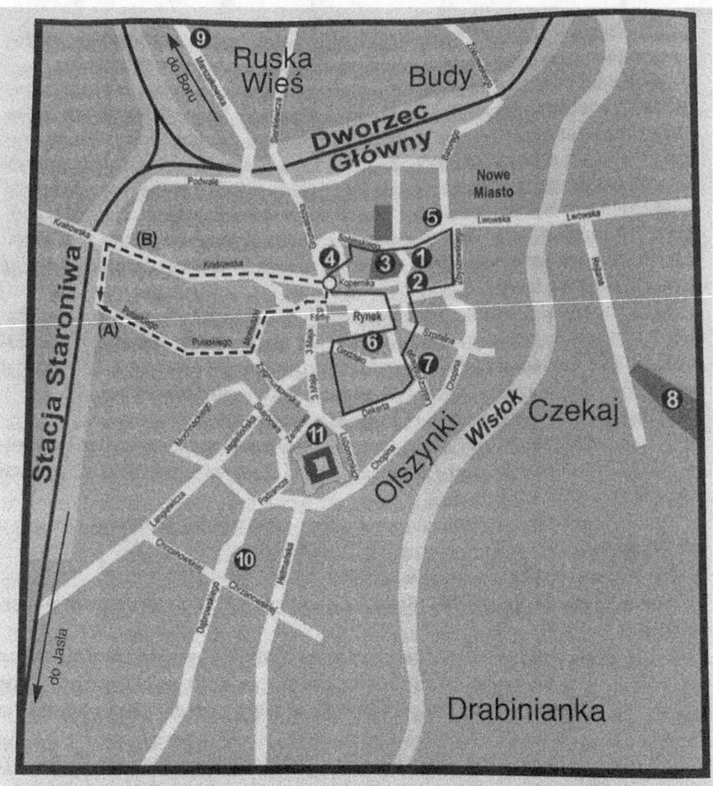

Główne drogi śmierci rzeszowskich Żydów:

Legenda:

O **Brama getta**

(A) **Przejście ulicami:** Kopernika, Grunwaldzka, Matejki, Plac Farny, Moniuszki, Pułaskiego

(B) **Przejście ulicami:** Kopernika, Grunwaldzka, Bernardyńska, Krakowska, Dojazd Staroniwa

1 Synagoga Nowomiejska
2 Stara Synagoga
3 Stary cmentarz żydowski
4 Żydowski Dom Ludowy
5 Dom Rabina
6 Żydowski Dom Starców
7 Szpital żydowski
8 Nowy cmentarz żydowski
9 Bór - miejsce straceń
10 Dom Ehausa
11 Zamek

Main roads toward death of Rzeszów Jews.
O: gate of ghetto, A ways to station,
1. New Synagogue, 2. Old Synagogue, 3. Old Jewish cemetery, 4. Jewish community house, 5. Rabbi's house, 6. Jewish old peoples home, 7. Jewish hospital, 8. New Jewish cemetery, 9. Bor site of killing, 10, House of Ehaus, 11. Castle.

Monument on the
site of mass killings
in Bor near Głogów

Monument to the
victims of the
Holocaust founded
by Rzeszów
survivors.
Dedicated in June
1995

AFTER THE FUNERAL

23rd July 1942. Life has seemingly returned to a normal pattern. How lucky for man that he can forget, to get over pain, that he has such a strong instinct for life. Jews go to work at various placings, building sites, road construction. They still bring something to sell. You can still buy a lot of good things from them. One has to admire their resourcefulness.

Jews found a lot less sympathy from the peasants in the countryside than in the city. Perhaps, because the countryside had not seen the horrors and truly believed that Jews were resettled somewhere to the east. Besides, Jews were never liked in the countryside. And the reasons were many, and of long standing.

Currently, the ghetto is being cleaned. How much wealth was left there! Sometime in the future it will be collected and sorted. But there are the brave, or rather the greedy, who despite death threats, squeeze into the deserted ghetto and take out many things. German police once caught two women and shot them on the spot.

Since the beginning of the war, a prophecy, of some Brother Louis, is often repeated. It foretells of the defeat of Germans in a Tartar country and the death of five million Jews. Regarding the Jews, the prophecy is being fulfilled, and the Germans have actually reached the Tartar country. Optimism about the end of the war is great, despite the German successes and their preparation for the winter campaign.

In the German army there is an increasingly strong movement against Hitler. Among many German civilians as well, but there is also terror.

Jews continue to be segregated, assigned to, or taken away, from less important firms, and given to more important companies. Ehaus threatens some other control, and announces that the district of Rzeszów will be the first to be 'free,' that is from the Jews.

Commonly it is said that what occurred with Jews in Rzeszów had also begun in the district Dębica. The ghetto is now closed. Some Jews, just before the action (of course, for a lot of money,) managed to obtain fake railway passes. They paid off Polish police and went to eastern districts where there was still peace. The Rzeszów action was attributed to the exceptional hatred by Ehaus. Meanwhile Ehaus was only the first, and the worst, enforcer of the general plan.

Rzeszów Jews seem to breathe a little more easily. The Germans have left them in peace after the last massacre. They themselves say that from the things left behind, even the poorest have arranged something for themselves, so that they are no longer destitute. Therefore, trade continues. In the evening, they return to the ghetto loaded down with parcels of food bought outside the city or even in the city. Nobody checks them, nobody takes away the food.

They cannot forget those displaced to the east and those 'deported.' They are the main topic of conversation, concerns, even dreams. Many people deceive themselves that it is a lie with this Belzec, maybe just another torment used by the Germans, maybe they are really alive?

A huge commotion was sparked by a rumor that someone received a card from his brother or father that they were alive and working. The writer did not indicate the place, only a number, as in a postal box. Is this true? A hoax? A German trick?

Polish German relations worsen. The attitude of Germans towards Poles is becoming more hostile. Rumors still circulate that the same fate awaits the Poles as Jews. It comes from idea that the Poles had shown no enthusiasm at all after the liquidation of the Jews, did not show their gratitude to the Germans. Quite the opposite. They do not hide their joy at the news that the Germans are doing badly. They do not hide that they believe in the ultimate defeat of Germany.

Food has become slightly cheaper, but vegetables are expensive. German women buy them all. Besides, vegetables have to be sold at official prices.

The centre of Rzeszów is completely Germanized. Everywhere you see a lot of women and children, young people in uniform of hitlerjugend, in German stores, you can hear much German language, and yet ...

Last year a large German telephone exchange was established in a huge house at number eight on 3 May Street. Suddenly the windows on the ground floor were covered in coarse mesh, and after a few days they doubled the guard at the entrance and strengthened them, even more, for the night. They are afraid of something.

27ᵗʰ July 1942. The ghetto is still being cleaned, but in reality, sacked. This is done under the supervision of German policemen. Naturally, these laborers share with the Germans, moreover, they have every right to do this. And if they can, they not only steal, but deliberately destroy a lot of things at least for revenge. The Germans send the more valuable things by car to the west. Inside the ghetto, depots of furniture were set up. The better ones are sold to wood stores for firewood. What destruction!

This prediction of this Brother Louis is a real psychosis. It was printed in the 90th issue of the 'Illustrated Daily Courier' in 1923. Many copies are circulating. The Gestapo already accidentally discovered it. Many people are now in custody.

Still come news of the Soviet landings, about partisan units, attacks on trains, shooting at them, of fruitless German expeditions against them, etc. This causes fear among the population because repressive measures were expected.

29th July 1942. In the east, actions against Jews are now also happening. In Warsaw also, but from there come news of the brave reaction of Jews, about the fighting and the killing of Germans.

In the fields and forests wander many Jews who managed to escape at the last moment out of fear. They wander like ghosts, they do not have the strength to fight or hide. They have no means to survive, Germans or Polish police catch them, some come asking for death.

Recently, the Germans have taken to the Gypsies, as a non-productive people. They capture them and resettle them in camps near Mielce or Tarnobrzeg. Some of them offer large sums for their freedom, but Ehaus is adamant.

The 317th German police battalion has settled in Rzeszów.

31st July 1942. Traces of Jews are being eliminated. Things are exported, sold, stolen and destroyed. The Gestapo take the spoils directly for themselves, but the drivers, who take these things away from the ghetto, destroy them. The Jews themselves destroy things with a passion. Inside the ghetto, huge warehouses have been set up where works the Jewish co-operative. Many things are distributed to Jews who remained. Wagons full of suitcases and trunks are driven out, locked and sealed and signed by the new owners. The names of all the leading Germans could be seen on them, who together with Ehaus, had entered the ghetto on 6th July. The furniture taken from Jews is stored in a local furniture warehouse, where it is assigned to Germans who arrived to Rzeszów. The Germans have lined their pockets, and how.

1st August 1942. The Polish community is living in great turmoil and suspense. Terror is growing. Raids and arrests are more numerous. Somewhere, a radio broadcasting station was found, and again the landings. Again, raids and arrests of people, interrogations, beatings. Police officers ride around in the area where they brutally rob food. Such an atmosphere was not seen since 1939.

To all the small towns and larger villages, units of German police came ostensibly, to ensure that the quotas were delivered, but really in order to keep an eye on each village. They introduced a curfew from eight in the evening.

5th August 1942. In the 'Deutsches Tuchhaus' [textile shop] there are a lot of previously Jewish owned things. They will be sold through ration cards.

In connection with Soviet landings and partisan groups, among the German settlers in the area Sokolow, Raniżow and Majdan, there is great panic.

Among the remaining Jews in Rzeszów, no one pretends that 'those' are alive. Now what happened in July in Rzeszów is happening in the Przeworski circuit and therefore in Łańcut. The Jews already know what to expect. They run away in hundreds. They drift in fields and forests, where sooner or later death awaits them.

Rzeszów Jews were recently not admitted to work. There are delays in the issue of passes for them. Once again, there are rumors of plans to further reduce the ghetto, of some other purge.

7th August 1942. A very naive announcement was posted yesterday in the ghetto that on 7th August in Arbeitsamt, will take place a registration of women with children who are capable to work. At the same time, they posted a list with several hundred names. When the men went to work the women took the children and went to the appointed place, punctually, according to the German mode. When all were in place, suddenly from somewhere, the German police rushed out and surrounded the crowd. A terrible scream arose. A cry of fear before death. These people, who had set out of the house for half an hour, were divided into groups of several hundred people and were driven to the Staroniwa Station. This procession was escorted, no longer by the SS, but by Schupo. They escorted one, then came back for the next group, and at noon to speed up this basest of actions, the rest of the people were transported in cars. Five hundred women and seven hundred children were transported in this manner. Also a few older men and boys up to 14 years.

The women and children made on the Poles a tragic impression. Many wept and cursed, asking God for vengeance, and a punishment equal to this crime. But the smartly dressed men did not induce sympathy. Everyone knew how they had tried to save their skin. But money also failed.

None of transports was as hideous as this last one. Especially because of the children and women. It was hard to imagine the feelings of weary husbands and fathers coming back from work to family, to a meal. What will they find? Empty and cold nests. One can share the feelings in the soul of these people ... How will they react?

The chief of the Rzeszów Arbeitsamt was a certain Feiler, a professional hairdresser, said to be the type like Pavlu and Ehaus. During the liquidation of the ghetto he was on leave. He had been replaced by Fuss, an SS man, but a good man. Feiler, on his return, made a hellish row for leaving the children and women in the ghetto. He was the one who created such a purge.

There are Germans who actually loathe Jews, there were also those who were just ordered to hate. The former, also despise the Jews more because they are humble and they are afraid of them. They consider them to be docile slaves, and treat them accordingly. So it is almost hard to believe, that in Warsaw, Jews staged an armed opposition, though they died in an unequal battle, but with honor. And even anti-Semites express respect about them.

Germans say:

'If we win, the destroyed Jews will not matter, but if we lose, then gain is also on our side, because who would apply a revenge on us the most?'

People who heartily sympathized with the Jews, who immediately after the July tragedy watched their elemental despair, were convinced that never again would they recover, that they will be psychologically ruined and broken for the rest of their life. And today they say:

'How wrong we were. They got over it quickly, even too fast. They laugh, act without care as if nothing happened. Because the Jews are a nation so old, that it has become childlike. It is greedy and mean, like old men, and at the same egotistical like children. Soon, like children, they return to equilibrium and thus carry on despite the many tragedies that they have sustained. There is no need to sympathize with them and help them. They will certainly manage on their own.'

An order came for the requisition of bicycles in the GG. Seemingly for military purposes, but people were generally aware that it was the fear of the partisans who might use them.

Germans began a campaign of 'Re-Germanization,' considering that at least half the population in the GG was of German origin. They should return to the bosom of the 'homeland.' They canvassed, spread leaflets, urged people ... peas against a wall.

8ᵗʰ August 1942. The bereaved men retuned to an evening meal. They found empty houses, cold kitchens. They soon learned about the German deceit. A dozen men, among them many married police officers, some recent ones, ran to the station to share the fate of their families. They left into the unknown.

The trick was truly diabolical. To remove suspicion, on the list were placed names of boys and girls drawn to work, and a few protected men, so they all went.

Germany, as a 'humane' nation again, allowed the establishment of a hospital in the ghetto. But then they repeatedly took away the sick to Glogów, or liquidated them on the spot. Even after transports, 22 men were found in the hospital, not sick, but bruised or injured at work. These, Ehaus also sentenced to the cemetery. Among the hospitalized was a Jewish policeman, possibly sick, a man like an oak. Seeing what was coming, he jumped out the window and disappeared. Ehaus announced that if he was not found in a quarter of an hour, things would be bad. The policemen ran like crazy and caught him. He stood before Ehaus, still in the uniform of a policeman, and reported that he was healthy and reporting for duty. Germans however have no sense of humor, and not a bit of generosity, so that nothing helped the fugitive, and he went to die like a sheep. If only he had kicked the scoundrel. If something similar happened just once, Germans would feel more respect for the Jews.

But Ehaus and Pavlu still feared Jewish shrewdness, while at the same time they were not sure of their own countrymen. Ehaus seemed to fear that the Jews, at the last moment, would persuade someone, just as the train was moving, to rescue a deportee. Therefore, before departure of the train, they personally controlled the closure and sealing of the wagons. They stood on the station until the train started.

Ehaus said in the past that Rzeszów would be the first district in the GG without Jews. And it seems they were not idle threats. Even the Jews themselves said it was imminent, and soon there would no longer be a ghetto. Germans would do just one more purge, and the workers would be put into barracks like in the PZL. Hundreds of Jews are working there, living in the most appalling conditions, behind barbed wire, under guard, as in a camp. Some companies already started to build barracks. There will be such conditions there, that the Jews will die of hunger and exhaustion.

10th August 1942. Yet another registration, and yet another deportation, are planned for the following week. Jews look for poison and pay well for it. Many men still lament the loss of their families, but already, some seem to come to terms with it. The instinct of life is often stronger than family.

Fantastic rumors circulate about the power of the Allies. And here, so many tormented people are waiting, praying, for the coveted second front, connect to it so much hope.

More and more, talk about landings and their numbers. Legends are created. Is it something to do with this second front? When will it be, when? It is so hard to wait for change.

The enemy fist is heavy, hard as power, but there are things worse than this: widespread demoralization, envy, denunciation, greed. And that hurts the most. Drunkenness is increasing. Under the influence of alcohol, the tongue is loosened and the informer listens. Many Jews, who had been in hiding here and there, fall victims of this drunken chatter. This and that one knew about it, and for some time kept silent, but finally gabbled it out.

11th August 1942. In the life of individuals, as in nations, occur crucial events, shocks, which should make people reflect, cause them to examine their conscience, look critically into their own soul. And after this terrible catastrophe, some Jews look critically at their nation.

Jews, deprived of their families and wealth and turned into slaves, come to the conclusion that one reason for their tragedy was materialism and a deluded attachment to the golden calf. They talk about a Jewish woman who was taken to Glogów, and was already led to the grave, clutched something tightly in her hand a moment before her death. One of the Germans noticed this woman pulled open the hand of the old woman and saw the gold. Gold, the strength and curse of the Jews, as said some, from the depths of their soul.

There are people in the ghetto who, after the loss of their nearest, screamed all day, but the very next day lamented over the loss of clothes, furniture, gold and jewelry. It was so hard to suffer over it.

'Cursed, cursed gold! We need to go to a country where it is unnecessary, where it is held in contempt,' dreamed out loud young rebels. 'Palestine. There a Jew can be a farmer, a laborer, healthy, tanned.'

When under the eyes of husbands and fathers, women with children were taken away, there were some who, despite the beatings and threats of shooting, jumped into cars and went with their families. But there were those who stayed. When asked why, they answered that they had to save the rest of their belongings, because when the family contacted them, they would need to send them things, to help.

Again, ten Jews were shot, caught somewhere in the area. They are so helpless outside the city. If a man saves himself, it is rather the village man, half peasant. Some of the more enterprising and determined, form gangs and rob the peasants of food. This again makes the peasants hostile to them. A vicious circle.

There are still about three hundred Jews hiding in the ghetto. They tremble at the thought of barracks for workers, because then they will be lost. And what will happen to the rest of the children and women? There are about seven hundred of them. Many women work on the railroad, and even Ehaus does not dare to remove anyone from there. The work is hard, but the Jews probably feel safer there. But there are wives with young children ... What will they do with them? Same as with those on Friday?

All the people employed at PZL, were settled in the barracks. Before that, everything was taken from them, even money. They faced hunger and lice. Even before the deportation, many Jews lost their Kennkarte, so they were issued with new ones. They no longer used the Kraków stamp, but the stamp of the Rzeszów Gestapo. They already sensed that the person who had such a stamp could be bought. Efforts already began to save this way, those in hiding.

Yesterday, a great danger loomed over these people. An incident occurred which did not lead to unpleasant consequences, only because of a fortunate coincidence that escaped the attention of the Germans. Yesterday, a fire broke out in the basements of the ghetto. The fire brigade arrived to find the source of the fire. In the vast cellars from the seventeenth and eighteenth century, they found crates of goods, some porcelain, notebooks, and a large quantity of food. The firefighters went through them, but came to the conclusion that it was in these basements that non registered Jews were hidden. And that they probably caused the fire.

For a long time, one already heard that in Germany there is much perversion and sexual abnormalities. And especially among the party. Ehaus, certainly belongs among those. He is a man, thirty something years old. Very elegant, impeccably dressed, either in uniform or in civilian clothes. Always polite and courteous. Apparently, he never raises his voice, but this man has something in him of the basilisk, something reptilian. He moves quietly, his face pale, puffy, expressionless, dark rings around his eyes. His lips are constantly quivering, which makes a strange impression. He is a nudist, which is confirmed by the Polish maids. The whole family goes around naked at home. He urged the Polish girls to do the same, without success. His sadism against Jewish women is well known who, though innocent, are beaten on naked buttocks by Jewish police. At the same time, it happens that he gives one or another bread with ham or cheese and even treats.

Ehaus hates blond Jewish women because they remind him of German women. Recently, going to the office in the Castle he arrived in the square in front of the Castle being levelled by a group of young Jewish women. Seeing him they urgently dug the clay soil. He came to the back of one, a blonde, and said:

'This evening you will be beaten because your work is bad.'

'Mr Kreishauptmann, she is the best worker,' interrupted the warden.

'Quiet!' he yelled at him and turning to the victim said: 'You will get what you deserve, and tell others that if they work clumsily they will also get a beating.'

The girl knew what it was to get to get a few dozen blows with a whip ... Maybe he would forget? He did not forget. Exactly at six o'clock in the evening he came to the yard, he knew that the guard did not dare to come down even a minute earlier, and ordered the victim to be led to the ghetto and handed over to a Jewish policeman, who had been previously notified.

'So it will be a Jewish policeman beating me,' she thought, shivering. 'There will be blood. The skin will be torn into strips..' She walked terrified in a panic.

In the ghetto they were waiting for further orders. Soon Ehaus himself arrived. He sought out an old abandoned and half ruined shed. He ordered a chair to be brought there and for the German policeman, who assisted the guard at the gates of the ghetto, to move away. Ehaus, with quivering lips and staring eyes, was relishing the fear of the girl victim. Perhaps he waited for tears, pleas for mercy, kissing of feet?

The girl clenched her teeth, mastering her crying. She stood muddy and sweaty after a hot day and fear. She waited. At some point Ehaus, always as fresh and perfumed in impeccable white gloves, sat down on the chair and told the girl to lie down on his knees. He picked up her dress. Holding the girl with his left hand he hit forcefully and precisely with his right, holding down the girl's buttocks with his palms after each blow. She knew that the sadist was waiting for her crying and moaning. She decided he would not enjoy it. And he did not enjoy it. After about twenty blows, extremely politely, he told her that if she did not work properly she would get it again. And others as well. She has to warn them.

Another type of pervert is Pavlu. Tall, broad-shouldered, with small often wild looking eyes which he never turns to the speaker. He is a drug addict. He walks around gloomy and with a constantly pinched face. He gives a grim impression. He also likes to thrash. He selects only the fat blubbery women, and beats their naked buttocks until they became purple, and the victim screams vociferously.

After that bloody Tuesday when 270 corpses of men, women and children were sent to the graveyard, Jewish policemen buried them all night from Thursday to Friday. The corpses, in a state of total decomposition, emitted a terrible stench. Pavlu assisted in this dreary rite all night, driving the workers. That night he shot two policemen, who in his opinion worked too slowly. Did they really? Or maybe they had no strength left, or the stench overcame them?

In the morning when the corpses were evenly stacked in the grave and had only to be covered with soil, he told an old gravedigger to lie down on those corpses, and shot him too.

'There were there so many Jewish policemen and only a few Germans. Could they not have paid them back, slit their heads with shovels, taken their weapons and escaped into the fields and woods?' said a girl, weeping bitterly from regret and frustration and impotent rebellion.

The above narrative is from, Miriam Hertz. She graduated in 1939, and for a long time worked at the Museum. A very intelligent girl and of strong character (footnote - F.K.)

People of like disposition, especially perverts, find one another and become close, even a German with a Jew. The terror of the Rzeszów ghetto was a seventeen year old slight Jew, still with a childish face, who already had been a policeman in Kolbuszow where he was a pet and right hand man of Twardon, an exceptional sadist. What was more, he was the 'mistress' of Twardoń, a homosexual. When Jews from Kolbuszow were transported to Rzeszów, Hahn, a German magistrate official and a manager of a department, also a homosexual, took him under his wing. This perversion was very common among the Germans. In recognition and reward for the abuse of his brethren, the brat was allowed to walk with a whip, the symbol of power given to the Jews by the Germans. He was called 'Iciale,' contemptuously by the Jews. He beats them with extreme satisfaction, and while beating he becomes berserk, insane. He beats until they bleed and faint. Jews are terribly afraid of him and loath him at the same time.

In Kolbuszow, Twardoń had whole detachment of such janissaries who made their mark on the Jews. Now they rage in Rzeszów like a pack of rabid dogs.

An eminent person in Rzeszów was Dr. Herbert Troschke, the head of the economy department in the Kreishauptmannschaft. Not a bad type, also a homosexual. He ran around as if he had a propeller in his ass. During the action he also shot at the Jews.

Another myth about Jews was dispelled during this war. Once they were regarded as an ideal of discretion: 'stone in water.' People said: 'You can kill a Jew, he will say nothing.' And now those famous brakes of discretion have suddenly ceased to exist. The Jews have 'wilted' like old women. They hide nothing. Some mania of sincerity has swept over them.

Maybe the Jews became so open with the Poles because, as they say, that in the ghetto they are afraid to speak out. There, walls have ears. Between German policemen and Jewish women there were sincere friendships and also love affairs. This was not strange, if one compared the German women to Jewish women. Totally different. Even today, some maintain correspondence with the Germans, which seems to indicate serious intentions after the war. And in the opinion of those policemen it will end very badly for Hitler. They tell that even before the deportation action, the Gestapo 'discovered' photographs of German police in friendly interaction with Jewish women. Someone informed about this, or maybe sent the photographs? The Jewish women were arrested and assigned to other work. One was so disturbed by this that she became insane. What happened to the Germans is not known.

The Jews themselves say with regret that Jewish women are attracted to the Germans, and the Germans to Jewish women. They say that among Jewish women and Germans there was friendship, love, and quite close relationships. They tell one another, which German hides a Jewish woman, and which one proposed to hide her but she refused. Some Germans tried hard to rescue Jewish women and saved them.

Where did this come from? German masculinity appealed to Jewish women and to the Germans, the special femininity of the Jewish women, which is so rare in German women. This was wholly human.

And that was why the German command murders Jews, because they not only desire their wealth but also their women. And maybe they are also somewhat afraid of them.

And the Jews? The Jews, that is the men, are also impressed by the power, and even the brutality of the Germans. If the Germans turned around and just wagged their finger at the Jews, they would have had the most loyal allies. Fundamentally, they are similar on the point of feeling their own worth. Both sides claim to be superior to others.

If the Germans did not find collaborators among the conquered people they would have been deaf and blind. They bought a Pole here and there, why would they not buy a few Jews. Jews are keeping an eye on them. They consider the worst spy Dr. Ben Kahane, whom the Gestapo openly uses. There are also high class parties at Ben's.

One heard that in few places occurred atrocities such as in Rzeszów. This was thanks to Ehaus, who was so unrelenting and inaccessible. Many Jews are trying to leave Rzeszów in some way, to get a fake pass, even just to Bochnia, or get Aryan papers and merge with the Poles. Or what many considered the most reliable, and what some have already done, to go to work for Germans as Poles of course.

Many Jews finally have come to believe that money

is not just for hoarding but for spending. Suddenly they become generous and straight out spendthrift. They throw money around, derived from the sale of their goods or from those deported, of those they still have enough.

They eat as never before and unlike anyone. They reason and rightly, 'What I eat is mine. Do I know what will happen tomorrow?' These epicureans until recently were bringing in with them huge bundles of food, which the Polish police did not want to see. This again came to the ears of Ehaus because suddenly a search was arranged, going out of the ghetto and on return. The Germans take everything that is worth more than 20 złoty, but the Jews, after so many ordeals, are well experienced, they manage well, especially since many German policemen during the search also looked through their fingers.

Some Jews whose families were deported and who had no possibility to go with them are still wild with despair. They are black like the earth, waiting to die.

German police deployed densely in the area in connection with the landings, still catch some Jews. They take them directly to a Jewish cemetery and shoot them. The majority are women.

They continue to bring in Gypsies. They are also taken directly to the Jewish cemetery and shot.

Today, just before the gate, six gypsies jumped from the wagon and began to run away. The police, escorting them, shot and killed two of them. Three, who first hid in the wheat field, surrendered after being called. As a reward they got only one bullet. Only one Gypsy managed to save himself. He fled to the Wisłok. For how long?

THE WAITING

17ᵗʰ August, 1942. In Russia, a very important conference is taking place, to which Churchill himself has come. No doubt the most important matters will discussed there. Maybe finally the second front?

In parallel with the conference, the German resistance in the Caucasus is growing. In the north, the great Soviet offensive was crowned with success. Soviet success was confirmed today in the 'Krakauer Zeitung.' So maybe?

Many Germans have clearly lost their enthusiasm. Lately at the gates of the ghetto, through which the Jews go to work, Jewish policemen are placed alongside the Germans. Big astonishment. Why is this?

Between the Jewish 'slaves' and the German police, some talking has begun. The policemen said openly they are Communists, they condemn Hitler, the regime and the war. They say that in Germany it is very bad, there is hunger that may lead to revolution. It was revealed why Jewish policemen have been placed at the gates. They are much worse than the Germans.

18ᵗʰ August 1942. During the night, Jews escaped from Polish arrest. In the morning there was a big raid. They searched everywhere, in gardens, sheds, under the stairs ... Were they found? And the Polish police? Did they have a part in this?

A number of people from the Aryan side indulge in an adventurous sport. In particular, small urchins take part, although they would face death if caught. Through various passages known from the time of the 'great' ghetto, they squeeze into the abandoned section and they scour the area. They take out a lot of things which they then sell. A whole system has been organized for this project. How many ideas are used, courage, audacity. How much satisfaction in cheating the Swabians. As after a victorious match.

The Germans announced that they wanted guardians for the abandoned houses of the Jews. There are many volunteers, not just because of work, but at the prospect of finding treasures.

19ᵗʰ August 1942. Finally! A powerful, but silent sigh of relief escaped the tortured breast of millions of people. The Allies are landing in France, so a second front. God! People walk as in a spell.

Will the war end in a few weeks? Huge war ordnance is on the move.

At the same time, the press comments on the question Frank expressed, on the occasion of some speech, whom would you prefer, Germans or Bolsheviks?'

This barking was taken up by smaller dogs, the kind of Ehaus, who toured the country asking mayors and other officials whom do the Poles want? Are they pleased about the transports of the Jews? Imagine the situation of the people who had to answer such questions...

20ᵗʰ August 1942. Another drop, or rather a whole bucket, of bitterness. It was not a second front, just some practice.

And this morning, over the whole city, even the Gestapo building and at the headquarters near the castle, unknown hands have painted letters PW, it means Poland is fighting. A clear demonstration that Poland has not surrendered.

How people are crushed from this disappointment. For Jews, the second front was far away, the Germans very near.

Pfeifer the head of the Arbeitsamt is a skunk, of the type of Ehaus. Ehaus, stands taller, in that he does not take bribes. Pfeifer takes bribes, big ones. Recently, he brawled with a German who employed many Jews, and took away one hundred girls. At the same time, he ordered that the girls had to assemble in the morning to be transferred to the camp at Huta Komorowska. They will work in the forest.

The girls became terrified, not because the work was hard, but that they were destined to a camp where they would be robbed and left to a fate of hunger and vermin.

From the beginning, it was known, that many girls would not obey this order, and there could be a resulting tragedy. And so it was. Less than half came to the assembly place. Ehaus, accompanied by Mack, the chief of Gestapo, arrived and the search started. Those selected, hid so well that not one was found.

So some dozen stragglers, who were not in hiding, and who for some reason did not go to work, were assembled. They were shot on the spot without mercy. A young married woman among them, a famous beauty, and eight months pregnant. What can be more dreadful? Maybe it was not about her life, but that of the child. Ehaus was unrelenting. It was well known that he hated beautiful Jewish women. Maybe because he himself is repulsively ugly, and his wife and daughters are also unattractive. The unfortunate woman had to stand against a wall... Her body was shaken for some time by the movements of the live and choking foetus. And the Germans, the fathers of children, were looking on. For such a crime, God has to send a terrible punishment.

Yesterday, one of Jews working at the Agricultural school in Milocin, picked two tomatoes. He dropped one. A German saw this and shot him. For two tomatoes!

Today, further details of the previous day's pogrom circulated through the city. Ehaus and Pfeifer always played a heroic role, of officers and commanders, like on the battlefield. Grotesque and macabre figures. A pregnant woman, who was after all quite legally in the ghetto because her husband worked, though he was not there on the spot. Begged for her life on her knees, kissing the feet of the murderers!

The husband was mad with grief, he saw the corpse of his wife. Today he did not go to work. Will he take revenge?

21ˢᵗ August 1942. Cheering and joy in the German press. The press shouted about the defeat of the second front. But people were already familiar with that...

During the night, two sisters, fifteen and twenty years old, were caught. During the pogrom they had fled to the Aryan side and were returning 'home.' Both were shot.

Besides the ones shot, 60 people, fully legal residents of the ghetto, working on site, were taken away. They were locked up in the basement of the Kahal. Maybe because of the rage that those girls were not found. What would happen to them? It was assumed they will be beaten. Although, who could predict what would get into the scull of such as Ehaus or Mack?

Still it was not the end of the madness. In the afternoon, when groups were returning from work, Ehaus personally stood at the gate with Pfeifer and conducted a rigorous inspection. It was permitted to bring bread, some vegetables and fruits, but not milk, butter or flour. After these products were taken away, the 'guilty' man or woman received at once 25 mighty blows on bare buttocks at the hands of Jewish policemen. The beaten women yelled frightfully. For Ehaus, it was certainly enchanting music.

Ehaus decided to reorganize the district in which the ghetto had been situated. The budget amounted to many thousands and Jews had to cover the expenses. There will be fleecing again.

23ʳᵈ August 1942. The ghetto calmed down. The Jews have recovered also. They said that they had become accustomed to something like this. 'Fear is only during action, but then, sir, you have to continue to live as long as you live,' said those who survived another massacre.

Perhaps it is the best philosophy? They were again

laughing, joking, made plans to smuggle and sell something, considered how to carry something out from the ghetto.

The larger group of Jews worked in Hucisk and Jasionka. They were so ravaged by hunger and work that they looked like veritable skeletons. Once, an overview was conducted of these human rags, about a hundred healthy and stronger ones were selected, and they were sent elsewhere. The remaining ones are shot, a few dozen a day. Airforce and police making a game, a sport, with human life. It was still good style to shoot a Jew. And one does not want to be worse than the other.

In the Caucasus, in the terrible heat wave, a fierce battle is taking place. Already during the sweltering summer, preparations for winter endurance of the German army in Russia are in full swing. All sheet metal workshops, and there are many of them in Rzeszów, do not produce anything other than iron stove pipes. Surely they would not be needed there now. So yet another winter...

Vehicle columns still move to the east but no personnel any more. They say that they will start taking Germans out of the administration, that many of them have settled, they live comfortably and do nothing or very little. And people are waiting for as many as possible of them to leave, to get a taste of the Caucasian war. There are rumors that in the forest in Głogów, large pits are being dug again. Will they finish off the ghetto? Are they shooting Polish hostages?

26th August 1942. In the ghetto, again five Jews were shot, and they are looking frenetically for a sixth one. And the reason? Would the world believe that something like this was going on? Two weeks ago, Jews, returning from work, entered a small shop to buy some vegetables. A German policeman stopped them, took their ID cards and announced that he would give them to the Gestapo. They only remembered about it the previous day, sixth will definitely be found.

The digging in the woods in Głogów has become clear. On the night of Sunday to Monday, from 23rd to 24th August, from the airfield in Jasionka, 65 Jews were brought, those 'rags and bones,' and shot. An eyewitness, a worker from Rzeszów, working in Pelkiniach, said that a few weeks earlier there arrived two trains of Jews, mainly women. One from Sieniawa, and the other from Rzeszów. Firstly they were stripped naked, then murdered. A number of them were buried at the bottom of a huge cesspit formerly dug by Soviet troops.

More and more German women with their brats arrive in Rzeszów. They get homes vacated by Poles, but no furniture. They get this from the warehouse of former Jewish belongings. Those who arrived earlier, got reasonable goods. But the latecomers complained loudly that they are given damaged dirty duvets and pillows. Maybe they do not know that they are from the ghetto?

It is said that the Soviets were drawing the Wehrmacht to the Caucasus. Also there is constant talk about Stalingrad, and about the decisive battle there. It must be a key position in this war.

Hospitals in Rzeszów are overcrowded. Those recuperating are taken to the west, whole trains arrive with new ones.

29th August 1942. For some time, the whole city is talking only about Ehaus that he got into conflict with some dignitary who was selecting redundant people around the office. Then again, that he went to war with the Gestapo, on whom he wanted to impose his will, that he committed suicide ... Ehaus had great self-esteem, a megalomaniac, a man absolutely overbearing. In addition, he is a member of the SS and has the rank of Sturmbannführer, the rank of major.

A note in the 'Krakauer' nr. 204, on page 5, sparked wild joy, that Dr. Heinz Ehaus, in Reichshof [in Rzeszów] (no longer written Kreishauptmann,) with effect from 1st Juni [June,] will be moved to the General Government [to the GG.] Is this possibly a disgrace?

Later came other rumors that a Gestapo agent drove Ehaus from Rzeszów. And when he did not get out in Kraków, but wanted to go further, his escort examined his luggage, which had a lot of gold. There was a huge row in Kraków and his dating from the first of June. How typical.

Now it is finally becoming clear that the Gestapo had been giving him trouble for a long time, they bothered him, and he denounced them, and they got rid of him. Has this something to do with the Jews? Or maybe it was caused by the ghastly procession of the deportees of 7th June? The transfer is dated 1st June, so before the action. This means something.

Pavlu walks around sad and angry.

30th August 1942. The Germans also believed in the death of Ehaus. But they were pleased. How they bad mouth him, what nasty tales they hang on him. This man had to be terribly hated.

Jews say loudly that this is God's punishment.

1st September 1942. Third year of war. Enough. Calm in the ghetto. Jews are constantly driven to work. Suddenly the joy of Jews and Poles is greatly dimmed. The gossip about the death of Ehaus is not at all certain.

In the ghetto, order is being restored and houses are cleaned. And the Germans, during the searches for gold and dollars, unstitch the feather duvets and spill the feathers on the floor. Today there was a strong wind which blew away the feathers, one got the impression, as if on 1st September, fluffy snow was falling.

4th September 1942. Something sensational occurred in

Rzeszów. Around 11 o'clock at night, over the city flew four waves of aircraft. Only after they passed the sirens rang out. Panic among the Germans. Poles ran out of their homes and looked in the direction of PZL, whether there would be explosions. But nothing happened. This flight however, raised the spirit, though it was not really known what kind of aircraft they were.

There is growing concern about Ehaus. He was supposed to be healthy, and he sent a telegram to his wife that he was returning. That would be.

A Jewish woman was caught on the street without an arm band. They shot her. The Jews said that she walked out deliberately to find death. She just did not want to die in the ghetto as a slave, but as a free person. Terrible!

In the ghetto, whole houses are being converted for the storage of various goods, so in one there is bedding, in another linen, clothes, watches and clocks, in yet another container glass and porcelain, metal pots, etc. Jews sort them meticulously. The better things are for the Germans, the inferior are sold to the dealers, whole mountains. They in turn sell to the needy.

The director of the ghetto, because that's what he insists on being called under threat of beatings, is an official of the Kreishauptmannschaft, even quite a decent man, but half, a half idiot. This power had gone to his head. He has whims and moods, sometimes he condemns someone to a beating. Once he even shot someone. Maybe not even from desire for blood and murder, but to pass the test in this subject, to complete his qualifications.

In fact, two Jews govern the ghetto for him, Gross, formerly a Rzeszów cabby, and clever, and the other a Jew from Germany, married to a German woman. She joined her husband in Rzeszów, she was here for a time until she was told to leave. These two wind the poor 'Director' around their fingers, and are working wonders with him, because the director is a fool, doesn't know anything. They take full wagons out of the ghetto and bring in food.

It is known that Jews have a special weakness for copper and silver. Often old cleaned copper utensils used to hang in kitchens, and silver, often very valuable, and of great historical value, shone in cabinets. Whole basements are now filled with these things. They are systematically exported to the west. Tens of tons of silver, copper and brass.

In pre-war auctions of mansions and apartments, Jews eagerly bought silver and copper. Now, smart Gross 'secretly' sends large baskets of 'antiques' to the Aryan side, which somehow return to their previous owners.

9th September 1942. There are more than 500 Jews working in the PZL. The factory had to insure them and pay social insurance. Is this not a most shameless irony? Today, Jews were led to the bathhouse, of course under guard. They are pale and haggard, and to stigmatize them, they are painted with yellow paint on all sides, so that they look like escapees from a circus. One cares more about hygiene...

Two days ago, two wagons of Jews, half naked, were driven east, it was not known where they were caught. One of them even had water. A railway worker brought a cup he had asked for. Both were shot on the spot.

During the 'holiday' of Ehaus, near the gates of the ghetto, stood crowds waiting for the Jews coming out, whom Poles followed to work and brought them back. So trade goes on. The buyers pull apart the rags, look them over, and haggle. Jews again take food. How much, in spite of everything, Jews are able to take out of the ghetto?! 'But it's ours,' they say, at some point selling even huge carpets. How were they saved? And moreover, in spite of controls, those working in stores take out many things and immediately sell them.

10th September 1942. Ehaus has 'resurrected' and is back. Not only alive, but still as Kreishauptmann. Still, he must have had a dressing down in Berlin. Today he drove all day around town to show himself. He was also in the ghetto. Immediately, rumors spread, that would be the end of the ghetto around 1st October, and even the Jews believed it. Perhaps some would die, but in the ghetto, there was so much work. Who would do it?

In recent days, two Jewish 'havens' have been liquidated. Bochnia and Wieliczka. Bochnia, this year, was like a Jewish Mecca. Their Kreishauptmann was humane. Jews fled there from other ghettos, there was production of false Aryan papers, and from there you could go out and mix with the Poles. And now, that was finished. Those 'lucky ones' were already driven through Rzeszów.

One scorching day, a train full of Jews arrived. They begged for water. Finally the guards gave permission to give them some, but took over 50 złoty for half a litre. The others paid, paid, paid ... They had to be honest, because the Germans had their eye on them. Later, the Germans took the lion's share of the money for themselves.

For some time now, every night there are air alarms. Tonight also. News come about bombing of Polish cities, which kill a lot of people. So a large part of the community becomes anxious. At the sound of these sirens, people flee from their homes into cellars and shelters. But not all Poles have to act like this. Germans do. They have 'pleasant' nights. Many Poles sleep happily saying that it will be what God wills.

Stalingrad is still on everyone's lips. It is called the 'Soviet Verdun.'

12th September 1942. The return of Ehaus had to be

celebrated somehow. And it was. That night, a police car drove into the ghetto and took more than twenty Jews, some of them women, a few Jewish policemen, and some lawyers and doctors. They were brought to the Gestapo. It seemed to be a serious matter. The Gestapo reportedly found out some scandal about the passes or official stamps. This meant that false red stamps were detected on the Kennkarts, also fake passes for railway crossings, to safe ghettos such as Bochnia. Those arrested were supposedly involved in it.

When the detainees were being transported in the direction of Glogów, one of them escaped in Grunwald Street.

Most Jews still want to save their life, the Jewish way. And these ways, in relation to the Germans, have become completely useless. But they do not know any other means. And it is not their fault, because of their way of life for so many centuries, and it is tragic.

14th September 1942. The affair of the stamps turned out very unhappily. Ultimately, 206 people, including six women, are involved in it. Included are the 20 people already arrested and sitting in jail, and more than 20 arrested in the ghetto, mostly lawyers, doctors, and educated women. The majority were rounded up from various institutions and barracks. They were the ones who had already received, or were waiting for, the false pass. Many of them were actually quite innocent. There was even a performance of hearings, which for Jews was something completely new. Was this not after the affair with Ehaus? Yesterday, many lawyers speaking German well, were interrogated. They gave a formal speech in their own defense, proclaiming their innocence. It did not help at all, neither pleas for life, nor the despair of young pretty women.

They looked especially for a policeman, who went into

hiding. Therefore, the other five were summoned, and were given the task of finding him by four o'clock in the morning. They won't find him, they will go. But they did find him. It happened on the night of 12th September.

How did they discover this affair? Who provided or compiled such a list of names?

These people were not driven to Glogów, although they went in that direction. It was when passing Grunwaldzka Street that one of the Jewish policemen jumped out of the car. He managed to escape, although he was shot at. This time, unusually, the condemned were taken beyond Kolbuszow, to the New Village, and there they were handed over into the hands of the sadistic torturer, Twardoń. Twardoń carried out the murder ritual at night, as was his custom. The victims were taken to the forest, where there were already pits dug by the youth brigade. Like in Głogów, they were forced to collect the clothes and bury the corpses. They reported, that the condemned, driven by blows into the woods, were allowed to sit and 'rest,' of course under police guard. Meanwhile, Twardon invited the executioners to his home where there was a four hour drinking orgy. And the people in the woods waited four hours for death. It became light and a magnificent day dawned ... Almost all the prisoners wrote letters to their family and to their friends, which the youth brigade brought to Rzeszów and delivered to the addresses.

Finally, the executioners came in excellent spirits and cheerful. They were sure that they will be shooting again at the terrified, helpless, people. Meanwhile, something unheard of happened. Whether it was because the condemned had time for reflection, or whether during those hours of waiting a new strength awoke in them... As a result the Germans met with protest, although only verbal. Not from all, but from many. A young Jew shouted with exaltation in German, that Poland will remain and that Germany will lose the war, that they were victorious only against defenseless naked Jews, that they were cowards and many will meet horrible punishment. The executioners reacted with beating, They beat the boy for a long time and in the end he begged for death. Finally they kicked him to death, the descendants of the nation's knights, poets and philosophers.

Some Jews still begged for life, it was so precious.

The 'heroes,' foaming at the mouth, shot at those already dead, and chopped them into pieces.

The youth brigade, who took letters often marked with tears, which told those still alive not to hope, not to wait, but to run. Some listened, as if from beyond the grave. Quite a few actually escaped.

The human soul is fascinating. Young and beautiful Jewish women, who were told about this, listened appalled. But after a moment, they laughed and joked.

Rumors of the imminent liquidation of all Jews are circulating again.

Near Debica, is the village of Pustków. On the land of the village, after the residents were expelled, a huge concentration camp was established, or rather work camp. Until recently, there were about six thousand Jews from various counties in it. The ones who had some dollars or money managed to survive, while others died of hunger and exhaustion. Some escaped and wander in the countryside until they get a bullet.

One such escapee from Pustkow, with his remaining strength, crawled to Glogów, to his village and to his house. When he learned that his entire family had long since been taken away, and only one son was working on the site, he asked someone to call his son. They called him. He exchanged a few words with him, because the son had to go back to work, after all he was a slave. The father lay in the garden exhausted. With his last breath, asked that German police be notified, because it was a torment for him to live any longer. A policeman came, and with one shot shortened his torment. Fate!

15th September 1942. Today, Ehaus called in the priests, teachers, governors and mayors of the area. Again, the workers destined to go to Germany, went into hiding. The lord governor raged, banged his fists on the table, shouting that Germany will win the war, and finally that they must denounce the Jews in hiding, because they were the greatest enemy of the Poles.

And the Jews are still running away, the more so, because of the constant talk about their transfer to barracks.

The Germans are raging. They imprison and even shoot peasants for defaulting on quotas. They catch dealers, take the goods and send the detainees to work in Germany. All this does not indicate a good situation for them.

From Auschwitz, reports come constantly about the death of inmates. Do they shoot them there?

21st September 1942. The Day of Atonement, the most important Jewish holiday. Yesterday there was an evening of prayer. Even former non-believers took part in the service. They prayed and wept. Although this could have caused a catastrophe, they prayed out loud, very loud.

Somewhere there has to be an entire industry for forgeries, because many Jews were living on Aryan papers. This and that old friend met a Jew who asked only for discretion. And there was no instance that someone was denounced.

In recent days, there was a battle around Sokolow and Przewrotne. Apparently with a unit. Bandits? A German officer and a Polish policeman were killed. What great mourning took place! For the German left four children.

The dollar is worth 37 to 38 złoty. That is bad.

29th September 1942. The dollar and gold are rising. There is great demand for them. Generally it is said, that the Germans themselves are buying them through their agents for worthless pieces of paper.

At night, still air raid alarms. They are becoming boring.

The Germans catch masses of people in towns and villages.

The work in Rzeszów city is in full swing, a barrack from the former ghetto was given back. Little is left of it.

Recently numerous transports, with Soviet soldiers who had joined the Germans, arrived for the winter. They say openly that they would have died of hunger, so they preferred to risk it. They say that hunger is terrible. Some cry in despair. On their shoulders they have all sorts of insignia, indicating the nationality to which they belong. They look for every opportunity to talk. When asked if they would fight, they answered 'uwidim'(we will see.) One could see that even now they are starving, because they eat raw cabbage.

30th September 1942. Many Jews, who lost everything, were suddenly consumed, not only by the desire to live, but to live it up at any cost. It is obvious that they are completely insensitive to the dreadful state of their coreligionists. This is thanks to the Germans. Today the Gestapo caught a whole group of gamblers. On the table lay a kitty of 15,000 złoty. And how much more did they still have? It was all from the sale of the possessions of those deported. All were arrested. The Germans want to know how they got so much money. Will they see the light of God's world again?

2nd October 1942. Hitler again made a speech, seething with rage. After that, it may really be the end of the Jews. They themselves are well aware of this. They run away, because in flight, there is always a little hope. They all dream of Hungary, where Jews still live quite well.

Scharführer Bacher rules the ghetto. Syphilitic, alcoholic, tubercular. Without an ounce of humanity. In his reasoning, most likely, he is there to torment the Jews, and does his utmost to do so. He gives horrible beatings. Day after day, all day long, he beats the same man until he is just in shreds. Only then he shoots him. And he is a bad shot. He is drunk and not in control of his hand. The victim is in agony for hours.

Jews themselves understand perfectly, that their innate separateness of which they were so proud, is now their undoing. Apart from their appearance and circumcision, their biggest problem is with language. It is rare for a Jew, even if he is educated, not to have a specific Jewish accent. Many also understand that hiding in Polish territory means death, not only for him, but for the one who hides him. The more so, because no subterfuge is possible. A Jew can be recognized at first glance. In the countryside, a peasant usually only has one room to live in, so how to hide someone there? Is it at all possible to hide in a village? The more so, because everywhere, Germans have scoundrels who denounce. And in town, it means an endless moving from place to place. Jews well understand that asking someone for help and exposing them to death is inhuman. And the end of the war does not seem likely soon. That was why they dream about Hungary, where you could mingle with fellow believers in freedom, and still survive. So some of the wealthier, establish contacts with Hungarian soldiers, who smuggle them to their country.

War in the east is still concentrated around the 'Russian Verdun,' Stalingrad, despite the fact that Hitler declared in his speech that it will be taken and the Volga will be crossed.

6ᵗʰ October 1942. Ehaus is really raging. He rounds

up thousands of people at the market, in churches, in the schools and houses and sends them to Germany. Very often, he carries out searches at the gates of the ghetto. For a potato or an apple, he beats mercilessly. Jews subsist on what they eat at work. For them, an unfavorable wind is blowing. Different institutions rid themselves of Jews, and take the youth brigade. These are quite openly used for military work. The PZL has replaced the Jews who worked there with machines. The municipality approached the labor office for 50 women to sweep the streets in place of Jewish women.

In the ghetto there is fear again, but after the previous events, it is largely a deep resignation. The most important concern in the ghetto is to get food for today.

In his own opinion, Bacher, is organizing some clever tricks. In truth, it is sophisticated torture. For example, a whole section of the ghetto is going to the bathhouse, as they stand but only with towels. After the bath they are settled into other houses, perfectly empty, even without a handful of straw. All they had in their previous houses, and which was so hard to acquire and preserve, is lost. As if they are just newly born into this world.

Food robbery, continues under the guise of collecting the requisitions. In addition to the official thugs, roam real ones, also who are a scourge for the population. The standard of living is much lower compared to the previous year, everyone dreams about surviving physically.

10ᵗʰ October 1942. Among Jews, anxiety is growing. There, the brains are truly struggling. The main effort goes towards gaining Aryan papers. Frequently someone escapes from the ghetto. Mostly to Hungary. Often with the help of Germans, for much good money.

Once, five Jews conspired with a German officer who got 5,000 zł for the transport to Hungary. On the night, with every precaution, he took them out of the ghetto and they set off. But after a few minutes he stopped and called out:

'Get out! Budapest!'

They looked out, and they were at the castle, and saw Ehaus with the Gestapo. They went to jail, and from there?

'Those five thousand was nothing, but what else did they have with them?' ... say others about them.

After this event among the Jews there is fear. What sort of information will be squeezed out of them? What will happen to others? Older Jews, hiding in basements, are dying. Who can bear such a life?

The city Building Office was ordered to renovate barracks in Lwów Street. They are to be like a concentration camp for Poles avoiding work. They are to replace the Jews.

The Germans are really short of people so they look eagerly for replacements among the Poles. There will be an action to select Stammdeutsche (descendants from the Germans,) and therefore lower caste Germans. It is to be a tough action, not voluntary, but compulsory.

It is already an open secret that in the nation of 'masters,' something is amiss. Among the Germans, rampant bribery has spread. This looks bad for them and for us as well.

Great news about Stalingrad, it had withstood the German siege. That is most important.

15ᵗʰ October 1942. In the city there is depression. Germans are living separately, Poles separately. Previously, someone or other could listen to London or Moscow over a German receiver...There were news, there were encouragements... Now nothing. People feel it very painfully.

Ehaus personally plundered Polish houses. He searched in pantries, attics, basements. He became furious if he found 'forbidden fruit,' and at once took it to the German hospital.

Pavlů stalks like a cat around the Jews, who are now

levelling the area in front of the Castle, so that no one should rest for a moment. Because the Jews are paid for work, 10 to 25 cents per hour. Women get 10 cents, and 1 kg of pears costs 10 złoty.

A book has come out in which are names allegedly formerly German and later Polonized. These are to be changed to German. This is a special 'Polka' for the Poles. People are afraid. They fear the inclusion of GG to the Reich. This concern is deepened by the change of the sign: 'Issuing Bank of Poland' to 'Issuing Bank.' There are rumors about changing the złoty to the mark. And even worse ones.

15th October 1942. Today the press announced that German planes are bombing English flotillas of boat landings. So a second front? People are running with joy. Meanwhile, trains full of food go to Germany. This indicates hunger.

20th October 1942. What nonsense is Ehaus talking about, these air raids! Exactly the opposite of what they are. He lies dreadfully. There delight, because it has to be grim if they resort to such measures. The role of Himmler is not enough for Ehaus, he play Goebbels.

Hospitals are being vacated, apparently to make room for new casualties. Will there be another soviet offensive? German planes are flying en masse to the east. Heads are raised. Good signs.

Houses, which are allocated to Poles displaced from the German district, are in a very bad state. There are no doors, windows, kitchens, door handles. 'Treasure hunters' destroy houses the most. They rip up floors, ceilings, and punch holes in walls. Often they leave an actual ruin. They really find 'treasures.' Yesterday they found two more hidden warehouses, one with men's clothing, the other with metal goods.

Pavlů seems deranged. He stands over Jews, who work near the Castle, from dawn until late at night, like an executioner over a sinful soul. He does not allow workers to go to relieve themselves nor does he go himself. So many people are tormented by this unbridled cruelty. Some ask for death, because it is impossible to live like that. Those in the barracks also beg for death, because of damp, cold and hunger.

Wounded and sick Germans arrived to the hospital in a terrible state. Often half crazed. There must be a 'celebration' over there!

25ᵗʰ October 1942. Ehaus recently announced that there would be no more round ups. Some suckers believed this. The police went crazy again today and caught people en masse. Like once the Tatars.

From the area of Kolbuszowa, hundreds of peasant carts bring in huge quantities of wood from dismantled huts. Only for the Germans.

28ᵗʰ October 1942. Two offensives, one in Africa and the other one in Rzeszów. Ehaus organized it here against the Poles. Yesterday at a meeting he was frothing at the mouth. He shouted that, as priests and teachers were hostile to Germany, therefore everyone under the age of 35 years would go to Germany. Former students, who had been caught and destined for Germany, escaped somewhere. These people were shot straight away. Germans were not only after workers but also to remove the young intelligentsia from the villages. They are afraid of them.

Today, Ehaus burst into the commercial school and took a section of young people away to work. He slapped the faces of the girls who resisted. He visits shops and factories in person and takes people away to Germany. He really behaves as if demented. He announced that there will be no round ups, but if he meets someone in the street, he takes their documents and gives them to the Arbeitsamt. In a few days the chosen gets the call to go to Germany.

30th October 1942. The transport of the intelligentsia was to leave today. Out of eighty teachers, not even half registered, of ten priests, none. Ehaus was foaming at the mouth.

Once again, a transport of Jews from Kraków was being deported to the east. Some wanted to escape in Rzeszów. Several people were shot. Thirty corpses were removed from the wagons. Is it any wonder? In such a cattle car are crammed one hundred and fifty people. In Tarnow they brought out fifty corpses. So some people jumped out. Many are killed, many wounded. Those are finished off.

Squadrons of the SS ride to the east. Real punks.

1st November 1942. Today was created a Polish 'Beirat,' something like an advisory body. The stories that Ehaus told them! That Germans are defending us against Bolshevism, that they are creating order on earth for us, and similar drivel. Does he by any chance want to do the same with the 'Beirat' as he did with the Judenrat ? People are anxious because the Germans are 'caressing' the Poles.

3rd November 1942. What a story! The teachers were brought back. Ehaus got a dressing down, and at once went on vacation. Germans said he will not return to Rzeszów after this embarrassment. It is clear that the Poles are being placated. But that will be a vain exercise.

Africa. Great events are happening over there!

HOPE

For so long the town had been quiet and sad, suddenly it has become noisy and cheerful. Somehow it happened spontaneously. Hitler's promise to take Stalingrad is not fulfilled. Rather something quite the opposite. People talk openly about the victory of the British in Africa and the superlative role of Poles in the campaign. The Americans beat the Japanese. The belief, that this year the war will be over, is widespread.

Recently, German reserve troops went to the front. My God! Children and elderly, grandparents with grandchildren. Now excellent units departed from the area of Poznań. They speak Polish. Others speak Czech. Are the Germans short of people?

Ehaus is very discredited. Germans enjoy this because they do not like him. He got a scolding from Frank himself, that he was spoiling his politics. That one caressed the Poles, the other one slapped them, and screamed that they were of the worst.

The teachers and students from the commercial school returned because in Kraków, they revealed that they did not go voluntarily, but under the threat of beatings. Ehaus went away, it was said he would not come back. The Poles and Jews alike pray for this.

Unheard of high prices. There was a real lack of food. Meat quotas increased sixfold. In Germany, hunger.

In the ghetto, hope is mixed with great anxiety. They are afraid that this month 'something will happen.' Simply to reduce the quantity of stomachs, and still get something from the murdered victims.

10th November 1942. The Führer was again being idiotic and shouting: 'Wir werden nicht kapitulieren' [We will not capitulate!] And the distance between this reassurance and the former, that they will win, is very great. So the

Germans are going about as if in shock. The Volksdeutsche are rapidly becoming Polish patriots.

The Germans are not only depressed but also frightened. The city is lit up all night, though until now, it was only until 10pm. Numerous patrols circulate in the city. Robbery of manors, rectories, forest lodges and rich peasants is commonplace every day. The Germans are just powerless.

Among the Poles, there are numerous arrests. A secret radio station has been found.

In the last speech of the Führer, there were again threats directed against the Jews. Hence the consequences. Jews from Belgium and France and also from Kraków are transported east. Is it any wonder that the Rzeszów Jews are very anxious? They are afraid, above all, for the women and children. In the ghetto, they drink ... like the condemned, because, what is left for them?

Pavlů is like a stubborn maniac in his barbarity to abuse Jews. His eyes are clouded, he is screaming. He does not enter the town hall. From morning till night he stands over Jews near the Castle. The workers there faint from fatigue and exhaustion. They intentionally flee, so he will shoot them. Meanwhile, Pavlů orders them to be caught and given fifty lashes for trying to escape, and then to keep working.

11th November 1942. In the ghetto, the mood is terrible, crazy, sensing menace. Trains with Jews constantly go to the east. They are escorted by unusual police. They are friendly to the Jews, but what can they do? Any day now the deportation of a large part of the ghetto is expected.

The former, one hundred percent Jewish, Galezowski Street, later the centre of the ghetto, has suddenly become a central Polish street. All the shops from the German district have been moved here. Premises are renovated and repaired. It is becoming a truly European street.

Many Poles have been arrested as hostages.

12th November 1942. For a number of days, German police have been on a strict emergency duty. What will happen? Many Jews, owning Aryan papers, are escaping to the German side. But many are caught and shot. Several Poles, city officials, were arrested and deported, among them, Tadeusz Woloszyn. It was about the supply of those lifesaving papers to the Jews.

14th November 1942. It is known that the Gestapo have been sitting for days in the registration office and writing addresses. Will there be further arrests? Terror?

The Germans are afraid. In the German district, gates of the apartment houses are shut day and night.

Something quite unheard of has happened. Into a very secret German office, located on the corner of Podzamcze and Kraszewski Streets, entered three men. They terrorized the German clerks, took some papers and documents, destroyed weapons and escaped. There occurred unprecedented confusion. Such crazy turmoil, searches, checking of identity documents, as Rzeszów had never seen. Then it became quiet. A rumor was spread by someone, whether or not by the Germans themselves, that they were prisoners who had escaped from prison. A very clumsy lie. It is a common opinion that the attack was done by the English underground. Or perhaps, a Polish organization? Such a case will have a depressing effect on the Germans, but will also double their vigilance.

15th November 1942. Tonight, from Saturday to Sunday, the dread of the Jews, unfortunately, came true. For a number of days, there had already been a lot of information, that there would be a deportation. Some census was done, records, shuffling. Finally, in the night, all the inhabitants of the ghetto were driven out to the square. There it was read out, who was to stay and who must leave. The whole stunned crowd were then divided to the right and the left.

At the same time, a special branch, searched the whole ghetto for those gone into hiding. And again, they shot around thirty people.

Among them were many homeless and abandoned children, who even had no one to take them to the square. Finally, all the money was taken from those on the left, and they formed a long column of fifteen hundred people, many men, but above all women and children. And in an already familiar way, they were marched to the Staroniwa Station.

And again, no reaction. Only, that a certain number from the right side, much smaller than in the past, voluntarily came forward to go with their loved ones. Children were separated from their parents, the younger children or elderly parents went. How to explain this passivity, this resignation? Selfishness? Destroyed humanity?

The deportation was directed by some selection, but in many cases it was decided by fate, often cunning. And again, went the least clever. Among those remaining, there were many wheeler dealers, crafty people and people without scruples. Once more they drifted to the Gestapo and back at their service.

They say that a quite lot of people fled, smelling a rat. Even a Kahalnick ran away. The remaining ones are constantly crying for the children.

23rd November 1942. Poles do not know how to hide their mood. The Germans immediately saw their joy, and extinguished it by arresting hostages. They say that they were deported to a camp.

There were several death sentences for hoarding food.

25th November 1942. In the last deportation, Dr. Kleinman, president of the Kahal, was finished off. Apparently by 'his own doing.' Did he not withstand, psychologically? Or perhaps, he realized that for his existing patrons, he had become uncomfortable, that he knew too much and had to be removed?

Previously, he had obtained Aryan papers for his wife, son and daughter. The night before the final deportation, he sent them out into the world. He could no longer remain alone in the ghetto, nor to leave with his family. And significantly, he was a slave to his looks ... So he wandered aimlessly, senseless, without any intention to hide. Perhaps, to be free in the last few hours? In the morning, they caught him in Rudna. They brought him back. When asked why he ran away, because after all he was in no danger, he could not answer. And the Germans were consistent, according to the 'law,' he got the bullet. Maybe, just without beating, and questions as to where his family was.

27th November 1942. Soviet messages speak about the great victory at Stalingrad. There has to be something in it, because aircraft are constantly flying to the east.

In the latest German daily, there is a confirmation of the 'Jewish Quarter' in Rzeszów. Naturally, after those deportations and shooting. Speculation is, that who remained would be left, that the ghetto would stabilize at this level, so the remaining Jews breathed sigh of relief.

1st December 1942. The Bolsheviks are boasting that they had closed the Stalingrad cauldron. What was more, they had chopped it up. The Germans deny this ... but there is something to it.

Goebbels called for savagery. Laughter. As if Germans did not resemble cannibals!

In prison, people are dying of hunger.

One hears about attacks every day. It already said loudly that, among others, there are also Jewish squads who raid and steal to survive. The German hospital has expelled all Jewish workers, and in their place they enlisted Polish help. Before their dismissal, the Jews were robbed of their money and whatever else they had. They were sent out with nothing, as a reward for their work.

Jews are selling up whatever they can, because food becomes more expensive every day. Hunger. Yesterday, a few people, who came out to beg for something, were shot.

3rd December 1942. Polish hostages were released today. In the city, there was great joy.

However, Ehaus came back. He is bursting with pride, that he is the feudal lord in Rzeszów again. And power is delicious.

From the surrounding region come tragic news. The Germans had begun hunting down Jews in the area. They realize, that in the fall, or in summer, even a group can hide in the fields or in the woods and survive somehow. But in winter? Life without the help of the population was impossible. It therefore became important to search for the hidden, and those hiding them. Surely that, for this purpose, they enlist spies as well counting on chance.

Once searching purposefully, or maybe just accidentally, German police found in Przewrotne, in the woods, a bunker dug in the ground, where they found a local Jewess. Whether under threat or as a result of beatings, she revealed who built the shelter for her, who brought her food. The betrayed six people were immediately shot. The old woman confessed, that in the bunker existed other Jews, and actually her family, including several sons. The Germans prepared an ambush and caught them all. Before dying, one of the young Jews, who spoke good German, taunted and insulted the captors, predicting defeat and punishment. He was shot when he began to sing 'Poland has not yet perished.'

Today, there was a meeting of the Polish Beirat, which Ehaus wanted to make into a tool, similar to the Judenrat. The Beirat has to go around town and find people to work in Germany. In the town, panic.

8th December 1942. All night, people were arrested, to be sent off to Germany. They were literally pulled from their beds. Families were torn apart. Slavery. One heard, that you could ransom yourself, but for big money. Only traders have it, especially those who, in spite of death threats, deal with Jews who manage the stores in the ghetto. This is their revenge, that they can steal the loot and sell it. Only to eat and eat, because that was all they have left. And they rob one another, if someone has put away something for the dark hour.... The Germans actually have no power in the ghetto. They do not have the people.

11th December 1942. It is now widely and loudly said, that the assurance of the Führer, that Stalingrad was taken, was not worth a cracker. How far are the Germans from the 'Second Verdun?'

13th December 1942. Ehaus and Pavlů are keener Hitlers than Hitler himself. They rage with round-ups, and send people to Germany. Who knows, perhaps they are more afraid of defeat than victory. They used the Beirat to select people for deportation. They got a scolding for it, even the Gestapo got mixed up in it. But that will not benefit them.

16th December 1942. German police are plundering villages in a horrible way. If they find something forbidden, they beat the owner to death, and take everything out of the house. They fall into a frenzy, they liquidate whole hidden units, using bribed polish informants. And they know all about them. There is no doubt, that a well-functioning organization is doing this. News come from different locations, that the Germans murder entire Polish families, when they find hidden Jews. When someone, who had hidden a Jew and told him to leave, the Jew, captured by the Germans, usually revealed where he was hidden and who supplied him with food. And he knows that death awaits him anyhow. Among those who helped Jews, there is panic and they flee into the woods. Even if a Jew escapes from the ghetto, he will not find refuge in the countryside, not even a nook for a moment.

German sadism shifts to the Poles. In Kolbuszow, like in the Rzeszów ghetto, villages are surrounded and the residents are sent to places, distant from the village. Among the screams and beatings, those capable of working are selected, then rushed to the nearest station and into the wagons to Germany. Who would take care of the farms if only the elderly and children are left?

More than a thousand Jews were brought to Rzeszów, the remains from the ghettos of Krosno, Sanok, and Jaslo. Certainly, the Judenrat with their families and their nearest, because among them are some elderly, and some children, whose parents were murdered long ago.

19th December 1942. A squadron of the SS arrived in Rzeszów. Poles are afraid of them, because Ehaus, still uses them as a threat. The Jews are even more afraid, especially the new arrivals. Because, at the Arbeitsamt, they drawing up lists again ... People here realize that Ehaus and the Gestapo will not tolerate an element in the ghetto that does not work, and yet they have to have something to live.

22nd December 1942. In the ghetto, the mood has improved. It seems there will not be any transports.

Worse news come from the street. Police catch former petty thieves, people slightly mentally disturbed, and shoot them. As if for fun. They have tasted blood and they must have it.

23rd December 1942. Today, a village woman was selling something near the Castle, to a Jewish woman working there. Some Germans noticed it and both were shot.

24th December 1942. Before Christmas, I think on Christmas Eve, one of the polish officials went to Ehaus with good wishes for the holiday. Ehaus was oddly nervous, he could not restrain himself. Instead of thanks, he said that if a bomb was dropped on Rzeszów, like the one on Kraków (which killed many Germans,) Rzeszów would surely remember him.

This year, there were three days of holidays. In that time, all the Jews were free from work. Extraordinary!

31ˢᵗ December 1942. Jewish fighting units have appeared in the area. They have even obtained arms from somewhere. But in order to live, they have taken various things, especially from the peasants whom the Germans plunder mercilessly. The robbed farmers indicate to the Germans likely hiding places, and sometimes they capture the fugitives themselves.

In addition to the German gendarmes and police, the Sonderdienst is also operating. It works as a police auxiliary made up of Volksdeutsche and Ukrainians. They wear black lapels and collars. Once, three armed Jews caught a Sonderdienst in Turza, near Sokolow. One of the Jews wanted to shoot the captive, but the two others opposed it. In the end he was properly beaten up.

Year 1942 has passed. A terrible year. In history, it will surely be recorded as the time of the greatest crimes in the annals of mankind. But perhaps, it will become a turning point in the history of the Jews that the revival of the nation would follow at breakneck pace.

18ᵗʰ January 1943. The term, 'people of the forest,' had already gained the right of citizenship, and it is also increasingly being used and understood. Among the 'people of the forest' are gangs of common robbers, but they are thrashed by the real ones. The true 'people of the forest' are actually the underground, Polish army which has not yet declared war on Germany, but only so as not to direct revenge on peaceful and unarmed people. On the other hand, it relentlessly punishes Poles who let themselves to be bought and serve the Germans. If the charge was serious they eliminate them, if less serious, they beat them.

The Germans are using a new method against the Poles. They surround a village and carry out a thorough search. They are looking for people hiding, Jews, secretly kept pigs, grain, butter, etc. It often happens, that one or another policeman does not see it, or does not want to see, for purely humane reasons. Others again 'do not see' for a bribe. Among these, tend to be real criminals. Sometimes, during such raids, a Jew falls into their hands. Then it was very bad.

In Rzeszów, 52 houses belonging to the ghetto are to be demolished. They were damaged badly by the lack of fuel and overcrowding.

15th January 1943. Jews are still being segregated. Will they once again eliminate people?

Suddenly, one sees many very well-dressed Poles. In many cases, they wear Jewish clothes, which the Poles took for safe keeping. They had often been given to this or that person as a conditional loan. If they returned, they would exchange them again, but often things were given to storage with the words: 'If I will live you will give them back, sir. Better that you take them than the Germans.'

Some are doing quite well, trading with Jews. But this is a dangerous trade. Many were killed, many had gone to camp.

18th January 1943. Germans increasingly repeat, 'If Germany loses, let other nations be lost first.' And indeed they act as deranged. Because it is bad for them.

19th January 1943. A German, a Bahnschutz, was found and shot in Budy. He was a monster, not a man. People are pleased, but also afraid, because 59 people were arrested. An investigation is in progress.

Many Jews who worked there were also arrested. One, who was found eating a meal in a Polish home, was led to the Wisłok. There he was shot and pushed into the water.

21ˢᵗ January 1943. Former Soviet prisoners of war go east again dressed in German uniforms. Only Mongols. This looks very strange!

26ᵗʰ January 1943. Last week they began to demolish several houses in the streets Mickiewicz, Galezowski and Copernicus, which were once Jewish houses. Suddenly, demolition was stopped. The district was closed to vehicles and pedestrians. Yesterday and today, many shots are heard from small arms, grenades and cannon. They were just exercises in street fighting.

The Mongols are still passing by, also in buses. They laugh toward the Poles and wave their hands. Is it because they move against the Bolsheviks? Or maybe they are tricking the Germans?

German soldiers are given very bad food. They curse and have enough of war.

The Gestapo, with help from the locals, seeks out pre-war communists. Someone was even shot for harboring a Soviet prisoner.

28ᵗʰ January 1943. Here is an excerpt from a street conversation:

'Did you know that Germans won Leningrad?'

'What? What are you saying?!' The listener become wide eyed and looks terrified. 'Leningrad?'

'Oh, not Leningrad, only Lewingrad.'

'Oh, yes! It's true. It's only interesting that this was not in the news.'

That is an allusion to the exercises in the ghetto, which was filmed at the same time, as an example of strreet fighting or maybe the capture of some of the city. And Lewin, is Dr. Lewin, who was a rabbi in Rzeszów, the president of the

Kahal, a member of parliament, a big fish.

Despite setbacks at the front, the administration is working as always, as if nothing has happened. There is preparation for a census in the GG. Its main objective will be to demonstrate that in the so called Poland, there were never any Poles, only Polonized Germans, Stammdeutsche.

1ˢᵗ February 1943. The Soviet radio announced that their troops are chasing the Germans out of Stalingrad. In the city, there is Aryan and Jewish joy. They are drafting Germans into the army. Ehaus is sick. Maybe he wants to avoid the army?

The urban construction department drew up a plan to link the cellars in the German district. The Germans, civilians and Volksdeutsche, conduct exercises in defending and winning, among the ruins of the ghetto. They are very brave there.

4ᵗʰ February 1943. 'Krakauer' came out yesterday with a black border, after the defeat of the German army at Stalingrad. And the things they wrote there! That the rebounding Soviet wave, even beyond the Oder.

'German mourning' was ordered, because among the 'indigenous' population, there is jubilation. In Rzeszów, they are drinking to excess.

In the past week, from the Rzeszów prison, hundred and twenty Poles and several Jews were deported to labor camps, perhaps to Pustkow. That means death for 90 percent of them. From a labor camp, a group of people, drained by work like squeezed lemons, half corpses, victims of the method, were returned to the ghetto.

In the surrounding area, they continue to shoot people formerly convicted, and to catch communists.

The Polish underground seems to be going on the offensive. Arbeitsamt, the dispatch department of workers to Germany, was burnt after Polish policemen were first terrorized. Eight masked men came in from the road, released the captured workers and burnt the office. And they shot the German secretary. Probably the same unit. There is a lot of talk that Polish partisan units were now circulating openly. A new front?

8th February 1943. The previous night, on the walls of the city, was painted: 'Deutschland liegt an allen Fronten .' (Germany falls on every front.) To paraphrase the slogan: 'Deutschland siegt an allen Fronten.' (Germany wins on all fronts.)

Despite victories, despite waves of hope in the ghetto, the mood is tense. Lately, fanatics of Hitler, mostly local thugs, have a free hand over the Jews. Again, they make some inspections, rob the apartments clean. What will happen now? What will happen when the work in the warehouse is finished, when everything is sorted, put in order and sent off? So the workers drag the work out as long as they can.

That evening, shots came from the ghetto again. They have not been heard for a long time. Is this an echo of Hitler's oration?

9th February 1943. They have again 'cleansed' the Jewish hospital where, last week, a few dozen Jews, half dead from exhaustion and hunger, were brought in. And immediately, wagons, which bring food to the ghetto, took their bodies to the cemetery. When today one of these food cars drove through the city, it was completely covered in yesterday's blood.

It is now clear what kind of divisions they are doing in the ghetto. The ghetto was divided into two parts: Ost [east] and West. In the West, would live all those who work in the ghetto, in a variety of workshops, pompously called cooperatives, and more than 150 Jews belonging to Stadtvenwaltung [the municipality,]who work in various city institutions. This will be the privileged district. They will live in allotted homes with their families, they will even have their own council. The president of the new Judenrat, is the infamous Beniu Kahane. The Rzeszów Gestapo has taken over command of this ghetto, with Mack at the helm, whose favorite is Beniu. In the ghetto, there is a terrible struggle to get into that section. It is a promise of calm and some kind of life there.

Ostgetto is to be one big labor camp. There will be no families, no households. Joint housing and a communal bath house. These people work in various centres in the city and beyond. Everything is taken away from them, everyone has only what they are wearing. They are placed in empty rooms into which only straw was brought. And so it is the most primitive prison life. Now there will only be hunger, misery and vermin.

That camp was divided into male and female. The authority over the whole was covered by two unknown people from the SS. They are supposed to be dreadful! Pavlů and Ehaus look benign, compared to them.

11th February 1943. Bloody news arrive from everywhere. Every day, here and there, people are dying. From the stories, it is assumed that the Germans have bribed various criminals who report to them. The police, or the gendarmes, arrive at once and shoot those indicated. Such informers are too stupid to pretend. In turn, they die at the hand of the resistance organization.

In the surroundings of Hyżneg, twenty Jews were killed and also ten Poles, who hid and fed them. For hiding Jews, they killed three sons of a forester from Hadli glassworks, five peasants from Grzegorzówka. Jews cannot not withstand beating. Although they know they will die, they betray their supporters. So many tragic acts and situations.

There is much talk about the navy blue police, which is

Polish. They are mostly honest Poles, but some are also the worst villains. The power they received from the Germans has completely brutalized them.

19th February 1943. Today, young people from the commercial school, were deported to Germany.

Also today, in broad daylight, five armed men took 152,000 złoty from cash in the 'storehouse.' Everybody knows that it is the organization. We hear more and more often of similar attacks.

24th February 1943. A strong partisan unit, after disabling the guards and the Polish police, occupied Glogów, destroyed the post office and burned down the town hall where the administration and the municipal office were housed. The Germans arrested many people and shot six old men so as to spill some blood.

Whenever partisans commit something, the Germans shoot people indiscriminately, whoever they find. It is a system of intimidation.

5th March 1943. A census was conducted in Rzeszów. It showed there are 20,648 Poles, 2,939 Jews, but it seems not to include those who are in barracks and work in the PZL, the State Aviation Works. There are around one thousand of them. The Germans, including the Volksdeutsche (without the army, police and gendarmerie,) are 1,095, 169 Ukrainians, and 41 others. You can calculate, that through the Rzeszów ghetto passed about 30,000 Jews. So 90 percent were murdered!

Ehaus announced a draft for the front, among the Germans of course. After long persuasion, two reported for duty. Patriots!

Since almost no one of the Stammdeutsche has reported, it is said:

'If anyone has a German name he may be German or a Jew but never a Pole.'

And so they must present themselves. This is called volunteering.

In the ghetto, blood flowed again. Apparently, it is not allowed to dry out, so the Jews can breathe. They found a Jewish woman who had not registered, who hid actually in the ghetto, in a box under the floor at the home of her acquaintances. Did someone report her or was she found by chance? The fugitive, and fourteen people, who were hiding her, were shot in their apartment.

10th March 1943. Bacher, the syphilitic and alcoholic, has gone away. He was a man half insane, he murdered people en masse. He went as a result of efforts of Pavlů.

The ghetto is ruled by two SS-men: Sturmfůhrer Schupke and his deputy, Untersturmführer Ester. At first sight, it seemed that Schupke will be bloodthirsty, the other, good-natured and gentle. Actually it was totally the reverse. The head of the ghetto Schupke, does not beat, not shoot, not even shout. He pretends not to see the incoming food, only cares about the economic side, that the ghetto should bring income. So the work in the cooperative is going well, it is put in order, cleaned, and packed. However, his deputy is simply a monster. He is a drunkard, and when drunk, he will not calm down until he has shot someone.

10th March 1943. Ehaus is just raging. He searches for people. He imposes fines on the fugitives, chases communists, and threatens with shooting. In a word, inconceivable terror.

Gold fell again. On 10,200 złoty for a gold 20 dollar coin, they now pay 8,000 złoty, and it is interesting that there are now as many on the market as in June 1942. This was explained, that in spring, in the hope that this year the war would be over, the Jews were preparing to flee. So they drew on their last resources and sold them to have liquid cash. The Germans are also aware of this. They increased the ghetto guards. The ghetto is watched by the 'blacks,' the auxiliary police made up of Volksdeutsche and Ukrainians. But the Germans are perfidious and treacherous. They do not say openly, but they imply, that they will apply a collective responsibility. Finally, that these Jews who are left, have great chances to stay alive, unless of course such accidents may occur, as an escape from the ghetto, etc.

Accidentally or intentionally, in the ghetto, on the one side, are individuals, completely stripped of everything, and next to them, are whole families, wife and children. Fathers of the families tremble at the thought of someone escaping. They monitor whether there was a conspiracy planned by those who are single, who are not tied to anyone. They are therefore under the control of hundreds of eyes, they are as on a leash ... It is hard to imagine a collective action, an escape. Maybe a single individual. But this is not a good prospect. Escape would be easier if outside the ghetto there was an organization that would develop a plan for the escapees, organize a safe haven, and from the ghetto would be sent only orders and ready plans. Some dream of something like it. Unfortunately, centuries of abnormality of Jewish life, which results in a cultivated sense of individualism and a lack of social sense, today gets its reckoning.

Yesterday, the city was witness to a macabre procession which consisted of about eighty Jews. At the front, on a stretcher, was carried a dead man or maybe just a sick man. Next, followed men in chains or rather, shadows of men, under a strong escort of PZL factory guards. They were those Jews who, hoping to save their lives, pretended to be metalworkers and were assigned to the factory. When placed before the machines they were completely ignorant. They were escorted back to the Ostgetto. Their fate is well known: hunger and hard work will finish them.

17th March 1943. Ehaus personally directs the collection of enormous requisitions. What is happening in the villages is terrible.

Uniformed military and armed units of the 'people of the forest' appear here and there and ravage German institutions and draw the Germans into a game like blindman's buff. In Przewrotne, near Glogów, a special operation murdered dozens of people suspected of communist sympathies. News come from various sides about similar murders.

21st March 1943. Tenth anniversary of Hitler's coming to power. The city is sparsely decorated with dirty flags. No obvious enthusiasm, although it is a holiday.

In Przewrotne, there was a second massacre. Again, thirty three people were shot, moreover they were taken straight from the church after the service.

On the eve of Hitler's holiday, the city was again 'painted,' namely with '1943 = 1918.' These symbols are now obvious to the Germans. Germans, in many cases, used provocateurs and false 'men of the forest,' so the Poles are very careful.

22nd - 23rd March 1943. The ghetto experienced hell once again. It was an echo of Hitler's recent speech. Several dozens of people were shot, including several women.

One of the best placing for Jewish labor is the Ostbahn, the work on the railway. A few hundred Jews worked under the supervision of German railway workers, by no means hostile to Jews. You could buy everything there. The Polish women brought in cooked dinners. One could even eat something decent in private houses. The guards were on good terms with the Jews.

Suddenly, like a bolt from the blue: an order to dismiss a part of the Jews from work at the discretion and wishes of a German engineer. And because, on the railway there worked mainly Rzeszów Jews, disposing of certain means, they came to an agreement with this engineer. He left those, who gave him a bribe, alone. Anyone who did not have enough to pay the bribe returned to Ostgetto. Most likely someone, as a revenge, reported this to the Gestapo. The engineer was arrested. But he had no scruples and denounced all those who gave him money. They were at once sentenced to death, but first they were beaten in a beastly manner. This incident became the spur for some brave souls to risk escape.

They hid at first on the train, then disappeared into the world. And as it is already spring, maybe they will succeed to survive.

Even the bloodiest deed, past and gone, is not as terrifying as a nightmare lurking in the near future.

At the same time came news from the Kraków ghetto, that about four thousand people died, mainly women and children, partly on site and partly gassed at Auschwitz. A new spectre is hanging over the despairing suburb. A large unit of Mongols, the former Soviet prisoners of war, has come to Rzeszów. But they are not German soldiers, even though they are dressed in dyed German uniforms. It is said that they are voluntary teams, working in the service of the Wehrmacht. They do not walk under guard, just under a German command. Their faces are like wax. They do not reveal anything, veritable masks. Jews suspect that this squad has come to replace them at work, and they themselves are becoming now unnecessary and will be murdered like the Jews in Kraków.

In all, the towns units of Schupo have been settled.

27ᵗʰ March 1943. Poles not only resist, but go into action. This makes Germans furious, because they have to keep a lot of personnel here who are needed in the east or in Africa. The Gestapo are applying truly medieval torture.

Today the 'Pol-Wacht-Dresden' are leaving. They have

been in Rzeszów almost one year.

29th March 1943. It seems that the railway operation is still continuing. At night, some wagons of Jews were taken to the woods near Glogów, mainly women, and were shot there.

31st March to 1st April, 1943. At night, the German police surrounded the Polish police precinct building, which faces the Gestapo building. In the basement of the police building were detained criminals and Jews. Polish police were forbidden to go outside. From the police basement, as well as from the Gestapo, dozens of people were led outside and executed in the courtyard. At once, Jewish hearses were called to carry the murdered victims to the Jewish cemetery. In this group there were only a few Jews.

Recently, the 'people of the forest' stormed the prison in Mielec and released all the prisoners. As a reprisal, many people were arrested, brought to Rzeszów and transferred west, perhaps to a camp.

German duplicity knows no bounds or restraint. Recently, the German press, published in Polish language, called on the Poles to take part in the reinforcing of a barrier against the east. Should the Poles contribute to the maintenance of this monstrous Nazi terror? It must be going quite badly for them, both in body and mind, if they have the audacity to write something like this. And Poles are laughing and rubbing their hands.

HOPE AGAIN

Hope in people's hearts stirred a little. A wave of optimism suddenly swept among people, like when during cold weather a south wind will blow. Although ... nothing concrete is indicated to logically justify this optimism. But still...

In the east it is quiet, but everyone knows that both sides are preparing for the final encounter, as soon as spring has dried the soil. Germans are pulling in reinforcements to the rear of the army, mainly members of the party, because the rear is only manned with such forces. How they defend themselves and evade being sent, because it is easier to fight with women and children than with the Soviet army. And so they mutually support one another.

The situation in Germany is disastrous, food shortages and constant bombardment. Polish workers write home about it.

In Africa, it is obvious that the situation for the Axis is catastrophic.

A unit of the SS came to Rzeszów to replace the Dresden battalion. They began their rule in Rzeszów with a massacre which killed eight men and one woman. The Germans are furious, because now, deep behind their lines, swirls partisan warfare, attacks and sabotage, then bloody retaliation. Hell is beginning, but the Jews say, 'The worse it is, the better.' Panic has gripped all informers and spies, because they are being systematically liquidated.

15th April 1943. The governing unit, which came to Rzeszów, hung a board in its quarters, 'II/SS Pol. Reg. 23,' meaning, the second battalion 23 of the SS Police Regiment. Very pleasant company.

27th April 1943. Germans carefully avoid encounters and clashes with the forest units, but willingly send Polish police against them. After the departure of the unit, they abuse and murder civilians. This is true heroism!

Recently in Staromieśc, the Wisłok brought to its shore two women, an elderly one and one very young extremely pretty. The young one had been strangled. Presumably, these were Jewesses, whom someone had murdered on hearing of the Glogów tragedy and was afraid of the same fate for those people in the event of being discovered. How many tragedies are happening!

In Rzeszów, there is incredible building activity. Some apartment houses are being finished, others are renovated, and some telephone centres are created. It looks as if they are hoping to stem the Soviet resistance.. People worry about it, and also about the breakdown of the Soviet-Polish diplomatic relations.

There is an uprising in the Warsaw ghetto. Or, perhaps, a desperate impulse to die fighting rather than in the gas chambers? Miracles are told about this hopeless battle, with admiration towards the Jews who are fighting without a shadow of hope.

1st May 1943. Since yesterday, heavily armed, German three man patrols, circulate in the city. Do they fear a Jewish uprising in Rzeszów? Or maybe a May Day demonstration?

Epics are told about the battles in the Warsaw ghetto. There is mounting respect for the people dying there.

4th May 1943. Today, Ehaus has called in the Beirat. Probably, in order to calm down the population.

Military forces and great numbers of planes surge to the east.

The Germans are forming a Ukrainian SS division.

7th May 1943. A military unit from Azerbaijan arrived in Rzeszów and then drove off to Glogów and was quartered there. They are to fight the communists.

The Gestapo worked the whole day yesterday in the ghetto. It seems they were looking for suspected communists. They took many people to the Gestapo. Their fate will be terrible. After torture, death. Gestapo is definitely afraid of a reaction in the ghetto.

Among the Jews there is some mysterious illness. So say the Germans. What kind of mysterious illness? Is it a pretext? People suffer from hunger and typhoid fever there. Yesterday, two wagons of the sick were taken out, naturally to die.

8th May 1943. The war in Africa is over! The Bolsheviks have broken the Kuban front!

Enough for today.

Joy, however, was dampened by the announcement that the old curfew from 9 pm to 5 am will be restored, and once again the Azerbaijan company, whose purpose was nothing else but to frighten, march through the city.

11th May 1943. On the night of 8th to 9th May, Przewrotne again experienced an inferno. One does not know how to call this operation, what it is about. That is not important. It is important that the Germans have again killed dozens of people. They took a large number with them to Rzeszów. Is this not the German reaction to the increasing number of operations by the 'people of the forest?'

Azerbaijanis from Glogów participated in the action in Przewotne. First of all, they stole or took away food. They also raped the women. Fear fell over the area.

Yesterday 10th May, at 7.30 pm, at the cinema door erupted explosions causing great damage. This was also a campaign by the 'boys from the forest' to prevent Poles going to the German cinema.

A wave of optimism that the war will end this year has surged again.

On Mount Lisa, a German, the Baudienst inspector, was found shot. The corpse had already been lying there for a few days.

Many people have noticed that Germans, working in offices, are polite and gloomy. That is something very new.

13th May 1943. Ehaus is sleeping in the 'Burg.' He is afraid. At one workshop, the Gestapo are putting powerful window grilles in the building? Are they worried?

In the Central Co-operative Bank, armed men took away 47,000 złoty in broad daylight.

15th May 1943. Last night, the Germans surrounded the district behind the barrier on Kraków Street and took away dozens of people. It was said it was a raid on communists.

There were arrests at the PZL and throughout the city. They were really hunting leftist activists.

Since several days, there is deportation of Jews from the west ghetto, that is the civilian one. In it, live or rather starve, die people, men without a permanent or temporary employment, women and children. They are supposedly transported to work in Mielec, two hundred people per transport, but all know it is to their death. How desperate they are!

17th May 1943. In the ghetto, they choose specialists, and take them to Kraków. What will happen to the rest? Especially after the uprising in Warsaw ... They say that whoever is left would be finished off where they are.

21st May 1943. In recent days, several German soldiers were shot near Rzeszów. The authorities are raging.

Ehaus called in officials of the county, both Poles and Germans, and declared that he has received full authority, and that if there occurs an attack on the Germans, he will order the officials to be shot. People are terrified.

23rd May 1943. In Rzeszów again, numerous arrests. Those arrested are brutally treated. Beatings and abuse.

25th May 1943. In Glogów, the Polish population has managed to communicate with the Azerbaijanis. They say that the Germans defeated them by starvation. When you talk with them about the Caucasus they cry.

Italians are returning from the east. They are extremely happy. They greet Poles heartily. Germany has nice allies!

In observing the Germans in Rzeszów, one does not know what to think. They renovate old buildings, arrange excellent shops, and create, at Pobitnem, a special cemetery for the Germans. Are they crazy? When will the roof collapse on their heads?

28th May 1943. Polish underground is eliminating Polish informers. They thoroughly thrash the less dangerous accomplices of the Germans. Apparently, this brings results. Zealous citizens of the GG were given warnings. Some Germans too. It is not only a local, but an overall action throughout the whole terrain of the occupation. That is why the Germans are really frightened. The villa SS, in Jagiellonian Street, is a small fortress, the windows of the Gestapo building are shielded by powerful bars. Further arrests are taking place. Are they not dictated by fear?

1st June 1943. At Staroniwa, 52 people were shot for damage to a transformer. A monstrous horrible crime!

2nd June 1943. There is constant talk about Soviet landings. The Germans look for them without success. Ehaus announces, that if the Poles do not eliminate these paratroopers, they themselves will perish.

Tension that something big will happen, fell like sunken dough. Silence. Only the market reacted, with a big drop in the price of gold and dollars.

4th June 1943. In the civilian ghetto, or the 'west,' there is hunger and typhus. Jews are dying en masse. The hearse is running there and back constantly.

How desperately people are trying to avoid grasping the razor accidentally! Hopes of the Soviet spring offensive have failed. The Jews invented another consolation for themselves. They believe that in the near future, in Germany, there will be a military coup that will remove Hitler and his party. The military government will immediately start peace negotiations. That will bring freedom for the Jews. Will they live to see this?

7th June 1943. In the Rzeszów prison there is typhus. People are dying. They are taken to the Jewish cemetery in the Jewish hearse, under the pretence that they are Jews who have been shot.

After Warsaw, the Germans had plans to begin the liquidation of the ghetto in Lwów. There they reportedly also encountered resistance, but weaker and less well organized than in Warsaw.

In Rzeszów, there is again a rumor that Jews, working in PZL, are to be driven back to the ghetto, where there is hunger and death. Are there plans to liquidate the Rzeszów ghetto, leaving only the cooperative?

8th June 1943. Last night, two villages, Boguchwala and Zwierzyca, near Rzeszów, were surrounded. Some stated that this is an operation against the communists, and others, that it was against railway saboteurs. Some dozen people were shot and many taken away somewhere.

From all sides, one hears of such pacification and mass murder of people. The Germans still hide their crimes behind an alleged struggle against communism. But we know that this concerns the murder of the Polish nation.

10th June 1943. It was not clear who caused the rumor that the various acts that provoke the German reaction are the work of the Jewish gangs. What nonsense!

11th June 1943. The Germans massacred and burned part of the village Hucisko, near Przewrotne. What a rabid madness!

15th June 1943. Still murder and murder, village after village. Is this not the Jewish prophecy coming true: 'Firstly us, and then you.?'

17th June 1943. Lately, they shot three young Jewish women, who had been hiding on Aryan papers. They were spared for so long a time, but finally they lost. Did someone denounce them?

The rumor has it that in the forest units there are many Jews. Memories from last year are revived, that young Jews from the provinces did not go to the ghetto. They went into the woods. Some of them died, but many remained and were alive.

There is a persistent rumor that a large part of the Rzeszów ghetto will again be eliminated.

22nd June 1943. One hears that a number of Azerbaijani groups, and the SS, have again arrived into the area. The Germans, apparently, considered that area unsafe for them. The Azerbaijanis do not hide their hatred of the Germans, but at the same time, they grab food from the Poles and rape the women.

Increasingly, mysterious aircraft are flying overhead, according to a general opinion, they are Soviet ones. Germans, who laughed heartily at Polish anti-air raid trenches of the year thirty nine, now mark out many of them in different parts of the city. Are they expecting raids?

Still a tense silence. German troops are driving through Dynów to the south. Will there be a second front there?

Again hope. And fear ... They shoot and shoot people. Every day comes dismal news.

7th July 1943. The German newspapers scream that the Germans have begun their offensive. But one knows it was just a counter offensive, the German way of defense.

8th July 1943. This morning, everyone is talking of nothing else but that, during the night Rzeszów was surrounded. There was supposed to be a purge. During the preparations, came a telegram that thirty Jews escaped from the camp at Pustkowie. So all the troops immediately went there for the manhunt. Was it true? God knows. Something must have happened, because today in all the streets, identity documents of people are being checked.

From early morning, light combat aircraft rumble to the east. They are probably needed there. Unhelpful unfriendly wishes are following them, sent by a tormented people.

9th July 1943. Yesterday there was a massacre in Stobierna. According to whispers, mostly communists were murdered. Houses were meticulously searched where allegedly, Jews were hiding, who constituted the majority of the local forest units. Those are the whispers, but is it really so? Rumors however must be based on something, as indeed in those areas, Germans captured a few Jews.

Control of identity cards is still ongoing and it is very thorough. Last night, around sixty people escaped from the ghetto. They were the most daring, and most convinced that the war will end this year.

In the ghetto, a list of Jews, of citizens from different countries, is being drawn up. A rumor is running that they will be sent back via Portugal to their places of origin. Is this a new German deception? Who knows? After so many trials for many, even a spider thread of hope seems to be a cord, provided at the end with a safety belt. One of the Rzeszów merchants, an Argentine and Brazilian citizen, was so moved by the possible travel to Portugal, that under the influence of sudden impulse or affinity or gratitude toward the ghetto commandant SS Hauptscharführer Schupke, he revealed a cache where he had hidden textiles and ready-made clothes worth several millions (naturally in present value.) Herr Hauptscharführer took it quite differently however. In the office, seeing the mighty loot, he indicated that the Jew was crazy.

Other Jews cursed him, and wished him on the road to hell. Because he awakened German greed, and sparked suspicions that the Jews still have more hidden treasures. They expect hard repressive measures.

10th July 1943. Germans have openly begun blatant robbery. Those inspections on roads take even the slightest amount of food, releasing alleged suspects and prisoners of the Gestapo for big bribes. The various requisitions and fanciful taxes show that, among the Germans, there is increasing anarchy.

PS: Jubilation. The English are landing in Sicily. So ... second front?

13th July 1943. Tonight, a squad of 'insurgents' passed through Przybyszovka, going towards Rudna. The peasants called them real partisans, in contrast to various gangs who mercilessly rob villages. The insurgents give the impression of a real army, and pay for everything.

At the news of insurgents, German troops drove to Glogów, apparently in pursuit of them.

14th July 1943. News come of mass massacres in the area of Sokolow.

16th July 1943. A legend has grown around the insurgents. The Germans are furious and hunt for them in various directions. The exits of streets are blocked with bollards, stopping cars and people, and yet there are a thousand other ways into the city.

Before noon, a number of cars were driven from the prison to an unknown direction and destination.

Lately, more escapes of Jews from the ghetto are due to rumors that on the 15th will be its final liquidation. The escapes sparked concern among the Germans because, those who flee, either form a new gang or increase an existing one. An order was sent out to forbid Jews to work outside the ghetto.

That was not all. The head of the Gestapo, Mack, called the heads of institutions employing Jews, to his office and emphatically denied the rumor that anything threatened the Jews. In this spirit, he ordered to influence public opinion, and said that spreading disturbing rumors will be very severely punished.

The tightened control of the ghetto had results. All Rzeszów knew, that organized smuggling of food into the ghetto was taking place. With weaker supervision it was possible, but now that they caught a number of smugglers, women and boys, they say that someone has already been shot, the guilty were beaten and they disclosed others who are being captured and arrested. The result will be, that hunger will increase, in spite of money owned by the Jews.

On Slovak Street, on the side of the ghetto, a number of houses in quite good condition are being demolished. Mainly, to obtain building materials at low cost, or rather at no cost at all.

Jews were harnessed for work, to give them something to do. How many idle hands there are in the Ghetto?

20ᵗʰ July 1943. From everywhere come news about murders, fires, robberies. It is total oppression of the people. They not only rob, but impose a monstrous use of torture, inhuman abuse. Terrible to think about it!

26ᵗʰ July 1943. Mussolini has dropped out of the game. The Axis has collapsed. People are wild with joy. They do not even hide it before the Germans. The latter walk around with aggrieved faces. The vision of the end of the war becomes more and more real.

30ᵗʰ July 1943. In the farther and nearer area of Rzeszów, several Jewish 'gangs' have been formed, who in order to exist, have to steal. They attack cooperatives, shops, and peasants. Following any such attack, a German punitive unit arrives at a village and brings order. They shoot and take people away. Villages defend themselves. Several groups always guard the village. It comes to fighting.

Bodies fall on both sides. So the Germans, unable to reach the runaway Jews directly, fight against them indirectly.

3rd August 1943. Ukrainians from Germany sneak over to the east, fleeing from forced labor. Germans capture and shoot them. It ends in death. Many, most, fantastic rumors are circulating! People simply revel in them!

19th August 1943. Yesterday, a miracle occurred, without a deadly event. A German policeman noticed that a boy was selling cigarettes to Jews who were wrecking houses in Slovak Street. The German wanted to stop him, but the boy took to his heels among people, in the direction of the Market. The policeman shot a whole magazine after him. The boy ran away and no one was even injured. A small but frequent incident. Or maybe he shot so as not to hit?

The Germans, because of their lack of success, continue to destroy the Jews. They hate them utterly. Hence the vicious extermination of them.

One hears all the time about the battles between the Germans and the forest units. Underground organizations continue to eliminate German spies.

31st August 1943. In the ghetto, great commotion. The remaining Jews were assembled, and were to be taken to some work camp. Among the 'selected' was the fear that they will be deported to the place from which no one returned. Anxiety is exacerbated by news from the east where mass murder of Jews is being carried out.

1st September 1943. The fifth year of the war has begun. What will it bring?

In Jasionka, Germans take new fields, and at a fantastic speed extend the airport, expand and lengthen the runways, build artillery positions and bunkers. And so, the war will be to the end.

Again, rumors about the liquidation of the ghetto in the next 48 hours, have spread. In Rzeszów, will remain only

Jews who work in a camp, something like the PZL.

Worried about the rumors, Jews living in the Ostgetto, or rather the official name of the SS in the Judenarbeitslager [Jewish labor camp,] went to the Obersturmführer Schupke.

He listened calmly to their concerns, and firmly replied that it will not happen so soon. The completion of work in particular sections would last at least until December, and then the 'Lager,' that is a team of professionals, could go to large manufacturing firms.

Schupke calmed Jews to such an extent that they began frantically to seek a transfer to Westgetto, in spite of the terrible hunger and terrible overcrowding there, so as to be able to go to a labor camp. It was always easier to survive in employment, and the end of the war seems close.

Jews were even more reassured by the fact that Mack and Ehaus took leave and went away, because until now, no transports occurred without them. Therefore, the market did not trade any goods still held by Jews, which always took place as a result of panic and rumors of deportation.

Other rumors circulate at the same time, are they not created by the Germans? That near Jaslo, Przemysl and Kraków, some Jewish settlements are being formed as evidence to the rest of the world, that the clamor about the murder of Jews is vulgar anti-German propaganda.

Recently, regardless of the great anti-Jewish propaganda cultivated in the press, the Germans, ever more insistently, apply a new propaganda as if to justify the cruelty. They circulate information that the pacification is the German reaction to the activities of the Jews who spread communism, and gangs who attack and destroy the work of reconstruction. At the same time, the propaganda explains to Poles the way to protect themselves is by their cooperation with the Germans in the extermination of Jews and Communists.

Nevertheless, they threaten with the death penalty, not only for harboring or assisting a Jew, but even for just seeing a Jew. And so, in the countryside, terrified and browbeaten by the monstrous pacification, peasants are ill disposed toward the Jews, not through lack of compassion, but to save their own life. And it happens that they are sometimes the proverbial sleeping agent.

2nd September 1943. Thursday. The ghetto is densely surrounded by positions of the SS, at some points with barrels of machine guns facing inward. It resembles entirely, July 1942. Without asking, without words, it is understood what was going on and actually what will happen. So the rumors were true, they must have come from a good source. On the Aryan side, people are moved to solemnity, a deep compassion and a sense of helplessness against the carrying out of the crime in cold blood. Already, it is a common secret that at night before the encirclement of the ghetto, dozens of young Jews escaped. Many saw this. They escaped without hindrance.

The ghetto is surrounded by a cleared area. From the windows on the Aryan side, one can see exactly what is happening there. So on the main square, the place of assembly and controls, a densely packed crowd of terrified people is surrounded by policemen, gendarmes and Gestapo. Violent shoving, pushing, kicking, searches, seizing everything, other than the clothes on their backs. A shot to the back of the head, in front of everyone, interrupts the monotony from time to time. In such a manner, were liquidated those who had been in hiding.

Many are curious what will also happen to Ben Kahane who, after the death of Dr. Kleinmann, became president of the Judenrat in Westgetto. This man is hated by the Jews and despised by the Poles. He used to say that he actually has nothing in common with Jews, only his unfortunate descent. From the time of the entry of Germans to Rzeszów, he was with them on perfectly good terms, and welcomed them and entertained them in his home. His extremely extravagant banquets were famous. He drew his wealth from the bribes for interventions with the German authorities in cases of individual Jews. He is obscenely bloated, when hundreds and thousands are dying of hunger. He has a permanent pass and often can be seen out on the town. According to general belief, after taking power, Kleinmann assumed total service to the Gestapo. He was an agent and secret tool of Mack. He was also a trusted agent for Stomacker, and other thugs.

At about 11 o'clock, a tragic funeral column emerged from the ghetto. In front walked dear Ben with the Judenrat, followed by the entire Westghetto, old men, women, children and even quite a few men. All without the smallest bundle. Apparently, everything was taken from them. And again ... as last year: kicking, beating, but without the screaming and shooting. The silence, broken only by the sudden and terrifying screams of children, seeking lost parents, was eerie. It made a profound impression.

The heavily guarded procession went from Slovak to Matejko Street and crossing the intersection of Grunwald, entered Kraków Street, then right on to Staroniwa, to the station. So a slightly different route than last year. Those marching, on seeing a Polish acquaintance, smiled sadly at them, or even slightly nodded their head to say goodbye. Many people wept, many clenched their fists.

At about 13 o'clock, a second column already markedly smaller, passed on Staroniwa. There was only a part of Ostgetto in it. This column may have gone to some labor camp or factory. Soon behind this column, drove Jewish carts with straw, which was put into the wagons. Interesting that the straw was transported by Jews without any escort. Railroad workers revealed to them, that a very long train to which they were taking the straw, would go to Jaslo. And there is really supposed to be a labor camp.

On the square, in the ghetto, remained a small group made up mostly of young women. A very thorough search was applied to them. They were searched even in intimate places. From time to time, from the group where the search was conducted, someone was taken to the side and shot. Apparently, something was found, which should have been unreservedly relinquished. But can you wonder at people who saved their belongings, the more so, that ahead of them was such an uncertain fate?

After 3 o'clock, the ghetto was shaken by shots from small arms and machine guns, and even strong detonations. They were shooting at the infirm elderly, the sick, and those who were still discovered somewhere else.

Several grenades were thrown into cellars. Apparently, those hiding there did not want to come out.

Compared to last year, they used yet another method. So the action inside the ghetto was carried out by local Germans, police and the Gestapo, whereas for surrounding the ghetto and guards, they used 'SS Asturia.' All young boys. They happily engaged in talking with the Poles, especially with the girls, and this in Russian!

3rd September 1943. Early in the morning, shots and explosions came again from ghetto. Before eight o'clock, a third group, just the girls, went in the direction of the Staroniwa Station. They joined the second group from yesterday, who were left all night in the field without water and food. Then both groups were loaded into a huge train that actually departed in the direction of Jaslo. None of these people had even a small bundle, only what they wore.

Also in the morning, wagons full of corpses, covered only slightly with straw, drove out from the ghetto. From the wagons on which warm bodies were still twitching, flowed streams of blood, marking their passage. People's faces froze at the sight. Older women loudly called for God's punishment.

Now there is general talk about the fate of Dr. Bernard Kahane. Feeling what awaited him at the Staroniwa Station, he was just ranting in despair.

'Where is Mack? Where is Mack!' He yelled wildly, looking for his protector. He could not come to terms with the thought that he deserved it, that he was treated like any other Jew.

From these events, it is clear that the leave, Mack and Ehaus took, was intentional. Dr. Kahane was sentenced to death. He knew too much. Therefore, he was shot at the station. Rumor had it that 60,000 dollars was found on him. He believed the Germans so uncritically that he did not even persuade his only son to flee. He did not look like a Jew and was not even circumcised. Provided by his father with the money, he could have saved himself. He saw his father die and he went to death with his mother.

About 250 people from the Eastghetto still remained in the ghetto, to clean out the houses, to sort out the booty and finish the job. And then ... Surely they do not have any illusions as to their ultimate fate.

The action was led by a depraved criminal, Hauptmann Wiese, who probably has on his conscience, thousands of people.

The guard in the ghetto was taken over by an unknown, and not previously seen, group consisting of very young boys, almost children. They are dressed in dark blue uniforms of the German police, but without eagles on shirts and caps. It was widely said that they are Ukrainians. They are stationed around empty buildings to prevent looting and theft.

Single shots and explosions were heard throughout the

day. Apparently, grenades were thrown into cellars and sewers. If somebody was hidden, he died.

In the evening, there was talk about a boy who sat on the roof the whole day, clinging desperately to the chimney. But no one could say if he was saved or he was shot.

4th September 1943. This morning, before eight, sound of shots came again from the ghetto. A little later, a truck full of corpses was transported to the cemetery. Who were they?

In the afternoon, the city already had an explanation. A dog, belonging to a German policeman, discovered a hiding place in some cellar or attic, in which lived fathers and husbands, with a large group of women and children. They were the ones shot this morning, or rather, another famous murderer, Gestapo Zielinski, shot them. This had a terrible effect on Schupke. He could not settle down after this incident.

Elegant Jewish policemen walked around town somewhat sadly, without the usual swagger. One of them said that Hitler was supposed to have announced: 'At five minutes before twelve, Jewish people will be gone'! Was the twelfth hour nearly here?

Looters have already rushed for the booty. In the night from Friday to Saturday, they caught two girls and a boy, aged between 15 and 17 years old, in the empty ghetto. Schupke had to ask Kraków what to do with them. The answer was supposed to have arrived, a public hanging. Will this happen?

The liquidation of the ghetto made a shocking impression in the city. Regarding the Germans, no one has any illusions. If the Jews were first in the plan, then in the other, will certainly be the Poles. Hence ominous forebodings. What will happen if the war drags on?

THOUGHTS OF ESCAPE

6ᵗʰ September 1943. On the same day as the 'action,' at 3pm, the official German news confirmed that the Allies have landed in Italy.

7ᵗʰ September 1943. Today, on the walls and fences of the deserted ghetto, red posters in small letters were glued for the first time in German, 'Die Plunderer werden erschossen,' then in large letters, in Polish, 'Thieves will be shot.'

What a shameless and treacherous announcement! Who are the real thieves here? But they may be a prophecy, that the thieves will be shot? Please God!

8ᵗʰ September 1943. Tonight there was an air raid alarm and some planes actually flew over. They may have been Soviet aircraft, or possibly English, with supplies for the 'people of the forest.' The raid was treated as serious, because the workers at the PZL were released beyond the limit of the plant, and officials were hustled into shelters. People were praying that at last the bombs should fall.

9ᵗʰ September 1943. At night. Italy has surrendered!

12ᵗʰ September 1943. The Italian thunderbolt, that deeply shocked the Germans, had an effect on the behavior of the Gestapo in the ghetto. And more specifically, relating to things stolen from the Jews. Jews themselves spoke of the stupendous wealth that the Germans amassed. Jews suffered poverty and starvation, and how much gold, diamonds and dollars were taken from them!

The Gestapo brazenly took much of the loot for themselves, even though it all was supposed to go to the Reich Bank.

Panic among the Volksdeutsche. Mass shootings of informers.

15ᵗʰ September 1943. For the second day, wagons with sides, take featherbeds from the ghetto to the station.

Yesterday, three wagons were loaded. Everything goes to the Reich, for the citizens being bombarded. If the Germans are greedy for such things, often so dirty, soiled, not knowing where they came from, it meant that over there must be 'fun.' But it was clear from this, that the liquidation of Jews in Germany had primarily economic reasons.

Only today it became widely known, that on the night of the 11th to 12th of this month, several Jews again escaped from the ghetto. Afterwards, several Ukrainian police were arrested, as they were suspected of facilitating the escape.

30th September 1943. Terrible arrests everywhere. At the same time, action by Polish organizations is more frequent. Confusion among the Germans.

1st October 1943. This morning, the Gestapo were escorting a priest, two women and a boy, through the market. But when they got a better look at the priest, the traders recognized a Rzeszów Jew, the goldsmith Singer. He was brought from Kraków and deliberately led through the city in a cassock, to evoke in the Poles disgust, for the use of a cassock. And the women, it appears, were Singer's wife and daughter, and the boy his son.

4th October 1943. In connection with Singer, several people who helped him to obtain Aryan papers, were arrested in Rzeszów. Singer, under torture, must have denounced them. They were immediately sent somewhere to the west. Several people disappeared, among others, a priest from the country, who gave or sold Singer the cassock.

One hears that recently a lot of Jews have appealed to Poles for protection. However Poles, now generally, refuse in spite of the urging of the secret Polish radio. The various betrayals have harmed others.

12th October 1943. More than five hundred Jews worked in the PZL. Barracks were built for them behind the huge factory. Again, the workers are surprised that, despite so many and such meticulous inspections, one or another has managed to keep some gold and diamonds.

In their relation to the Jews, Germans conscientiously use methods to annihilate them, like in other concentration camps. Thus, for some time, a group of the most exhausted are taken to the ghetto to extreme poverty. These people have nothing any more, and they cannot count on pity, even though for those remaining in the ghetto, conditions are again very good, because they arranged something for themselves. Again, one hears about feasts and drunken orgies.

Recently, two Jews were able to escape from the barracks at Mount Lisia. And the escape would have been successful if they had not come upon German workers. They caught them. One was shot on the spot and pushed into the Wisłok, the second was horribly tortured to reveal who had facilitated their escape. He did not reveal anything, because no one helped them.

In place of Jews, Volksdeutsche arrive from Romania and Hungary to the PZL. They complain and curse. They serve as guards. They don't care about anything. When one of them dozed off, the Jews escaped.

They remove everything possible from the ghetto to the station. Horrible goods and rags. Yesterday, thousands of old shoes, all wrecked, which had been lying in attics for decades, were loaded into wagons. You wonder how the Germans will utilize everything.

To think that, not so long ago, posters on the walls of the city, hideous in their various forms of lies, proclaimed that 'The Jew is dirt, bugs, typhoid.' Today, everything is zealously packed and sent to the cultured Reich.

Trade has resumed again on a large scale, because Jewish workers take whatever they can and sell it. But generally, there is now little of it, and in poor condition. So traders who made fortunes in this kind of shady business, sigh mournfully.

Granite slabs are brought to the streets of Kraków and Bernardyńska, and there is serious discussion about breaking a passage from the Sobieski Street, straight to Kraków Street. For this plan, a number of houses are to be demolished, mostly in Grunwald Street. Interesting, that it was not required in 1939 or 1941, and only now. Very interesting.

15th October 1943. New Italy has declared war on Germany.

26th October 1943. Germans use terrible reprisals against the actions of Polish organizations who are cleansing Poland of spies and traitors. Again, corpses and blood. The Polish fighting organization has excellent intelligence, and applies instant and unfailing action. Germans are powerless. In retaliation, they kill women, children, and prisoners. It is not so heroic.

A new military detail came to Rzeszów, Lord have mercy. There were selections of the elderly, children, and the really disabled. Is this supposed to stop the Allies?!

1st November 1943. Day of the Dead. And, as in normal times, near the tomb of the insurgents of 1863, people burn candles and lay wreaths. Wreaths were also placed at the site of the ruined monument of Colonel Lis Kuli, and on the graves in the new cemetery of those murdered. It was done in broad daylight. Later, the Gestapo destroyed it all.

It seems that the Jewish tragedy is coming to an end, a tragic end. In the past week, part of those remaining were sent to an unknown destination. Perhaps to work somewhere. Before that, however, a few escaped. Either they knew what would happen or only sensed it. They must also have had a prepared shelter somewhere. There are still about eighty people left. Really only the select few. The rumor has it that they were the lovers. Again there are monstrous acts. One Jew hid with a janitor, or rather with his daughter, a real villain. She dragged from him what he still owned, then betrayed him to her lover, a German policeman. They came, pulled him out of hiding and shot him like a dog in the yard.

Another fugitive lived for about a month outside the ghetto. He returned, like the prodigal son. Schupke pretended not to see him, as if the man had been on vacation. But as a typical urban Jew, not knowing well the Polish language, not knowing the village or the forest, he could not survive outside.

After cleaning, the Westghetto was opened 'to the public.' The urban poor threw themselves on the half wrecked fences and houses destined for demolition. They dragged out anything of any value, mainly for fuel.

Some dwellings will be allocated to the Poles for housing. It is horrible how these houses look, in what dreadful conditions the Jews had lived. People were crammed in there like herrings. And the smell there was also like a barrel of herrings.

The fate of the deported in September was made clear. They were driven to Szebnie, near Jaslo. The healthier and stronger were placed in a local labor camp, and the weaker, women and children, were shot. Reportedly about eight hundred people. The corpses were layered in a stack, with wood in between, doused with petrol, and set on fire. The stench over the whole area was terrible. After the burning of the stack was finished, the Germans rounded up the local peasants who carried away ashes and scattered them over the fields. Not even a trace was left.

When the Poles tell the Germans whom they trust what is going on, the Germans are not surprised. But they state that something similar is happening in Germany, with German opposition.

In the east, for a change, the Ukrainians are raging, the furious pupils of Nazism. The Polish refugees tell of terrible events, about murders and barbarities carried out by Cossack bands. Something like the days of Gonty and Zelezniak. The German culture has been sown widely.

6th November 1943. In Ukraine, near Kiev, the German front has stopped. Battles are already underway in the Crimea. And so, 'Deutschland siegt an allen Fronten?'

While the Germans show their worry in various ways, Pavlů, the commissioner of the city, behaves differently. He is nowhere to be seen. They say that he is fully ready to leave. Who knows if he is not the smartest, also the most cowardly. He knew well how to shoot defenseless people.

12th November 1943. In Kraków, they caught a Rzeszów Jewish woman, hidden by a Rzeszów nouveau riche, a married man as well. They transported him to Auschwitz. His Jewish lover was shot. But in connection with this again, they arrested several people in Rzeszów. From their identities, it is clear that it was they who helped the dead woman in obtaining Aryan papers.

In the Rzeszów ghetto, there are still about a hundred Jews, some of whom almost every night escape without too much difficulty. Those who remain are those who are no longer able to run away, for a variety of reasons. Usually they neither have the courage or strength to risk a hard uncertain fate, or just afraid to fall into the hands of precisely those Jews who escaped and live somewhere in the area, and who have a score to settle with those who were too cooperative. Those remaining are tragically sad.

The cause of the numerous escapes, which occurred recently, and the sorrow of those left, are confirmed news that in the camp in Treblinka, Jews were totally annihilated in exceptionally dramatic circumstances. Hiding in the camp, and indeed as one time in the Rzeszów ghetto, were many 'illegals,' that is those who were condemned to be deported to die and who hid among those officially remaining. These illegals were to be captured, and at that moment, the Germans met with violent resistance, actually a rebellion. The Germans could not bear or tolerate it. They began a mass murder of the entire camp. In the confusion, they say a few hundred Jews escaped. They set off to their own territories, with which were familiar, and where they had friends. It was true, that they often paid big money for being hidden, but those caught, informed almost without exception. Poles were afraid to hide them. Germans capture the drifters and destroy them without mercy.

Those few remaining in the Rzeszów ghetto are in a strange mood. Schupke is increasingly getting milder. He does not even beat anyone, not to mention any shooting. At escapes, he looks through his fingers. Ostensibly, it seems that between him and the Jews, there is a friendly attitude. In fact however, it is not so, if only because he is German and belongs to the SS. The Jews do not trust him, and also hate him, though actually, for those remaining, life is very good. Only because of the ceasing of control and persecution. Some women, and in real women, even a few years of living in hell has not killed their femininity, walk dressed up to the finest fashion, as in the best of times. You really have to admire them, like those French aristocrats during the reign of the Convention.

Most recently, there is a veritable abundance of talks by leading European men. Some say that the end is near, others that they will not live to see the surrender of Germany, etc. However, for the Germans there, it is not pleasant. It shows. From the Ukraine, various units and German companies, still arrive. The local Germans tremble at a call up to the army, right now at the time of defeat. Under the guise of exercises, around Rzeszów, are built positions and field fortifications. Again, hope flares with a brighter beam.

Germans conduct a rabid anti-Bolshevik propaganda.

17ᵗʰ October 1943. In recent days, again, a few Jews escaped from the very small group left in the Rzeszów SS-Lager. Even women and older children, because there are still some there. It is widely said this was with the complete knowledge of Ukrainian guards who also take notice of messages coming from the east.

Schupke is very angry because he does not have people to do the work, they cannot not finish the work he planned. He is therefore very happy to accept returning fugitives. Among these are several escapees from Trebklinka. They report exactly how things occurred there.

Ukrainian guards, whether they received orders, or to receive some compensation or just praise, began to look for the illegals. Jews rushed at them with knives, massacred them, captured guns, and it came to a battle. The braver ones, if not killed, escaped. The timid ones stayed. It was only when an insane massacre started, whoever was still alive, ran away. These people have registered under the 'caring wings' of Schupke.

There is a lack of fuel, and it is hurting everyone. Therefore, a large number of houses are demolished, just to get fuel. In the entire area between the streets, Slovacki, Grodzisko, Baldachuwka and King Casimir, only a few houses remain. In reality, it will be of little benefit, because last winter, the Jews burned all that could be removed from buildings without fear of their collapse. Suddenly, in a very well built up district, is created a huge square.

Germans not only murder Jews and Poles. There is now open talk, from those who came from the Ukraine, that the SS murdered Italian officers who supported the king, and therefore the capitulation of Italy.

In the northern part of the district, dominated by communist groups, formal battles are waged between them and the German troops.

21ˢᵗ November 1943. A gloomy atmosphere in the city. News circulate about some lists and addresses being drawn up, which are carried out on the order of Himmler, because, in the event of an evacuation, all the Polish intelligentsia are to be taken away. The community is gloomy.

22ⁿᵈ November 1943. Despite the restrictions imposed by Schupke, individual Jews still escape. God knows what happened to them. One hears that many of them perish.

A few days ago, a well-known Rzeszów merchant, who lost his wife and son in Lwów, escaped. He himself succeeded, and was able to come back. A clever and unscrupulous man. In the ghetto, according to the Jews, he made a fortune. He traded in gold and diamonds. No liquor, no delicacy was too expensive for him. With power in the ghetto, he had mistresses and organized feasts. Feeling that the Germans had their eye on him, he fled. They caught only those who helped him to escape, a husband and wife. They robbed them completely and sealed the rest.

Whether it was to prevent further escapes, or maybe the Gestapo found some kind of escape conspiracy, yesterday afternoon, all the inhabitants of the SS-Judenlager were called to assembly. There were read a dozen names, mostly young people. Ukrainians immediately surrounded those named and shut them in a cellar. The prisoners managed to break the door and escaped. While they were scaling a fence, some fugitives were shot and Ukrainian guards rushed in pursuit of the others. They shot three near the synagogue and one in some doorway. The rest got away, only because it was already evening. One of the last few Jewish doctors died.

What these people have lived through! What impulses

of the human soul can arise in such a situation?

The Germans are increasingly frantic. Always raids, repressions, shooting. They plunder quite openly. Time after time, the names of those sentenced to death redden the walls.

24ᵗʰ November 1943. The latest escapes of the Jews have been explained. The Hungarians help them, and there are currently many of them in Rzeszów. For a fee, they willingly convey them to Hungary, where there are still a lot of their fellow coreligionists, among them, relatives and friends. The main issue is to find a temporary refuge in the house of a Pole, to which a car pulls up and takes away the 'emigrants.'

Only today, one heard what happened in the ghetto after the escape of those in custody. When the Ukrainians returned from the chase, the Gestapo again assembled all the Jews in the square. Fourteen were selected, that is as many who escaped, and they were shot in front of everyone. After this murder, they issued a regulation that no one is allowed to go into the city without a Ukrainian policeman. Indeed, if one sees Jews in town, it is under guard. In such circumstances, it will be difficult to make contact with those Hungarians willing to help.

Watching the Germans and Hungarians, one sees no fondness between them, but rather hostility. And it is the same everywhere, with all whom the Germans encounter.

28ᵗʰ November 1943. Most school buildings in Rzeszów, except two, were occupied for military purposes. The largest building, that is the Society in Hoffman Street, contained as many as six schools. That was the one the army occupied as a hospital. The school directors inquired what would happen next, and they were told that they will get the ghetto buildings. But the Jews are still living there, and there are also large warehouses. Can this be the announcement of the final liquidation of the ghetto in Rzeszów?

Once a Jewish doctor, a captain in the Polish Army reserves, managed to escape from the PZL in an extraordinary manner. He very cleverly devised the escape, and coolly executed it. For some time, with the permission of the guard, and under his watch, he used to come out of the main gateway to buy a couple of rolls or cigarettes. The guards had become so accustomed to this that they stopped taking any more notice of him. That doctor was only waiting for an opportunity. Finally it came. Just as the doctor was buying the cigarettes, something happened near the gate, perhaps it was about a pass. The preoccupied guard forgot about the doctor, who disappeared quietly. His absence was only observed after several hours. Search for wind in the meadow!

7th December 1943. The Rzeszów merchant who ran away to Hungary, wrote a note to Schupke, with greetings and an invitation for a drink of good wine.

'Well sir such a scoundrel was able to escape, and so many good people have died,' say the Jews, his good friends.

YEAR 1944

The new year began with news that the Germans were retreating, and the Soviet army was already on the pre-war Polish territory. In any case, there is great hope.

After the escape of the factory doctor, it was announced that if even only one man escapes, everyone will be shot. Yet last week, one managed to sneak into a car which was to drive outside the area. He wanted to play the hero, and left a farewell card that he was going to where the doctor was. One of the Jews found this card and immediately ran to inform the Germans. It so happened that the car was delayed and the fugitive was found. Under pressure, he divulged who provided the doctor with the Polish Kennkarte, namely a PZL employee, a Ukrainian woman. They shot her. Better not to talk about the fugitive.

9th January 1944. The remains of the smashed Armored Division Grossdeutschland [great Germany,] arrived in Rzeszów.

Evacuation trains arrive, travelling from east to west. Many Ukrainians arrived again to Rzeszów.

The atmosphere is of defeat and retreat.

In the streets, parade German Cossacks. The world had never seen the like!

Businesses and workshops drive away on and on. This is a wonderful sight for Polish eyes.

24th January 1944. The influx of people to Rzeszów is overwhelming. The Poles are expelled from buildings to make room for German civilians and the military.

Something unheard of must be happening. Germans recently sent the worst bedding and rags to the Reich, and today they are selling excellent wares from the stores in the ghetto, and very cheaply. It seems the purpose is to empty the buildings and obtain the space.

Despite the watchful guards, there are less and less

Jews in the ghetto. Last week, seven people again escaped. Among them, a well-known fat red-haired butcher by trade who drove the hearse, and if necessary, ordinary carts. He must have driven several thousand dead to the cemetery. Apparently, he felt that he himself could become a 'wolf,' who would be driven one day. He managed to escape, even with his children, who had up till that time survived.

What will they do with the miserable remnant? Murder them? Move them to PZL? Smuggling Jews to Hungary has become very difficult. This was said by the 'king' of smugglers, who conveyed Jews to Hungary and Slovakia, and transported various goods back. The border was strengthened heavily with Ukrainian policemen, who had been withdrawn from the Ukraine. Together with their families, because they had nothing more to do over there.

30ᵗʰ January 1944. In the ghetto, there is feverish repair of homes, which were allocated to Poles displaced from their decent houses. Jews are even more crowded, but that is only a handful of fifty people. They whisper that they will be transported to Plaszow.

1ˢᵗ February 1944. Polish partisans are effective: they blow up trains, damage bridges. The community is afraid of a new series of rapes and murders.

6ᵗʰ February 1944. Germans still catch well hidden Jews. Again, they discovered a whole family, namely the dentist working in the health service, along with his son and daughters. They were complete strangers in Rzeszów, but still they succumbed. It seems that the Germans had special information in that matter.

For some time, people are telling the following story:

Somewhere around Wyzneg, a nun came to a hut, which stood on the outskirts, and asked for shelter for the night. The peasant initially was reluctant because it was very strictly prohibited, but finally he relented. In the morning the housewife prepared breakfast for everyone and went to call her husband. The nun took advantage of the opportunity and poured some powder into the breakfast. A girl saw it and told her father. The peasant called the neighbors. They seized the nun and found on her a revolver and some powder. She was told to eat the peasant's breakfast. She ate it and soon died. A whistle was also found on the alleged nun. One of the peasants whistled, and then six Jews came out of the woods, and came to the house. They were rounded up and shot.

Many people do not believe in this little story. It is quite clear that it is German anti-Jewish work.

Many Jews are coming out of hiding. A mild winter is favorable for them. Increasing numbers of robberies are widely credited to Jewish groups.

German retaliation for blowing up trains is terrible. Officially, a hundred people are shot, but in fact it is about five hundred.

Since yesterday, in Rzeszów, took place a drastic anti-Jewish exhibition named 'Judische Weltpest' ('Jewish world plague.') How much this has cost, how many people were hauled in for the work. What an event they made of it, and all the important people arrived for its opening!

Crowds of people are brought in to the exhibition, even from far neighborhoods. But the Poles are a discerning nation, and did not let others change their opinion. They know that the enemy was first and foremost the Germans.

10th February 1944. However, the Germans, at least Ehaus and his milieu, are very naive. They think that if they approach the Poles, as they do, the Germans, the Poles with joy and praise, will firstly rush into their arms, and then request German guns and uniforms, and millions of them will pounce on the Bolsheviks. The poor people!

For today, a great assembly of people was called

together. Crowds are actually driven to the market near the town hall. Even a simple orchestra was assembled, which played Polish melodies. Ehaus mounted a platform, began a speech from:

'Liebe Polen! Liebe Burger!' (Dear Poles! Dear citizens!)

What an effrontery! Or just stupidity? Furthermore that, to the Polish homeland, to the Vaterland, to GG, the Bolshevik avalanche is nearing. So everyone should cooperate with the Germans.

The blood of people was boiling. And he was yelling, screaming, asking questions to which the terrorized youth brigade and previously trained PZL school answered 'yes' or 'no.'

Polish melodies again. Ehaus, with an idiotic smile, bowed then he said in Polish: 'Goodbye,' and on leaving, nodded to the beat of the Krakówiak.

The crowd dispersed in silence, closely watched by the police and the Gestapo. And later, people laughed heartily and rubbed their hands that, with the little Germans, things must already be very bad if they were flirting with Poles.

Ehaus, previously used to tour various locations in the county where crowds of people were also driven to the meetings. In Glogów, a woman asked another:

'Why has the governor arrived?'

Because the speaker was somewhat deaf, the other answered quite loudly, 'To say goodbye.'

Maybe she said it at the right time.

13th February 1944. Yesterday, on Friday, the ghetto was actually liquidated, deporting men to Stalowa Wola, and the women to Plaszow. Only four men were left, probably to help the governor to pack.

Also, about forty men were taken from the PZL to Stalowa Wola. Before being transported, they were urged in different ways to disclose whether any of them still had anything hidden with the Poles. They were promised, that if they confessed, the owners would get a portion. So they used the method of Mr. Schupke. The Jews understood this in their own way, that the Germans were nearly finished, and did not reveal anything.

It is commonly rumored that about two hundred thousand Jews were brought from Greece to Auschwitz to be murdered.

On the subject of Soviet landings and their cooperation with the Poles, the Germans fell into a real psychosis. At any rumors they drive about frantically. And the partisans are there, that is true. That is where the bolting Jews are drifting.

16th February 1944. Out of the transport from PZL, forty weaker Jews were shot. Only a part reached the destination. These messages were sent by Polish workers, who worked in Stalowa Wola and returned home on Sunday.

THE FINAL ACT OF THE TRAGEDY

24th and 25th February 1944. On these two days, one can definitely say, that the final act of the Jewish tragedy was played out in Rzeszów. None of the previous events had such a dramatic sensation as just this last one.

After the final emptying of the ghetto, the houses were allocated to Poles displaced from good streets (for the Germans.) In spite of being winter, repairs to the horribly damaged houses were started immediately. Furnaces and ovens also had to be repaired. Stoves also had to be mended, which required clay. The necessary clay was brought from Rzeszów basements, because the city was located on loess soil.

During repairs of former Jewish homes, there was always some discovery of various hidden things, sometimes very valuable, and so certain legends arose about treasure in the former ghetto. The workers who went to get the clay, habitually examined and tapped walls for traces of fresh brickwork. Once, in one place, they actually found a new wall not sitting on burnt lime but on clay. So frantically they began to tear down the wall. A few bricks came out very easily, but just behind the bricks appeared fresh clay. One of the workers using an iron bar, began to dig it into this clay. The bar went in without any trouble, but then some force pushed it back. At the same time, behind the wall, there was movement and muffled voices. The excited workers pushed a longer pole into the clay, but this was also pushed back by something. By now they became very frightened and they fled in panic. But there were many of them, so the word quickly spread that there was 'something' in the basement. And maybe nothing would have happened if not on the night after this event, Bahnschutz caught a Jewish woman at the station who wanted to buy a train ticket. They took her to the Gestapo. Under torture, she revealed that in the basements of Rzeszów, hid 32 people, men and women, but after the event with the bars, some were frightened and fled. She also. What happened to the others, she did not know.

The Gestapo immediately organized a raid, precisely on the site of this mysterious fresh wall. The Jews, who supposedly fled that memorable night, just hid in the cellars. Now they could not stand the anxiety any longer and decided to run outside, through some opening in a demolished house on Mickiewicz Street. Eight of the fugitives, including several women, and the famous landlord of the ghetto, Gross, a cabdriver, who for several years had kept a firm grip on the ghetto and its German bosses, were captured by passing German soldiers.

By using their specific methods, the Gestapo soon learned everything. In the first place, who supplied them with food. He was the caretaker of one of the houses in the market, a Ukrainian. When the Gestapo arrived there, they found him sitting surrounded by Jews. The previous night they had escaped from the cellar, went to their supporter and took refuge there. On the table were several bottles of vodka. The caretaker was completely drunk. Naturally, the caretaker and his wife were arrested.

In the house of the caretaker they found 20kg of horse sausages and 15 loaves of bread, intended for the shelter. The caretaker had to say where he bought it. The butcher and the baker were immediately taken away. It was also discovered, that the contact took place through a camouflaged hole in a ruined building. The captured Jews were deliberately escorted through the streets. On the faces of those people, was evident, a horrible fear of dying. The expression on the face of people being led to their death is indescribable.

Among the captured, was also the young sadist from

Kolbuszow, the favorite of Twardon and Ehaus, who used to flog his fellow Jews. The Gestapo learned that some of the Jews had firearms. They had escaped in an unknown direction. In fact, one of them was running away near the Old Cemetery, when he thought that a man passing by wanted to block his way and he threatened him with a gun. Later, it became clear, that this was one of the Jewish police, who had on his conscience, a Jewish boy who had been killed.

The captives disclosed a lot. Actually, some people had already lived in cellars for six months, since the last great deportation in September 1943. Imagine half a year of living in a dungeon! Most however took refuge in 1944, just prior to the deportations to Plaszow. They were precisely the ones who had vanished, as if into the ground.

The shelter had been prepared for a long time, and very cleverly. Mainly by the Rzeszów people, because, only they knew Rzeszów's basement labyrinth. Only Rzeszów people knew that the cellars extending far below market, roads and streets, at the time of the construction of water mains in 1936, were cut off and walled up to form an entire system of separate cells. These sections were joined by small pathways, which formed the underground labyrinth. It was prepared, even at the time of the old ghetto, by a few trusted people. The commander and controller of the shelter was the same Gross, without whom, the project would have failed. After all had been arranged, the connection with the ghetto was bricked over. But in order that the wall did not resonate, it was blocked with clay from the inside. They forgot only one thing. They forgot to stain the new wall, and that was the consequence.

But the Gestapo was not sure if the maze still did not hide someone. No one dared to go there, in case they were buried or shot. It was decided to use gas to drive out any resisting ones. So, as to not poison the residents, smoke was first released into the labyrinth, and all the cellars were checked in the market, whether smoke was escaping from somewhere.

Only after this test, the gas was released. Finally, when in the opinion of the professionals, the gas should have done its work, a group wearing masks went into the underground. What they found there exceeded all their most extravagant expectations.

People in the shelter had prepared themselves for a long stay. With additional external supply, they could actually survive for many months. What despair must have gripped these people that so much ingenuity and effort was in vain! Thus, various items of furniture, mattresses, barrels filled with water, whole blocks of butter, boxes of bacon, primuses, lamps, a lot of gasoline and kerosene, and stocks of carbide, were found there. In general, everything that was needed for living. And since all that was permeated by the odor and gas in the basement, it was generously assigned to the needy Polish people.

Simultaneously, with great outlay of time, people, and valuable gasoline, the Germans organized a furious and ruthless pursuit of those missing. The manhunt continued on Friday, Saturday and Sunday. A few were caught as far as Sokolow, some 24km from Rzeszów. Someone was shot. The captives were held alive. It was certain they would be tortured, to get out of them, by every means, where the gold was, where the U.S. dollars, and where the accomplices.

On Saturday, at noon, in the Market Square in Rzeszów, a young and pretty woman approached a German policeman and said that she was Jewish. She was completely exhausted, and resigned, having lost the life instinct. Dreadful.

28th February 1944. Evacuation columns are endless. Simultaneously, masses of people are captured and deported to Germany for work. Those previously deported, report that there is hell there.

2ⁿᵈ March 1944. The sensation about the labyrinth has somewhat abated, but one does not know what the result from it will be. The Gestapo is still holding those eighteen captured people. By adding the ones shot, it is calculated that still nine people have managed to escape.

The butcher and baker were released as completely innocent people. But they are keeping the caretaker and his wife. They wanted to arrest someone else, but he escaped. Mainly, it concerns those, who at the time of the ghetto, supplied food to the Jews.

Masses of wounded Germans are driving by. It is interesting that the transports are moving to the south. It seems that the front is in the west, or maybe there is nowhere to place the wounded?

Currently, Rzeszów had a second sensation, but it was immediately suppressed. From a large section of the Ukrainian police, who guarded the ghetto and the Jews, thirteen escaped a few days ago. It is rumored that they found some great former Jewish treasure, only gold. From it, they gave a little to the Germans as a bribe and disappeared with the rest. And gold is expensive, valued at 300 złoty per gram.

4ᵗʰ March 1944. The tragedy of the Jews of Rzeszów has seemingly come to the end. On Wednesday evening, that is 1ˢᵗ March 1944, arrived Flaschke with another person to the prison. At night, eighteen dead bodies were brought to the Jewish cemetery, ten men and eight women. That would add up. The corpses had their heads mangled by bullets, were almost completely stripped of clothes, just in tattered underwear. All had ripped mouths from which gold teeth had been torn out. This gruesome sight was seen by the people in the vicinity of the cemetery.

Among those who managed to escape, some were actually armed. They took with them the cash of the unfortunate underground community, calculated at 3 million złoty. The Gestapo promised half a million złoty to anyone who would catch the escapees.

7th March 1944. Around Kolbuszow, Majdan and Raniżowa, it is already an open secret that the Germans conduct artillery exercises. Often from there comes a dull thunder, and in the sky you can see streaks of white smoke. This weapon was to be used against England.

Another Jew from the underground catacombs was caught.

19th March 1944. In Rzeszów, insane traffic. Columns of cars rush in various directions, entire streets are evicted, and the houses are given to the military. And to accommodate the displaced Poles, more houses in the former ghetto are being renovated, not from private expenses, but by the fund which was established from the rental of Jewish houses. The council, or more precisely Ehaus, administer this fund.

22nd March 1944. Today, posters were put up with death sentences for fifteen people. On it was also the name of the janitor, the Ukrainian Stachnik, who supplied food to Jews in the basement.

22nd April 1944. During the demolition of dilapidated houses and basements, a few days ago, around the baths, was discovered an almost warm Jewish shelter. They must have lived there since winter.

Lately, they caught a Jew somewhere in Słocina. Could he be the one from the hideout?

In the PZL, there still work a few hundred Jews. From time to time, under a strong escort of factory guards, they go in small groups to the baths in the city. After a bath, in the sauna, they slowly walk back. They are pale and emaciated, poorly dressed. Seeing friends on the street, they smile sadly, sometimes even with pleasure. Many however are foreigners. At the back of a small group walks a well-known Rzeszów physician, Dr. Heller, with his inseparable pipe in his mouth. He lives under special consideration. In the factory he resides with his wife and one daughter. He is always elegantly dressed and healthy looking.

Last week, at a time when the Jews were bathing in the steaming bath house, many soldiers arrived from various units. One realized that his revolver was missing. Only then they noticed a young boy who rushed out. The soldiers screaming 'Jude! Jude!' [Jew] ran after him firing continuously. And they found their target, but not the runaway, just a worker in the street, who later died. They captured the boy and, as a Jew with his hands clasped over his head, he was led to the Orstkomand. Along the way, the soldiers boasted that they had caught a Jew. Eventually, it turned out that he was not a Jew, but only one from the resistance. For the captive, it was his luck that he was not led to the Gestapo but to the Ortskomand, from where he fortunately escaped.

25th April 1944. An agent of the Polish secret police was shot, an older man named Stefanowski. He was one of those in whom the war had awakened, and developed, a desire for sadism and murder. His brother was involved in the shooting of both Poles and Jews, and he was also a Gestapo informer. He died miserably, as he deserved.

Many people who collaborated with the Gestapo had now been eliminated. All scum, and capable of anything. The Gestapo had used, and still uses, such people.

4th May 1944. In the woods behind Glogów, the Germans had amassed huge stocks of ammunition. Apparently, somewhere in the vicinity, they want to maintain the front.

10th May 1944. In Rzeszów, a Jew was again shot. He was possibly frightened by the banging during the demolition of the houses. He left his hideout, and so another corpse.

16th May 1944. It is not known how, but the police discovered a Jew in a German garrison church. He saw what was coming, slit his throat with a razor and died. In his possession were found two German military blankets, also three loaves of military bread, two gold watches, two diamond earrings and some money. In all likelihood, he was hiding in the church basement, which was used as a German depot. He could only hide there with the knowledge of soldiers, and he must have also acquired blankets and bread from them. Why did he go into the church? He will not reveal this secret any more.

Yesterday a young Jew was caught near Buda, and a Polish policeman, or a railway guard, was told to escort him. There are different stories. Along the way, the escort shot the boy, allegedly for wanting to escape. It was whispered that he did it on purpose. Because, the boy would die anyway, but before that, under torture he could disclose from whom he got help, and this could again lead to a lot of victims, as happened in many similar cases.

17th May 1944. The Germans shoot people at every opportunity. Today again. Among others, some convert, married to a Polish woman, who in the evacuation from the east, came to Rzeszów where he got a job. They took him away from his work place.

7th July 1944. One event is greatly intriguing the Polish community. For several weeks, in the woods near Głogów, in the so called Government Security Office (BOR,) where in 1942 several thousand Jews were shot, there are some very mysterious preparations. Apparently, something is going on, but for what purpose? It is known, because in the woods are working people driven from Głogów, and the surrounding villages.

A few domestic barracks, fully equipped, have been

installed there. A large strange building was erected next to them. Near it were dug a number of pits. An SS platoon is already living there. One of the SS men, speaking good Polish, and handling different matters in Głogów and, who used to get drunk in the inns, said something very vaguely about it. So it all looked as if in BOR was being built some camp for the extermination of people. On the basis of the revelations of the SS man, people speculated that perhaps they would bring in Hungarian Jews for their liquidation, or that it was for the Soviet prisoners of war. Some fear that this could be for the liquidation of Polish intelligentsia. A very strict order was issued, prohibiting approach to that area. Even the gamekeepers and foresters are not to come close.

12ᵗʰ July 1944. This morning, just after eight o'clock, the hearse left the prison gates. It crossed the castle square, May 3rd Street, both markets, going to the Jewish cemetery. A red trickle, all the way along, wrote on the Rzeszów pavement, a fresh German atrocity. Witnesses watched in horror. Many were tormented by the thought, whether it was not someone close, who had departed from this world. It all soon became clear. The Germans were settling old scores. Four criminals were shot, one of whom had been sentenced the previous year. In addition, among the dead was still another Jew caught somewhere near Kolbuszow. So they were still netting these people.

18ᵗʰ July 1944. The Soviet offensive is advancing at an unbelievable pace. The German retreat is in full swing. The German high command arrived in Rzeszów and occupied a lot of houses. The Polish Aviation Works is fully prepared to evacuate. The most valuable machines are being moved out already. As well, a group of Jews have been deported somewhere.

21ˢᵗ July 1944. One can clearly hear artillery shots.

22nd July 1944. PZL factory is practically shut down, and the Polish workers have been dismissed. Some Germans guards are left, and about five hundred Jews, full of anxiety about what will happen to them.

The situation has to be very serious, since the high command has packed up and gone further west.

Today, all political prisoners were removed from prison.

The night of 23rd on July 24th 1944. Sokolow is reportedly already occupied by Soviet troops.

Jews are still stuck in the factory. They are scared and prepared for the worst, because there is a lack of wagons. The Volksdeutsche have been waiting a few days for departure. The Jews are afraid that if they are not able to be deported, they will be murdered and not allowed to go to the east.

From 24th to 25th July 1944. Last night, a dozen Jews fled from the PZL. As punishment, a few others were selected, shot, doused in petrol and burnt. That night, in the direction of the factory, drove many camouflaged cars and armed men. Is it for the purpose of deporting the Jews?

25th July 1944. Indeed. During the night, the Jews were deported from the factory. Officially, there were none left in Rzeszów, but everyone knows that a number of Jews are hiding among the Poles, of course in the greatest secrecy.

The artillery fire is very close.

THE END

After a few days of fighting on the Wisłok line, on the night of 1st to 2nd August 1944, the German troops left Rzeszów, where at dawn on 2nd August, Red Army soldiers entered. Together with them came many Polish partisan units, which also had taken part in the battle for Rzeszów. Already in the morning of the same day, on the streets, one saw Jews. They were the ones, who in the last days of the occupation just prior to the deportation from the PZL, escaped and somehow survived somewhere in the fields or forests.

And shortly, when it turned out that the Red Army was settled for good to the west of Rzeszów, and that the return of the Germans was out of the question, all sorts of hiding places opened up. From them emerged Jews from Rzeszów, or nearby areas, who had been in hiding for months or even years, whom acquaintances or friends had sheltered. They survived in hiding places, burrows, and cellars in the damp and in the dark. So one could see all sorts of lame broken people, whose legs and hands had been deformed by the cold and damp.

Later still, from different areas, arrived more, many of them friends. I talked with them long and sincerely. I concluded, that the war and the ghastly events, had differing impacts. Some survivors were shocked, and deeply reflected on what had happened. Many completely changed their former positions, or responded differently to a number of issues. For others, it was as water flowing over glass.

Many understood, that one can only live fully and freely in a free homeland, and that one had to win that free homeland, even at the cost of blood and life. They understood, that in order to obtain the conditions for life, it was often necessary to save life itself. From these were recruited Palestinian fighters, who had to persuade the world. For them, money and gold represented a doubtful value.

In September 1947, two years after the war, the Jews of Rzeszów were almost gone. If you saw someone, it is just so 'on the fly.' This was explained to me by an outstanding expert of the Talmud, that where a great crime had been committed, the Jews were not allowed to live. And Rzeszów witnessed unimaginable horrors.

When I was transferring my notes of those terrible times to these pages, all of it seemed to me a gruesome dream. And yet it really happened. Today, it is hard to believe, but if one will let one's imagination work for a while, it is as if he has experienced it all a second time. Looking at those notes has drawn me back to those times.

I had no illusions when I was making these notes then, and I have no illusions today that what the Germans inflicted on the Jews, they were preparing for us Poles. Only at the right time, after winning the war. Because Germans are like a pack of trained dogs. They will lie very quietly, will allow to be stroked, will be even fawning, but if one or another Führer shouts: 'Halloo! Kill' the previously nicest and gentlest of creatures, will change into a pack of wild beasts and hungry for murders and blood. I will never forget these young Bavarian boys, in July 1942, happy, laughing, teasing Polish girls, who a few hours later were able to coldly kill people, cut up children and spear them alive.

Make no mistake! After winning the war, when Germany had a calmer head, they would have staged macabre fun with us. Unfortunately, there were, and are still, those who delude themselves. Let this absolutely true description be a warning for them.

AFTERWORD

During the Nazi occupation of Poland, Franciszek Kotula kept a general diary, but after several months, he decided to record the information about the Jews in a separate journal. It is from this journal that this book has originated. Writing a story out of those separate notes had a deeper sense than just a literary one. It was the author's wish to record distinct fates of two communities during the occupation.

After the war, the original notes were revised, supplemented and commented on, and, as a result, they are today a multi-layered text. This should be kept in mind while reading, because the boundaries between the layers, dating from different years, are at the same time the boundaries between different attitudes of the author; between presumption and certainty, guess and conviction.

Taking the notes during the occupation, and revising them after the war, Kotula hoped to create a historical document – the chronicle of the Rzeszów Jews. It was to be a very special chronicle, written by a Pole, based on accounts of the Jews he met every day, as well as on testimony of Polish people, including policemen and boys conscripted by the Nazis.

For the contemporary reader, the documentary value of this work goes much beyond its original boundaries. **'Fate of the Rzeszów Jews'** can, and should be, read today as the account of a Polish witness looking at the ghetto; the book, which is not only about what was going on in the ghetto, but also what could be seen on the other side of the wall.

Striking is the fact that Kotula records many scenes where the Poles are witnesses. Their accounts depend on places from which the ghetto could be seen. In the days of deportation, under the date July 6th 1942, he writes down: *'Through the windows on the Aryan side of the market place, one can see what is going on there. The ghetto looks like a field surrounded by merciless hunters, on which the encircled game toss.'* Or, under the date July 10th 1942: *'From balconies on the Aryan side, the life in the big ghetto can be observed. Silence and quiet. (...) Looking at this, one does not dare to speak up.'*

All those references about observation posts, windows, balconies looking out on the ghetto – so important for the topography of the town – are crucial signs of the author's own situation. They are signs of the distance. It is the awareness of this distance that dictates the chronicler's words about the essential limit of his account. *'Can a man who has not himself lived in the ghetto, with all its horrors, express the mood of those dark days? Never! You can know horrible facts, feel sympathy, but recreate the torment of these people ...'* (June 20th 1942.) The perspective of the witness, allows him to record events, but it does not allow him to grasp the dimension, which only experience can provide. The observer is thus deprived of their psychological and existential aspects. Understanding the fate of those who were shut in the ghetto is marked by the sense of distance.

It is important, for the authenticity of the observations, that the chronicler is an educated man from a provincial town, who finds himself, during the occupation, equipped with the knowledge of Polish-Jewish relationships and conflicts of the pre-war times. His personal point of view is supplemented with the local opinion. This, thanks to the author's interest in stories of the common people. These stories are regularly and precisely recorded, so the chronicle sometimes resembles a document discussing the impact of the Jewish fate on the awareness of the Polish population of Rzeszów.

Expressions like, *'It was often said,' 'It is rumored,' 'The news comes,'* are repeated by Kotula. His notes report what was said about the Jews during the occupation: gossip, rumors, suppositions, guesses, even jokes. They record a bit of what the Jews said about themselves: their voice from the ghetto. This way, the dynamics of the colloquial knowledge, and ignorance, is recorded as well as the accompanying undulation of public feelings.

The chronicle allows us to see how the information about the diplomatic game, on the major political scene, events on battle fields or the local events, reached the provincial community. This picture, which becomes quite changeable, because corrected every day, according to new facts, emerged from German and Polish reptile papers, stories told aloud or whispered in secret.

From those precise records of rumors, gossip and suppositions, we can assume when people started to realize the true German designs on the Jews, and how the certainty about the ultimate destination of the people, taken by *'trains to nowhere,'* was born and spread. In July 1942, foreboding and suppositions, concerning displacements to the East, change into the news about Belzec. Under the date, July 9th 1942 Kotula writes down: *'It is said that the Jews are transported to Belzec where they are killed with gas or current. Nobody has checked it though.'* Soon the truth would be known on both sides of the ghetto wall. On August 5th, the author wrote: *'The Jews have already learnt 'those ones' are not alive.'*

Both the voice of the chronicler, and the voice of others, make us aware of complicated and mixed feelings the Poles had for the Jews during the occupation. They make us realize how powerful the ethnical stereotypes, both the ones close to original, mythical sources, and the other transformed politically, were in perception, and understanding, of Holocaust. It is enough to put side by side recurrent expressions about *'the Jewish tactics,' 'the Jewish materialism,' 'love of the golden calf,' 'insane attachment to gold,'* to recall stories about the Jewish gold, Jewish solidarity, Jewish discretion or coquetry of the Jewish women, or to quote the statement, *'the Jews were like a foreign body in the Polish organism.'*

However, stereotypes also have a cognitive function. When treated as an attempt at familiarizing readers with the system of principles and values completely different from the one generally professed, the chronicler shows that the stereotypes could impose the course of life. *The Germans are capable of ...,' 'the Jews are capable of ...'* are the stereotyped statements often repeated and used to provide the justification for the behavior of both individuals and whole nations.

There are many typically Polish clichés, taking for granted, the opinions about the current events. The stereotype of armed resistance, is especially important in ardent glorification of *'human impulse of revolt.'* But the feelings aroused in readers, are often ambivalent because, of the one hand, we get the description of the ghetto's civilian protest and its everyday arduous, though inefficient, struggle for survival, but on the other hand, the Jews often seem to be passive, resigning themselves to their fate. *'What accounts for this resignation?'* This question asked on November 25th 1942 comes back very often. Trying to find the answer, the chronicler puts forward many assumptions: hope, instinct of life, faith in the power of gold and Jewish influences. Sensitive, to all sorts of acts of protest, as well as, to pro-Polish performances of the Jews, he reports the reactions to the uprising in the Warsaw ghetto, and tells us about boys, one of them shot as soon as he started singing the Polish national anthem (December 3rd 1942,) the other shouting, just before his death, that Poland will revive.

The power of stereotypes finds its expression, mainly, when the attempts at comprehending the extermination, are taken up. The author writes about the extermination of the whole nation, but at the same time, he maintains that, '*it becomes a popular conviction that the extermination of the Jews does not result from unrestrained hatred, but simply from greed and inclination to capture the Jewish riches, so that the war could be carried on*' (July 8th 1942.) For the provincial community, the sense of Holocaust can be reduced to manslaughter, but nevertheless, with the intent to rob. So, the myth of the Jewish gold and Jewish treasures comes back.

Kotula's chronicle also recalls another process, contrary to the described above use of stereotypes, as tools for creating the picture of the world. The author comes to the conclusion that some myths about the Jews, have dissolved before his very eyes. Thus, the stereotypes turned out to be deceptive in cognition. Furthermore, the language also proved deceptive. The chronicler becomes helpless, not only in the face of the meaning of events, but simply in the face of the choice of words he could use to report them.

Deceptive are the words relating to the reality of the old pre-war world. First named as pogroms, the Nazi actions in the ghetto far more resemble the scenes from the Apocalypse than bloody anti-Jewish riots. Kotula writes about '*hell of the ghetto,* German '*bunch of satans,*' the division into the right, and into the left, during the selection, and finally, about '*the Way of the Cross,*' of the deported. Eventually, the opinions can find the support, in the most significant and lasting religious notions. So, it is not surprising that Kotula quotes the Jewish religious interpretations of Holocaust, and refers to the notion, of the Christian conscience, while commenting on Polish attitudes towards the extermination.

The theme of Polish-Jewish relationships during the

occupation in Rzeszów is one of the most important for the chronicler. He treats the relationships as a part of all relationships between the Germans, the Jews and the Poles as nations. First, much more attention is given to the German-Jewish relations. Then, after the ghetto is closed and the German anti-Jewish propaganda increase, the Polish-Jewish relations are also analyzed broadly.

'It becomes clear that the Jews are destined to be scapegoats' – Kotula writes down under the date July 18th 1941. Thus, the Jews are perceived as victims, the Germans as murderers (he uses the notion of the German *'instinct to murder,'*) the poles as witnesses. The author credits the witness with much significance. He shows the horror of the deportation marches, and stresses the influence of this experience on the attitudes towards the Jews. He relates reactions of the German civilians, also accidental eyewitnesses, who, like the Poles, are horrified by the cruelty of the German squads escorting people to the trains bound for Belzec…

Exceptionally, the boundaries between the roles performed by the three nations become less distinct. For example, when the boys from the Baudienst squads are forced to dig common graves, assist during executions, collect the victims' belongings in the woods near Glogów, Kotula records: *'The boys from Baudienst were used by the Germans as their assistants in the crime' (July 15th 1942.)* So, they are no longer only witnesses but also forced assistants.

Apart from the witnesses' reactions, the justification of their attitudes is related, something other authors, writing about the occupation, do not often do. Kotula relates the witnesses' arguments with sore sincerity. *'The Jews demand from others to risk their lives for them, but none of them is ready to risk their life to rescue their own life.*

They would prefer others to risk their lives for them – this is what people thought in the recent days, when sinister, thunderous clouds could be seen over the ghetto' (July 6th 1942.) A few months later the author reports: *'The Jews know full well that it is inhuman to demand rescue from others and expose them to death' (October 2nd 1942,)* or *'The villagers, horrified and terrorized, by the horrible pacification, are ill-disposed towards the Jews, not because of the lack of compassion, but for the rescue of their own lives' (September 1st 1943.)* People face the choice of their own life, and somebody else's life; the choice of somebody else's death, or their own death.

Hopelessness, sympathy, terror, as well as passiveness, are the recurrent themes in the passages, describing reactions of the witnesses. Kotula reports, for example, *'On the Aryan side there is profound sympathy for the victims, and this awful feeling of helplessness, in the face of crime committed with cold blood' (October 2nd 1943.)* The author seems to be apologetic towards Polish attitudes towards Holocaust. Although the chronicle contains the information about common informers, cases of denouncing the hiding Jews, *'hyenas'* plundering the deserted ghetto, Kotula keeps on stressing, that *'the Jews themselves admit that the Poles show much kindness to them (...) and the Jews would not be so compassionate if the same happened to the Poles' (June 19th 1942.)* He says that the Poles are afraid to hide the Jews (November 12th 1942) but he also reports the cases when the Jews, caught at escaping from a ghetto, betrayed the ones who had helped them. No matter what the contemporary reader's attitude to these opinions is, the fact that these are voices from the past, should be taken into consideration.

Both, as the chronicle of the fate of the Rzeszów Jews during the German occupation, and the document of the

Polish attitudes towards the Jewish problem in that period, Kotula's work records, first of all, how the history forces its way into the everyday life of the provincial community, and how it leaves a stamp on it. The book also records how the *'normal'* life goes on, amid and despite of, the horror. The simplest and everyday rituals, the rhythm of everyday life, which seems indestructible, opposed to all the destruction the history brings: *'So many people have been killed, so much suffering has been caused, but the world looks as if nothing has happened. The sun shines, people do their jobs, eat, sleep - life is powerful' (July 9th 1942.)* The amazement with which the author observes this undisturbed rhythm, implies his understanding of the sense and importance of the events he witnessed.

EUGENIA PROKOP-JANIEC
(translated by Irena Progorowicz)